A MAN WHO
CAST TWO SHADOWS

By

Len Russell

Published by **Nun the Wiser Books** a division of
Dancing Tree Productions Limited
7 Ridge Road, Weston, Connecticut 06883 USA

ISBN 978-0-9571333-0-3

For Samantha, Eliot, Hunter,
Benjamin, Lucas and Nathan

To PHILLIP,
ENJOY THE READ
Best Wishes

Len N.
July 2012

PROLOGUE

I've been called a rascal a few times in my life, but I remember two in particular. My mother called me that when I was young and she meant it in that endearing way the word is now generally used. It sits alongside scamp and mischievous and it's a term of affection for someone you like who is perhaps a little bit naughty. Many years later I was called a rascal by a man who intended the word to carry its older meaning, a member of a 'rabble', a villain. So, there seems to be some agreement that I'm a rascal; but are they born or are they made? What I've written here is the tale of a rascal. I've tried to tell it honestly and I've avoided the temptation to leave out the unflattering and unsavoury bits. It's a warts-and-all recounting of growing up in England during the aftermath of the Second World War, going to sea at a young age, jumping ship and stowing away to reach my personal Mecca at the other end of the world. I thrived there, married and had a family. I succeeded in a range of businesses both legitimate and illegal and lived a life that was well beyond the imagination of my family and peers back in England. I took enormous risks and participated in some dangerous and criminal activities. In the end I survived.

I live in England once again and have the luxury of

looking back at the last seven decades, most of them spent in New Zealand, Australia and Asia. I remember with great affection all the characters that life threw across my path, the humour and the heartache, the thrills and the despair. And I've written them out as best I can in the hope I can honour the memory of the ones who've passed on and I record the great kindnesses that were shown to me, perhaps provide a cautionary note for any person thinking of making a career in the underworld and if I'm lucky, make a couple of retired policemen gnash their teeth in rage at chances missed. My editor says I remind him of the "Sixty-year-old smiling public man" in W.B. Yeats' poem. I apparently remind him of the character who after a life of rage and lust and passionate existence is bemused to find himself an elderly, respected figure in his community. He may be right. Life is certainly a quieter affair these days, but I am thrilled to have survived and to be surrounded by my family, particularly my grandchildren and to be living in the little Home Counties town of Rickmansworth, where my father's family settled in 1890 after living, working and dying as "Bargees" on the Grand Union Canal since around 1826.

Perhaps I should settle for retired rascal then. But my question remains: are they born or made? I'd like you come with me though this little tale and see what you decide. And as Yeats said, sometimes it's hard to tell the dancer from the dance.

Chapter One

Watching the searchlight beams traversing the night skies, listening to the warning sirens, then the 'all clear'. Picking up hot shrapnel, these were the normal pursuits of my childhood years. I have a clear memory of being one of a group of children standing in farmer Findlay's field. We were mesmerised as we watched the vapour trails of the dogfights and heard the distant 'rat-tat-tat' of the machine guns firing. This would have been after the Battle of Britain as our outnumbered Spitfires and Hurricanes fought the locust-like hordes of Messerschmitts and Dorniers, twisting and turning in individual fights to the death. We watched a live action theatre taking place above us in the warm summer skies of rural England. Cries of jubilation came from the older kids. "It's one of ours, one of ours," they chorused as a victorious Spitfire roared over our little piece of a troubled world. It must have been the summer of 1942 and I was not quite four years old. And then the moment was gone.

"The war is over, the war is over," I joined in with the other kids and adults who were shouting that out and dancing in the street. I shouted and whirled around too, although I didn't really understand the significance of what this mass outbreak of happiness, shouting and dancing meant. Old Mrs Newton and Peggy, her large daughter, reserved but nice people, were out there dancing and hugging other neighbours. The O'Briens, Coxes, Critchers, Cadmores, Puddefoots, Mathews, our next door neighbours the Collins's had all poured out of their houses after the official announcement on the radio. Then down the road to join us came the Philliskirks. Mrs. Philliskirk had great reason to be happy as her oldest son Georgie was a prisoner of war and now she knew for sure he would be coming home. Connie Beeston, her brother Wiggie and her mum were there. Mr. Beeston was a commando who had been on several raids. He came home after being wounded. As with all wounded men, once they were treated and restored to good health they were given some leave and then returned to their units. Their experience was too useful not to be used and so he was soon in the thick of it again and he took part in the Normandy landings.

We kids had plenty of local heroes to identify with. There were at least three prisoners of war from little Mill End alone and it was made up of only nine streets in those days. A friend of mine from Basing Rd, David Biggs, proudly told us about his Dad as we walked to school. He had been a prisoner of war who escaped and had crossed the Swiss Alps on foot on his long journey home. These were all people from my little world, centred on 35 Penn Road, Mill End. My Mum, my brother John and sisters Jean and Joyce, were all out there, dancing around with kind Auntie Grace who had come to live with us, while her husband, Uncle George, was on active service. I felt the glow of happiness springing from the adults that was so real and was so new to me. I was six years and eight months old at the time. It was a lovely day in May 1945. We had a Penn Road party. We had cake and drinks, even a few sweets. There were flags flying, streamers hung from house to house and bonfires blazed. We could leave the lights on at night. A grand outdoor dance was organised. How exciting it was to win a war, I thought. No more sleeping under the iron table, no more trips down to the damp air raid shelter at the bottom of the road, no more sitting outside watching the searchlight beams roaming the night sky. Great changes lay ahead.

"There he is, Mum, we can see him. It's our Dad. He's coming home from the war."
This Information was coming from my brother John and my sisters. The older sister was Jean and at only eleven years of age she was already a fussing and caring little mum for us. Wartime circumstances had demanded that my Mum work and the burden of looking after us younger kids had fallen to Jean. She made life tolerable for us; she was always there and someone to turn to. My other sister, Joyce, was two years older than me. She was the one who missed our father the most. I was less than two when he left and I was too young

to remember him, but I knew who the soldier was in the big framed photograph above the fireplace. We were crowded around the upstairs window, looking down Penn Road. I squeezed in; I could just get my head high enough to see over the window ledge. I didn't really know what I was looking for, but I could see a soldier coming up the road. This was a dad, my Dad. I knew because of all the excitement and chatter from my older sisters.

Dad was only of average height, but to me at seven years of age, this tanned man with his army uniform, his greatcoat and army holdall was a giant. Two of the boys I went to school with had a dad at home, but most of them were like me, their fathers were away in the war; so us younger ones had never experienced having a dad. He had volunteered for the army in 1940. He always said that they all knew it was coming and that the call up would eventually reach his age group. He wouldn't have had to go, as he was in what was a reserved occupation, but as a volunteer, he would receive higher pay and I am sure he took that into account. He was very English in his ways and as patriotic as the next man. At that stage he had four kids and I suppose he was concerned for their future. Both his older brothers had fought in the First World War. Jack the elder of them, with great distinction. The younger one, Bert, who had falsified his age to join up, was a Royal marine. He was in action in Russia in support of the Tsar in the early days of the Bolshevik Revolution. He again saw action in the Second World War being assigned as a Royal Marine Gunner on an armed Merchantman. I think they heavily influenced Dad. He may have felt that it was his turn now to answer the call, as his siblings had done before him. These were certainly amongst the reasons that had influenced him to leave his wife and young family and go to war much earlier than he needed to.

Chapter Two

Whoosh! was all that I heard followed by the sound of breaking glass. I was a light sleeper and had just joined Mary who was asleep in the upstairs bedroom. The kids were sound asleep and tucked up in their rooms. None of this had woken them. I jumped out of bed and ran to the front window. My instincts were kicking in. This was dangerous; this was no accident. I had an empty feeling in the pit of my stomach. I wrenched the window fully open and looked down at flames licking around the downstairs window. A petrol firebomb had exploded. It had been thrown from the front lawn and had smashed on the wooden wall near the main lounge window. Luckily, it had missed the glass. Had it smashed through the window the curtains and soft furnishings would have served as an accelerant and the position would have been so very, very different.

"Wake up Mary, get the kids and take them downstairs, there's a fire on the outside wall of the house".
I tried to play it down, but I didn't need to. Mary was great she didn't panic. She brought the kids down and sat them in the TV room. I had rushed down the stairs and outside. I grabbed the garden hose, which fortunately was nearby and played it on the flames. The cascade of water quickly

doused them. The house was a lovely two-storey wooden dwelling in Jervois Road, Herne Bay, a desirable property in a desirable suburb on the edge of the city centre. Neighbours had come out on hearing the commotion. They had called the fire service and the police. Even though the immediate danger had passed, it was still a nerve-wracking experience.

Fire, the very word itself conveys clearly what I am sure is the most dangerous and scary of all the elements. In its place, it has provided warmth, security and comfort down the ages. On the other hand, when it is used as a weapon, when it is indiscriminately used to terrify and to injure or kill, it takes on a completely different character. That was the nature of what was perpetrated on my family and me that night.

Instinctively, I knew who and what was behind this cowardly attack. My mind went first to protecting my family, then straight to revenge. I knew what I had to do; I also knew that I had to take care of it myself. The police would be of little use in dealing with these characters. I had to find a way of removing them from the scene.

Chapter Three

I was eleven years old and attending St, Peter's Junior School. We had had an addition to the family by then. He was one of the crop that later came to be known as the Baby Boomers. This was the name given to that great increase in numbers of babies, born between 1946 and 1964. I know historians will tell you that it was caused by higher living standards, improved expectations and a more equal spreading of incomes across society; but I much prefer the "cause and effect" explanation offered around the pubs of Ricky. Cause - the men were home; effect - normal service was resumed. Our addition was my younger brother, Edward. He grew up in a much more protected environment and being the youngest he was hopelessly spoilt. Probably all the babies of that age were. It didn't harm him however, as he turned out a fine well-balanced family man.

St. Peters was a Church of England school. This meant we were marched up to the Church, which bordered the school grounds, three mornings a week for a Church service. There were some who liked it. I certainly didn't. It was such a drudge, but those were the days when people, particularly kids, did as they were told and no arguments were tolerated. Our Head Mistress was a fearsome spinster called Miss Andrews. She was a martinet.

She ruled this little school as if it was her personal fiefdom and she bestrode it like that great warrior queen Boadicea. Miss Andrews took no prisoners and brooked no resistance. The world and all it contained was black or white to her. There was no room for grey. Not for her that vital area where opinions flourished, where matters could be keenly debated and progress could be made. For Miss Andrews any change was a change for the worse. Not a good or progressive way of thought for a school headmistress. I think this highly constricted situation helped propel me into my first real act of rebellion.

I was friendly with two boys of my age at the school. Both of them also had a rebellious streak as is evidenced by the audacious plan we concocted and carried out at the tender age of eleven. The background to this escapade needs to be outlined. As schoolboys often were, I was involved in a playground fight with a boy called Victor from a village further down the road, Maple Cross. I have to inform you that Maple Cross, along with a village called Harefield, were our natural enemies. And Maple Cross and Harefield didn't like each other either. It was something you were born into. There was generally an uneasy peace, but there were often scuffles between young males, mostly over our girls really. The lad I had fought was big, but not a real fighter and I had won against all expectations. It would have been better for me if I had lost. The next morning just as I was enjoying some hero worship, as was my right in schoolboy lore, a great shock came my way. My opponent from the previous day appeared at the gates of the school with a huge well-known scrapper from the senior school. Another Maple Cross boy called Billy Parslow. Shit, I was in deep trouble. The hangers on who had been showering me with hero worship disappeared into thin air; this lad was a known tough guy. He must have been a stone heavier than me and a year older. That's a lot when you are young. It's even worse if the big lad can fight as well and believe me he could. He went on to be a fighting legend in the district. It was no use waiting for someone to intervene, or say seconds out and ring a bell. Desperation can be a great asset and being the underdog can work in your favour, but not his time. Big Bill just rushed me swinging heavy punches and he was a bruiser. I had recently had two boxing lessons from Mr Wilson and Mr Edwards down at the Ebenezer Chapel on the main Road. Both of them were Chapel teachers and returned servicemen and they had started up a youth club for us kids. Those two lessons saved me from a real beating. My teachers were of the old school, they taught the basics: right hand high, straight left jab. I had a few scraps later at sea and on two notable occasions in the ring representing the ship, but that's a tale that comes later. This bout in the Junior School was as bitter and hard as any of them. That was because he enjoyed it and wanted to be the hero. For me it was to survive and not be disgraced. We went at it surrounded by shouting boys. He drove me back and he knew how to use his weight. I kept my hands high and kept getting him with the straight lefts I had been taught to throw. Although he was winning he was surprised how hard it was. I was clever enough to not let him get close and turn it into a wrestle, where I would have no chance. It must have gone on for a couple of minutes and that can be a long time in a scrap. Fortunately for me a Mr. Beckford, a teacher, stepped in and stopped it; nobody was more pleased than me. Big Bill was sent on his way, all the while unleashing a string of threats, promising to get me when I moved up to the Senior School. Those threats caused me a great deal of anxiety, but that was relieved in part by my well-wishing, but disappearing, fans returning in greater numbers. Mr. Beckford, it turned out, had watched it right through and stepped in at just about the right time for me, bless him. According to him I had done quite well. The fight that took place was nothing unusual really; in those days they were a regular occurrence amongst boys. I wasn't special or a troublemaker; it's just the way it worked out.

The two fights were a conduit for what came next. Schoolboys being schoolboys, the two contests became greatly exaggerated. Naturally I allowed the fights to be talked up to a noble battle where yours truly was the hero. What was worse than that, I started basking in the glory and believing the exaggerations of my sycophantic supporters; a very, very bad mistake to make. As boys are inclined to do, the exaggerated reports of the fights caused me to believe the praise that was being heaped upon me. We, that is, me and the other two rebels, started planning my new career as a professional boxer. It's worth remembering that we were only eleven. Looking back it was just a schoolboy playground boasting game that had got out of hand. The trouble was, not one of us would give in and pull out of it. Misplaced pride was now driving us. We had decided we should go to London and get this great career started. Then come back to Mill End famous and with a lot of money, which should only take a 'couple of weeks'! My support group and managers, as they had appointed themselves, were Ken Wilson and a certain Dave who wishes to remain unidentified beyond his Christian name, which means that there may be as many as half-a-dozen people in Rickmansworth who won't know who I'm talking about.

Money was now needed to launch this great plan. Our playground meetings were held in a secretive, earnest huddle. We had figured out we needed the train fares to London, about a pound all together, plus some money for food until we organized a fight for me. Simple really. Money!

How do we get the money? That was the question. Secretly I was feeling pretty safe; the fact that we had no money was my comfort factor. We thought we needed about three pounds in total. As a comparison, I think my Dad was earning about five pounds a week at the time. So there you are, I could enjoy the game and the hero worship and milk it as long and hard as possible.

I must now relate how we intrepid three secured the funds to launch us on this great adventure. It had been observed by us that Miss Andrews used to receive the money from the collections held at the church services. We were aware that Miss Andrews had an office in the schoolhouse, where she also had a safe into which she deposited the collections, along with other money paid to the school. We knew where the key to the old fashioned lock up safe was hidden. Three excited schoolboys, none of whom wanted to appear scared in front of the others, had talked themselves into deep water. Our next move was to get the money. The question was who would go in to actually get it. The time for big talk was over. I immediately claimed that this should be the manager's jobs, which astonishingly was agreed by the other two. Dave and I were both council house lads and lived in the same street. Ken however lived in a posh area in a private house and used to come to school in a blazer and tie, which caused him a bit of grief. I think that helped the decision,

14

Ken always felt the need to impress. Ken got the job.

We watched Miss Andrews' movements closely and spotted a time that she was regularly out of her office. She used to walk across the road every lunchtime to a little shop. It was only yards from the school and office, but she sometimes stopped and had a chat with the lady who ran the shop. We worked out that there were about three or four minutes for Ken to get in and get the keys, open the safe, get the money, relock the safe, put the keys back in the hiding place and get out. We also decided to create a diversion, to give Ken more time, as sometimes she was in and out quickly and the door of her office was always visible to her. Our diversion was simple. The school gates were right across the road from the shop door. Dave and I were going to start to fight each other right in front of her as she came out of the shop.

It wasn't quite the planning of the great train robbery, but it wasn't bad for eleven-year-olds. I can only say it worked like a charm. She did come out of the shop quickly. Dave and I went at it. I was pretending, but he didn't hold back. Ken needed the extra time as it worked out, because another teacher, I think it was Mrs Strange, was heading for the office. Fortunately she heard our ruckus and diverted to it. There was a planning lesson there for the future; you have to allow for the unexpected. We were lucky. Miss Andrews came across the road shouting, Mrs. Strange joined the melee and Ken got in and out with the money.

I often thought about this alternative scenario. We have done the job and got the money, but have no plan to run away to London. We split the money and sit tight. Presumably Miss Andrews doesn't go to the safe for a couple of days. The fight in the playground is a normal occurrence, absolutely no reason to tie it in to the robbery. Maybe it would have been that elusive rascal, the perfect crime? Over the years I have always had a wry smile when I visualized Miss Andrews opening the safe. I imagine her, after getting over the initial shock, scrabbling around in the depths of the safe and then searching the office and her desk for the money. Maybe questioning herself and wondering if at her age she was starting to lose it mentally. Then worse still, having so much difficulty explaining it, that she might have fallen under suspicion herself. She was a formidable woman however and it would have been a brave person who accused her of dishonesty.

That was it; we had to do it now. We didn't stop to think about the sensible alternative, to stay put and divide the money. If my memory serves me right we had about ten pounds, a fortune at the time. We intrepid three met the next morning at Clarkes Pitt as arranged. From this point we could easily make our way to the railway station without being observed. The tension was electric. I think we were all both excited and scared in equal measure. But the die was cast, we had to do it.

"Three tickets to Baker Street," Ken said to the man in the booth, Ken was holding the money. This was the start of an amazing day. We boarded the train and we divided the money. We were rich and free, for a while all fears disappeared. I had now learnt early in life that a pocket full of money creates options and that lesson, well learnt, stayed with me. We wandered around the Baker Street area. We found a Lyons Corner House restaurant, an absolute palace for us. Our appetites and choices knew no bounds. I went for something like beans on toast, twice, an egg sandwich, two cakes and a cup of tea and the others had something similar. This was the life. We had no further ambition but pleasure, so let's go to the pictures. School, Mill End, bullies, boxing were all forgotten. For in that moment of freedom a glimpse of another life was shown to me. We had engineered this moment for ourselves, by ourselves. Whatever way you look at it, it was a pretty good effort. Whatever you do, do it well, was the school motto. We certainly lived up to that.

The afternoon was spent in bliss at a picture house we found. This was the zenith of pleasure for us at the time, whether we were at home, or as in this case, on the run. Life and pleasure were controlled by money and for a short while we had enough. Lyons Corner House was beckoning again. We were drawn back to there to the comfort of surroundings we knew. It seems that in our understandable, but never acknowledged, insecurity, we felt a little safer in the familiar booth in the restaurant. Our money had almost run out so we couldn't order on the same lavish scale as before. On Ken's urging we ordered some slices of bread and butter. Ken took charge and with a great show of finesse and fairness he sprinkled salt and pepper on the slices making them into sandwiches, which he divided evenly amongst us. He spread out the remaining slices and sprinkled sugar on them saying they were his favourite sandwiches at home. It was food and shelter, something you don't put much of a value on until you don't have it.

It got dark and we were outside Baker Street Station. We had no plan and we'd run into a wall. As we walked the unfamiliar streets we came across a night watchman. He was sitting in one of those little round tent affairs that were always dotted around road works and building sites. He had a lovely warm fire glowing in a brazier in front of his shelter. The glow of the fire was a beacon of comfort and security and we nervously homed in on it.

"What are you boys doing hanging around here?"

he enquired in a kind, cockney voice.

We struck up a conversation with the night watchman and warmed ourselves by his fire. He was boiling a kettle and making some toast over the flames. He spotted our hungry glances.

"Wants some toast does yer?"

"Please, Mister," we chorused.

He put on some more toast and asked if we wanted tea to go with it. We couldn't believe our luck. He made us toast covered in beef dripping, which was delicious. He served us hot sweet tea in jam jars. Fine tea in bone china served at Buckingham Palace couldn't have tasted any better. We sat on a little bench, wide-eyed and temporarily secure. The man inspired our trust and we decided to tell him about our situation. He advised us with a conspiratorial wink to go back home and to come again when we were a bit older. It was just the push we needed and he made it sound as though we weren't giving in and so our pride wasn't hurt; in fact we felt we'd done rather well. We finished our tea and headed for the station in a much more buoyant mood.

I looked up at a big clock, it was half past eight. Not knowing what to do next and having virtually no money, we just hung around.

"What are you three up to?" asked a large railway policeman.

It transpired that a porter had been watching us. He had remembered seeing us when we arrived and thought it strange that we were unaccompanied.

"Okay lads come with me."

He sounded kind and looking back I realise he must have dealt with many runaways. We gave our names and where we came from.

"Why did you run away?"

Ken piped up and told him the whole story, but not about the robbery. We were held in the Staff Canteen. Tea and toast was loaded on us again. Another policeman spoke and joked with us. That canteen felt like a sanctuary, not a police station. They contacted the Ricky police, who advised our parents where we were. It was getting late, perhaps ten thirty when my father was shown in. My Dad rarely got angry; my Mum was the disciplinarian in our family. It was a different story now; he looked fit to burst. He hustled us out of the canteen and onto the platform; I think we just made the last train back to good old Ricky. Our parents dealt with us, as they felt fit. I got the strap, a good telling off and sent to bed. Ken's family, being a bit posh, just told him how disappointed they were and sent him to bed without his milk and arrowroot biscuits. Dave probably fared about the same as me. Discipline was much of a muchness in Mill End.

We still hadn't said anything about the robbery but it was bound to surface now. Fanny Andrews, as she was called by one and all, even the teachers, was beside herself. She really was red in the face with rage. She had obviously put two and two together, when she found the money missing and she had three well-funded truants to deal with. We denied it as long as we could, until she threatened to call in the police, who for her own reasons she hadn't yet contacted. We could well have finished up in one of those notorious 'approved schools' of the day. Anyway the story eventually came out. We were punished in front of the whole school (more strap) and received a very public dressing down. She and The Reverend Edwards, I think it was, delivered that with dire predictions based on our sinful ways and our blighted futures. We had to replace the money; I got myself a paper round and had to use my pay to replace my share. Fortunately I was about to leave the Junior School having surprisingly failed the eleven plus exams. My next school was Mill End Secondary Modern. I think they had prior warning about the robbery and the runaway. I think I was branded.

It was now 1950 and I was leaving St. Peters Junior School and Fanny Andrews behind, I can remember the relief I felt. No more of those mind numbing mornings at church service three times a week. Though to be fair, there were things that I had enjoyed at the school. My main pleasure had been my involvement in the school plays. My greatest triumph was as the lead in the Pied Piper of Hamlin, although there were some who might have thought I was more suited to playing one of the rats. I must have been good, as my mother said so! I later wondered; did Fanny ever see a connection, between me in leads in the plays and the leads in the playground escapades? There were a few of them besides the fights and the robbery. I don't suppose she did. To her it probably only indicated the extreme areas of my character. There have been many times that I wished that I had carried on with the thespian side of things at school and wondered where that may have taken me. The only times I ever used my acting skills were in playing the part of the innocent and put upon victim in courtrooms and police stations. Well, as any actor will tell you, you have to play the roles you're given. Unfortunately it was about then that I was attracted to the more wayward areas of life and once on that road there didn't seem any turning back. I didn't make a conscious choice to go that way and I didn't plan ahead. I just reacted to the situations I was in at the time. It seemed and it was, exciting. And that was enough justification for me. For better or worse it has always been that way.

This was it; I was now up there with the big kids and all the other failures. This was the school we went to on failing the eleven-plus. When the results had come through and I had failed, I was genuinely surprised, as were my parents. It was generally expected that I would pass, so it was a bit humbling for me to fail. I then felt I had to show off and make my mark some other way. That put me firmly in the ranks of the rebels and that's where I stayed. And I had another problem looming; I would have to face my nemesis, big Billy Parslow, who was lying in wait. There was no way a thespian type could handle him. It was quite a package to have to deal with and me not yet twelve. I was very nervous, quite close to crapping myself probably. It was all right being King of the Kids in the Junior School, but this was a different league. Think Manchester United v Ricky town FC, or The All Blacks v Merchant Taylors Old Boys. Woe was me.

This was the school where I met up with my Moor Park caddy mates. Though I have a strong belief in fate, I think you get choices on the way through life. Your fate still lies in wait, but you may get to it along any number of roads. I was attracted to these caddy guys; they were from Ricky and we had a lot in common. I got pretty involved with them, we caddied together, chased girls together, became public nuisances together. One of them, Gordon Cooper or Gorgy as we called him was, like me, a bit of a free spirit. Our great concern was money and how to get it. We were sitting in the pavilion of the King George playing field. It was a cold night in late September and we were thirteen by now. My Dad, bless him, used to make a bit of money on the side with scrap lead; it gave him his pocket money for his gambling. I had been involved in this a couple of times. My job required me to stay away from school when the scrap metal dealer was coming round and to deal with him. I had to watch the weigh in to make sure he didn't cheat us and to collect and hold the money till my Dad got home. All part of growing up I suppose. This involvement gave me some ideas and more importantly, a connection with Ernie the scrap dealer.

Chapter Four

Here I am, my first day in the Senior School. I find myself in one of the four lines snaking out into the boy's playground. We have been streamlined into class's 4a, 4b, 4c and 4d. I presume that the report from the Junior School has been the deciding factor in the placements. I make it into in 4a and believe me that was quite a relief. That went a little way in salving the humiliation of failing the eleven-plus. I recognized some of the boys, a few from the Junior School, but there were some new faces, they must have been drawn in from other areas. The Headmaster addressed us. A Mr Thompson, a stern disciplinarian and in this school he would need to be. Everything about him screamed out discipline. He was very straight-backed and very slim; he exuded authority. He moved around the school at an amazing pace. Mr Thomson always wore a long flowing black robe; it was his badge of office. He wore it with a grim determination and in it he seemed to glide, almost to float. He had one pace of movement and that was fast.

His opening address to us on that first day resembled what I had seen in war films. I was reminded of a German Camp Commandant hectoring the prisoners after some indiscretion, or insubordination, or escape attempt. The scene that was set up was no half-hearted attempt to instil discipline; it was more. It was a professionally choreographed routine, to demonstrate control, to state who was in charge and show the folly of bad behaviour and ill discipline. Many things are controllable in human interaction. But human spirit is not one of them; any success in that exercise is fleeting. I suppose you can understand the attempts to exert implacable authority in an effort to keep the school running efficiently. It couldn't have been an easy school to run. Fortunately there are always individuals of an independent nature and spirit, who see life and their place in it from a far different angle. That old chestnut, 'youth will out', proved so true and on so many occasions, that is the way it is and we are all the better for it.

After the address we were allocated to houses. This was a system borrowed from the posh public schools. It was a very good Idea. There were four houses and each was named after a senior teacher. The houses continually competed against each other, academically and in sport. It did seem to breed a degree of pride, support and loyalty, which presumably was its objective.

However it's back to my high noon and those first, but very nervous days waiting for the inevitable confrontation with Bill Parslow. I desperately hoped that it was a thing of the past with him. I was in a complete state of nervous apprehension. I really had nowhere to go and no one to turn to. I had to sort this on my own as best as I could. We didn't have a culture of turning to our parents, or worse still, to teachers. Playground fights, bullying, pecking order battles were things we had to live with. To have turned to a teacher would have made the situation worse and that would have been a slur on me for a long, long time. There must have been five or six hundred kids at the school, so it wasn't hard to lay low and keep out of sight and hopefully out of mind for a couple of days. I used this time to try to work out a strategy to delay the inevitable bashing coming my way. The couple of days stretched out into a week or more and there hadn't been a situation that enabled a confrontation. I started to get complacent and relax a bit and then the roof fell in. It happened as these things often do, just when I had a growing comfort level and should have been still on guard. I have often thought about it and other of life's traumas since. These thoughts have drawn me to the conclusion that perhaps we subconsciously allow, or even promote, endings to traumatic situations. In hindsight, one way or another, I believe I did then.

"Got you, you little bastard."
Bill had me round the neck from behind. My worst nightmare was about to unfold, but strangely a wave of relief swept over me. This moment had

been plaguing me for about six months. I struggled trying to make him lose his grip, but he was very strong. We were in a little area between two sets of large double doors. They were set up like that as a way of allowing access whilst keeping out the cold. It was an area of about three metres by three metres; an area that would suit Bill, because there was no getting away, this was it. We were on our own; it transpired we were both heading for the toilets, for him as an excuse to dodge part of a lesson and have a smoke. For me it was a safer time to visit as I thought it was less likely that I would encounter him. I think they call it sod's law.

We struggled around for a bit; he still had me from behind. When he felt comfortable in the fact that I couldn't get away he let go and tried to swing me around to set me up for one of his heavy punches. Now, I was no hero, or John Wayne, but the survival instinct kicked in. I wasn't afforded the notion of fight or flight, as there was no getting away and I wanted it finished now come what may. I was going to fight hard and hoped that would mean the bashing wouldn't be so bad. I knew he would try to hit me on the turn. Bill was a good fighter and to be fair to him, he was known to have fought bigger and older guys. He wasn't your normal bully who only picked on the defenceless, or those who couldn't fight back. Unfortunately I had become an enemy. I was from Mill End and a thorn in his side.

Unfortunately, my efforts against him in our previous encounter had become exaggerated in the telling and in schoolboy lore. It was a situation he couldn't allow. I understood that it was fight or flight and flight wasn't an option. As he turned me I quickly stepped back and his first flurry missed. I had determined to fight, so I threw two or three straight punches. It wasn't cold or calculating, skilful or brave; it was sheer terror that drove me on. I knew I had to get his nose; in schoolboy fights that often decides it. One blow did, or it might have been a collision, but this was Bill Parslow and it would take a lot more than that against him. He roared in anger. He was like a hungry bear and I was between him and his food. His nose started to bleed. It wasn't the pain that pissed him off even more; it was the fact that he was bleeding. We whirled around that space like dervishes, him trying to get in a finishing blow or in fact a lot of them. Then there was me, up on my toes defending for all I was worth and getting in the odd sneak punch. He got me with some real good shots, but mostly around the back of my head. I was tiring badly and he was really landing them. To his credit he did the right thing.

"Have you had enough?" he asked.

"Will that be the end of it then?" I gasped.

At the time I think Bill was in 3c, though I understand he went on to be successful in the building trades and developed properties. At that time however, he wasn't up to instant decisions. We were facing each other off. I could see it sifting through his mind. 'What's the best option? Bash this bugger some more and risk the others seeing my bleeding nose, if we keep going?' That would be dangerous, because boys would give the victory to the one who dealt out the bleeding nose, no matter how much of a hiding he got.

"Okay," he said "eff off and don't give me any more, shit, you got it?"

What a relief, it was over and I wasn't too badly hurt. I knew I had to keep schtum about the nosebleed. That's what he meant when he said, 'don't give me any more shit'. That was a face saving code for don't talk about the nosebleed. If you'll pardon the pun, the escapade must have been getting right up his nose. Anyway, all was well that ends well.

Chapter Five

"How about this Gorgy, why don't we pinch some lead waste pipes? I know where we can sell them." This was to Gorgy Cooper a friend from school and caddying. His family had arrived in little old Ricky from the East end of London to avoid bombing in the Blitz. He was a bit of a free spirit and always up for a bit of villainy to make a bit of money.

In those days the older houses had lead exterior plumbing and I knew lead was prized by Ernie.
"Okay, but where shall we start?" asked Gorgy, up for it straight away.
I had already spotted a good target; it was Gorgy's neighbour, the Clarkes. (The lead pipes in our street weren't nearly as attractive as the ones in Gorgy's.) Their house still had the two-inch external lead pipes taking the waste from her kitchen sink to the drain outside her kitchen window. I smiled to myself; it would be a good score; it was about four feet long and it would probably fetch fifteen bob, I calculated.
"Right come on let's do it, right now," said Gorgy.
"Yes, right now," I agreed.
It was about seven to half past, so we knew Mr Clarke would have been home by now and having had his dinner, would be relaxing and listening to the radio.

"Come on," I said, "we'll go to my Dad's shed and get his hack saw and a sack and some grease. We'll have to be quiet so they won't hear us."
We scurried off; crept into my Dad's shed and got the tools we needed without disturbing anybody. It was very cold but we were too engrossed in our work to feel it. What we were feeling was an adrenalin rush, but we didn't know that.

We were outside the Clarke's house. It was very dark; the street lighting was restricted at the time. Up the side alley we crept. We made it without being heard. We crouched down right under the kitchen window; the light was on, but nobody was in there. Gorgy was bigger than me and quite strong, so I got him to pull the pipe out a bit from the wall so that I could get a good cutting angle. This lead was gold to us. I put the grease around the cutting point to keep the sawing quiet and then got started. We were both on our knees keeping under the window ledge and kneeling on the sack. I was gently sawing away feeling very pleased with myself. Gorgy was smiling; he was already counting his share. I was nearly through the pipe when catastrophe struck. Mrs Clarke had come back into the kitchen and was finishing her washing up. Unfortunately for us that only required her to empty the sink. We looked at each other and I sawed the last little bit very quickly. The pipe came away in Gorgy's hands just as she emptied the sink. This was something we definitely hadn't planned for. It was like the arrival of Mrs. Strange - it was a message to me to factor the unexpected into my plans. The greasy dishwater cascaded out and over the crouching Gorgy and Len. We got such a shock we both yelled out in surprise. Gorgy shouted:

"C'mon, let's go, but grab the effin lead."

Mrs Clarke screamed. Mr Clarke came running and shouting:

"What the fuck's going on?"

He was a biggish man and we were just kid's. Wet, shocked and scared as we were, we still grabbed the lead between us. We scrambled down the narrow path, scratching ourselves on the sharp wire fence that separated the houses. Then we legged it down Basing Road as fast as we could. We were running with probably twenty pounds weight of lead swinging between us and that was a lot harder than it sounds. But youth gave us the edge and middle-aged Mr Clarke, shouting threats and abuse, soon gave up the chase. Fear and excitement really feeds the adrenalin, but it was mainly fear that drove us on. However, we were lucky, so we gratefully slowed down. We had a hiding place sorted out. It was under the Girl Guides' hut, only a few hundred yards away. Panting, we made it there unseen and stowed our prize safely. We had unscrewed one of the finishing asbestos panels that ran along the bottom of the hut from the ground to floor height. As we stood up Gorgy, who was drenched more than I was looked at me with wide eyes and said, "that was close, but I don't think he recognised us, do you?"

"I don't think so," I panted. "He would have called out our names if he did."

Gorgy grunted, I didn't know whether that meant he agreed or not.

So there we were, two thirteen-year-old would-be villains, standing by the hut in the pale moonlight. The panel was fixed back in position; nobody would ever know it had been taken off. There we stood feeling triumphant, but at the same time, soaked and caked in greasy smelly dishwater, on a very cold night. This crook business was proving harder and more difficult than I'd expected. But the upside was we would have a nice little pocketful of money out of it, plus a large dollop of independence. The downside was the soaking, but that was minor in the scheme of things. I felt I was a foot taller and definitely felt a growing confidence. We had to sneak into our houses and if we got caught tell the best story we could think up. I did get caught. My mum came into the kitchen as I tried to slip in. I made up a story about a water fight in the playing field, which sounded all right as there was a drink fountain there. So apart from a telling off, I thought I was home and hosed. I went to bed feeling smug and thinking of how I would spend my money. It turned out not to be quite the perfect crime.

It happened that Mr Clarke was a member of the same social club as my Dad. It further happened that Mr Clarke was in the club the following weekend, telling all who would listen, about the cheeky theft of his lead waste pipe. That wasn't the problem though. The problem was that as he told the story my dad was there armed with a bit of background knowledge on this particular subject. But worse was to follow. Mr Clarke informed everybody about how the villains got soaked in dishwater for their troubles, which apparently brought a laugh. Even worse still was to come. He next informed everybody about his new quality hacksaw that the villains had left behind. At that point my goose was cooked. My Dad knew his tools and knew that I had come in wet. He also knew that I could deal with Ernie the rag and bone man. You didn't have to be Inspector Slipper of the Yard to work this one out. Another real telling off came my way, but that's all, he was never violent with us. A real barrage of words and abuse were hurled at me. It was to the effect that I had to start behaving and that I was on a bad path and only trouble lay ahead. He was right of course, but I never felt capable of, or wanted to, change. Poor old Dad, he really had a problem in dressing me down on this one, for very obvious reasons. Gorgy and I laid low for a few days and then went to see Ernie with the booty.

"Hello boys, I have been waiting for you," he said with a chuckle. Not much happened on our patch that Ernie didn't hear about.

Ernie was a typical gypsy rag-and-bone man. He roamed the district with his old horse and colourful cart. His battered brown trilby hat was always perched on his head at a jaunty angle. His face had that ruddy look of a man who had spent his life on the road. He didn't suffer the pallor that comes from a lifetime of working in a factory. Or the lined stressed faces that usually accompanied the unfortunate souls who did those repetitive boring jobs, day in and day out. Contentment beamed out of Ernie's face, this was a man happy with himself and his situation. He lived in a caravan on a piece of overgrown land on the main road. It must have been about an acre in size, big enough for his horse, cart and dogs. It had a fenced off area where he stored his scrap metal, rags and scavenged building materials. Ernie disappeared off the scene quite regularly as a guest of His Majesty. My family were among the first to know if Ernie was away. We could always tell, as it had an immediate effect on our Dad's finances and consequently his gambling and therefore his mood. I think my Dad was amongst Ernie's biggest customers. Ernie's 'aways' were usually only for a month or two. They were never enough to stop old Ernie; he was soon at it again after his release. As he knew nothing else, his life choices were limited. His wife was a tall striking Romany gypsy woman. She struck fear into the hearts of us young ones and the adults when she was drinking. We had three pubs in Mill End; they were The Vine, The Tree and The Whip and Collar. Ernie and his wife were regularly barred from each of them, usually for fighting each other, or anybody else who was foolish enough to step in. It got so difficult that the landlords got together to find a solution. They didn't want to lose them as customers completely, as they were big spenders and good company when they were behaving. The landlords came up with a unique solution. They would allow them into their pubs separately, but never together. There were much debate and earnest meetings between the parties, including Ernie and his wife and our local tough guy, Nobby Brownsell who was well respected in the district for his fistic abilities. The Landlords had appointed him as arbitrator and peacekeeper. Eventually the compromise was accepted and honoured by Ernie and his wife. Peace was restored, all were happy, particularly the landlords.

Through all these machinations I got to know Ernie quite well. I seemed to get attracted to these people who operated outside the usual conventions and rules. I found them interesting. I remember at an early age being intrigued by their lifestyles. I admired their independence and their ability to survive surprisingly well. I admired the fact that they did it without having the regular type of job. You know the sort, out early and home late, everyday doing the same thing. I admired the fact that Ernie couldn't read or write; yet owned various fields and properties locally. I was always impressed by the large wad of notes, including those impressive white fivers he would pull out of his pocket, to make on the spot payments for his purchases. There are some who would say I got a wrong and dangerous message. Maybe that is so, but right or wrong, it saved me from what would have been the horrors of eight to fiving, just surviving. And for that, I am eternally grateful to Ernie and his like. Despite that, this crook lark was proving more difficult than I had expected. But this time I had kept the money from the Clarke's drainpipe. Anyway, no real harm done, the council would have to replace it, not the Clarkes. Independence, the Odeon picture house, ciggies, egg and chips at the café were all beckoning. I had money in my pocket, I felt good and things were on the up.

And while we are on this subject, another little scrap metal job by Gorgy and I deserves recounting. This effort had a funny side to it with no comebacks on us, which caused me to think there might be a future in this lark after all. At school my favourite period was the weekly afternoon metal work session with a Mr Dan. He was an ex-army man, a tall, athletic, man's man sort of a guy. He was also very popular. He was quick tempered, but had a sense of humour (most of the time). However it went AWOL shall we say, over this next episode. I was in a different class from Gorgy, but this escapade needed the two of us to pull it off. As usual when I broached it with him he was up for it. I didn't have to talk him into it, or any of the other jobs we did. I had noticed that Mr Dan was very careful about having the off-cuts of copper and brass gathered up and then boxed up in the storeroom of the metalwork class. Not a scrap was left lying around or unaccounted for; he was scrupulous in his attention to it. I had watched over a few weeks and was aware how it would build up and then mysteriously disappear. I had made up my mind to go after this very valuable prize. To pull off this bit of enterprise successfully and to get the maximum return, timing would be critical. I figured that to get the best result, we had to strike just prior to Mr Dan having his happy monthly cleanup. The plan was quite simple and as I knew that the stash was probably due to disappear on Friday night or the weekend coming, we had to strike. We did. Thursday afternoon's metal work class was the last chance to put it in action, or we'd have to wait another month. The excitement buzzed inside of me. I felt elated and in charge of my destiny. This must be the same feeling felt by soldiers before a battle, or paratroopers before jumping I thought. I suppose that was the limit of comparison available to me at the time. I didn't see myself in a heroic role, but it wasn't all about the money either. There was another unidentified driving force going on in my life, which was going to propel me into some extraordinary situations in the years ahead. This exploit, exciting as it was, was only another step down that road.

Impatiently I waited for Thursday afternoon, but at this stage I have to digress. About this time Mr Dan was organizing a school trip to Belgium for second and third year pupils. He was regularly involved in school trips and was the teacher in charge who travelled with the party. I had pestered my parents to allow me to go. They agreed to it, as long as I used any money I earned towards the cost. They were thinking of caddying and paper rounds, that sort of thing. However it's now Thursday afternoon and we were working away and it was bedlam in the metalwork room. Desperate Dan, as we called him, had us making brass fire screens. They involved a wrought iron frame with a brass circular panel hanging from it. Lots of off-cuts were building up. I was mentally calculating the haul. I had been into the storeroom and seen the great pile of brass and copper off-cuts and was working out how many sacks we would need to spirit away the loot.

"Okay," Desperate Dan shouted, "let's get tidied up".
He seemed particularly happy that day; I think he was doing a bit of mental arithmetic as well. It was

a quarter-of-an-hour before the bell would ring signalling the end of the day. We did the tidying up, swept the floor and put the tools away. Then took the off-cuts and put them with Desperate Dan's stash. I swear old Dan was smiling when he looked at the stuffed-full boxes lining the walls of the storeroom, I was alongside him and I smiled too. One of the boys had been detailed to check the windows, making sure they were all secured. They were those single pane push out windows, very small. The metalwork room was in one of those prefab classrooms designed to quickly alleviate the crowding that was starting to become apparent in schools in the early fifties. I had to get the lockdown catch on one of those windows free and it had to be one not too high so that I could scramble through the window. It would be a tight fit. I would have to do it, Gorgy would be too big. I knew that Mr Dan would go round checking the windows even after the lad he had detailed the job to had done it. He was careful, he always double-checked. I knew that he would then go into the storeroom to check that window. During those few seconds there was, as they now say, a window of opportunity. I had to slip the catch on the window I wanted and not be spotted by the other boys. I had taken up as good a position as possible to achieve this. I just got on the tail of the queue that was forming to get out. There was always horseplay going on so I joined in and pretended to stumble backwards and slipped the catch at the same time. I started to see how magicians worked. Nobody saw a thing.

"Okay boys, you can go now," bellowed Mr. Dan.

He definitely was smiling. That night we waited until Mr. Cox the caretaker had gone home. We figured we had about an hour to work in, as police had started patrolling Mill End and the school in particular at night. They didn't seem to operate to a regular timetable, but we thought that they would know Mr Cox's movements. There was a recreation ground that backed right onto the school. Fortunately it had an entrance gate very close to the metalwork room. The other entrance to the recreation ground was from Springwell Avenue and this was the road the Girl Guides' hut was in. Very convenient, as that was our usual safe house, our stash point where we would be hiding the loot.

We had been hiding in the recreation grounds near the rear gate to the school. It was dark now and quite cold and there was nobody about. We crept up to the metalwork room. Gorgy lifted me up so that I could prize open the window; it opened easily. I scrambled through and landed head first on a workbench. I went straight to the storeroom. I opened that window and started passing the off-cuts through. The main doors into the classroom were very heavily locked and bolted. It would take too long and be too noisy to prise them open, so we were restricted by the size of the window in what we were able to take. We worked feverishly for about fifteen minutes and got most of it outside. I scrambled back through the window. I pushed it shut, from the outside; nobody would be any the wiser. We bagged up the haul. There were three heavy sacks full. We had planned for that. We knew where Mr. Cox kept his wheelbarrow; it was just outside the boiler cellar, about two hundred yards away, Gorgy sprinted off for it while I guarded the loot. It took us another twenty-five minutes or so to wheel the sacks through the deserted and dark recreation grounds. We nipped across the road and stowed them under the ever friendly Guides' Hut, about three hundred yards away. Quickly back through the recreation grounds, replace the wheelbarrow. Hey Presto, job done.

To have seen the look on Mr Dan's face when he discovered his loss would have been such a bonus. The thought crossed my mind that if I had been an artist, I could have painted the shocked faces of Mr Dan, Miss Andrews and Mr Clarke, plus a few more as I progressed further afield. A naughty thought that I suppose won't please all readers. Later on that Friday morning, we heard from other boys in his class, that he went ballistic. Apparently he ran out of the storeroom, yelling about kicking the arses of the thieving bastards who had taken the scrap. He was yelling that he knew who it was (he didn't) and they would be very sorry. He then gave himself away by asking the class if any of them knew who did it and offered a pound reward if he was told, using his words, "the dirty little shits' names". No chance of that as only two people knew and Gorgy and I couldn't be bought for a pound anymore. Everybody was talking about it in the morning break. We saw Desperate Dan, striding through a corridor; his face was black as thunder. That normal cheery grin was no more.

One might well wonder why he took it so hard. After all, wasn't it school property? The answer to that lay in the following conversation overheard by a couple of the boys.

"The effin little bastards got my Belgium trip money," said Desperate Dan to Mr. Gough the French master, who was a mate of Dan's.

"The wife will go effin crazy when I tell her. She always said they're a pack of thieves in Mill End and that I should get a better position. I'll be getting flack off her."

He went on, "would you believe it, I was going to pick it up on Saturday morning, there was about forty or fifty quid's worth there at least."

He was irate, cursing and haranguing those 'dirty, little thieving bastards' who had taken it. I felt quite proud as the boys laughingly told the story.

The next clue as to why he had taken it so personally showed in the fact that the police were not called in. I suppose if they had been it would have become public knowledge that he had been getting a nice side earner out of the scrap. And good luck to him would have been my sentiments, but that's life. You win some and you lose some. I was about to discover that harsh lesson when we took the scrap to Ernie. Again he was expecting us.

"I thought it would be you two. Okay lads, ten quid," he said, starting to count money from that big roll of notes he always carried. We were paralysed.

"Come on," said Gorgy, "it's at least forty quid's worth".

"Yes," I chimed in, "come on, Ernie, be fair".

We haggled as best we could. We had nowhere else to take it as he smilingly pointed out. We pushed him up to fifteen quid and really were happy to take it. It was a fortune for us. But I wasn't going to waste it on Belgium.

Chapter Six

Sometime around 1929 a pretty, sixteen-year-old lass arrived in Rickmansworth. She had come down from Newcastle to work as a domestic in one of the grand houses of Hertfordshire. This was a common practice at the time. Many years later I was struck by the thought - who was the main beneficiary in this migration? Was it the southern employers who often exploited these girls, paying very low wages and working them long hours? Or was it the northern girls; girls who saw it as an opportunity to change their lives, to travel and to expand their horizons? It's not often that life allows both parties to win, as I think it did in this case. The families in our large country houses found Newcastle a fine source of cheap domestic labour. A consequence of this was that Rickmansworth was good naturedly dubbed the 'Geordie capital of the south' because large numbers of Ricky men fell for these, mostly attractive, Newcastle girls and often married them. A fact not always approved of by the local females at the time and over the years. However, looking at things fairly and considering all the angles, this situation has worked extremely well for all parties, not least the town of Rickmansworth itself; my mother and father being just one fine example of these unions. Yes, as you probably guessed, that sixteen-year-old girl was my mother.

The contribution made by these Geordie girls to our little town, can scarcely be over stated. One very good example can be seen in the Geordies' devotion to enhancing and expanding the local gene pool and it must be said that in the twenties and thirties the Ricky gene pool certainly would have needed some help; particularly when you consider that Mill End was dominated by only five or six families and most other families had a marriage, or blood connection to them. I'm not saying that good old Mill End and Ricky was breeding a crowd of look-alike banjo pickers with eyes suspiciously close together in the manner of the movie *Deliverance*, but we weren't exactly cosmopolitan. If anyone had enquired what we were doing with our gene pool at the time it would have been fair to say we were only dog paddling in it. Nature in her wisdom, may well have decided to intervene.

Sarah Gilchrist, my mother, had spread her wings at a very early age. I believe it was to escape the extreme poverty of Newcastle at that time and the rather sad environment she was living in. Byker was then a dreadful slum. It was typical of most British inner city suburbs in those days. Some still say bring back the good old days. They obviously didn't have to live through them. It must have been a huge step for her to take. She arrived here with very little support, maybe a shilling or two in her purse, which she grimly clutched. I often wondered whether she saw the parallels between her questing out so far from home and the journey I would undertake. She often spoke of the unhappy and miserable time she had to endure in her first position in this area. Her problems were compounded, as outside of her employer and his family, who were not particularly kind to their servants, she knew no one. She had an older cousin, Amy, whom she barely knew. All that she really knew about Amy was that she worked locally in a very large house - the old Moor Park Mansion.

The house that my mother had been assigned to was a splendid property called Clutterbucks; the home of a local family of landowners. The property had its own church adjoining it, where the family enjoyed the luxury of its own pews. My mother often told us of the difficulties she encountered there and how sad she was on her own. The house stood in a very rural location; she had little opportunity to get about, or means of transport to enable her to find her cousin Amy, or any of the other girls from the north. She was very lonely and still a child. One day Sarah could bear her isolation no longer. She impetuously set off to Rickmansworth to find Cousin Amy. The grand house she was in service in, stood on the very top of a beautiful valley. That valley divided the village of Sarratt from the main road that ran down to Rickmansworth. She knew that if she could get to

Rickmansworth then Moor Park Mansion and her cousin Amy would be close by. The walk from Sarratt to Rickmansworth, even today, is a very testing one. From Sarratt it's down an extraordinarily steep hill. It's just a country lane, which in those days was more of a horse and cart track. Upon reaching the bottom she was faced with a climb up a very steep gravely hill on the other side of the valley. These two hills are so steep, that they presented major problems for delivery of goods into Sarratt at that time. A popular local story authenticates this. In Sarratt, there is a public house called the Cock Inn. Its name obviously lent itself to many a joke with the locals; apparently it was a Morecombe and Wise type favourite. This is more so, as the Cock Inn, Sarratt is situated in the county of Hertfordshire, known as "Herts". The pub was named because in the days of horse-drawn drays there was a special breed of horses used for heavy, hard hauling. These horses were the famous shire horses. The top Shire horse, the strongest one of the pulling team, was always celebrated as the cockhorse. You are probably familiar with the nursery rhyme 'Ride a cock horse to Banbury Cross'. The best cockhorse was needed to deliver the all-important cargo of beer to the pub atop that very steep hill. In appreciation of their efforts it was decided to honour them by renaming the pub the Cock Inn. And so it was a difficult walk that Sarah faced. She often told us she felt it appropriate that she should wear her best boots, not knowing whom she might meet along the way. Those boots were the heeled, lace-up, highly polished, black ones, so popular at the time. Fine looking boots, but certainly not conducive to country walking. We can only imagine the additional difficulties that they must have presented. Apparently they were a prized possession, so she didn't want to run the risk of losing them by leaving them at Clutterbucks. Sarah eventually reached her first goal, Rickmansworth, after a two-mile walk. Not knowing anybody she could ask for help, she wisely went to the Vicarage in Church Street. There she sought something to drink as it was a warm sunny day and she was by now very thirsty. She also wanted directions to the fabled Mansion. At last she had some good fortune. The kindly Vicar listened to her story with great interest, comforted her and gave her a drink. Realising her difficult situation, he offered to take her on to the Mansion. Another mile and another hill, but this time she rode in comfort in the Vicar's motorcar. Upon arriving there, having been driven up through the magnificent parkland entrance, Sarah, was absolutely taken by the house and grounds, which had been fashioned into a first class Golf Club and course. The Vicar realising how lost and distressed my mother was still feeling, took it on himself to go and find Amy, leaving Sarah waiting nervously outside. She waited and worried; then to her great relief, out of the beautiful columnated entrance and down the grand steps, strode the Vicar. He returned triumphantly with Cousin Amy and the golf club secretary. Amy cuddled my mother, who, overcome with emotion, was sobbing and blurting out her story. The Vicar took his leave and motored off back to Rickmansworth after assuring Sarah of his continued help and support and telling her his door would always be open. He was a very kind man, who very obviously practised the Christianity he preached. Even to this day when I pass the Vicarage, which is almost daily, my mind is invaded with images of a sad, but determined, sixteen-year-old Sarah, knocking on that vast, solid wooden door with a its huge black iron knocker. I applaud her resourcefulness and when I consider the many difficult situations that I have conjured up for myself I think that thankfully I must have inherited some of Sarah's survival genes. Those Geordie genes have made me resourceful and kept my eyes the right distance apart.

Amy, whom mum always said was very kind and supportive, was naturally very angry and upset at the treatment and loneliness that my mother had been forced to endure. Now here the story takes a fortunate turn. Cousin Amy held a senior position on the house keeping staff and being something of a beauty, enjoyed a liaison with the previously mentioned Secretary, a man of some importance. The upshot was that my mother was invited to join the live in, housekeeping staff. This was a coveted position at the time and certainly a godsend to Sarah, which she very gratefully accepted. Meanwhile the secretary, ever eager to please Amy, dispatched a member of staff to retrieve Sarah's meagre belongings. Sarah, now happily installed in the staff quarters, enjoyed a feeling of security that I suspect she had not felt for a long time. Mum always spoke of her times at the Mansion with fondness. In her time there, she cleaned, she polished and she was happy. The fondest and the most lasting of her memories were of waiting on the tables at the many glorious high-class dinners and functions that were so often held there. She told us of the times that she and Amy were allowed to sit on the balcony and watch the lords, ladies and gentry parading in their finest clothes. Sarah remained happily ensconced there for three years. During that time she met my father and she stayed there until her marriage.

Chapter Seven

I believe fate plays a very important part in life. But fate doesn't work alone. It has assistants. Fate may be pointing you to a future that has no appeal to you at that time, but which in hindsight can be seen as both benign and inevitable. As a young boy, I was, like my mother before me, enthralled by Moor Park Mansion and all its mystery. My friends and I explored what were once secret escape tunnels. The tunnels ran from hidden entrances within the Mansion and out onto what was now the golf course. One of them had its exit on the left hand side of the twelfth green on the west course. We often sheltered there if it was raining, or if we had to hide for a sneaky smoke, which was frowned on at our young age. I was filled with excitement and moved by Moor Park's splendour and mystery. My mind filled with thoughts of daring escapades down the tunnels. I could imagine the round heads and cavaliers as they fought there centuries before. I could hear the sounds of the swords clashing and amour being struck. I heard the shrieks of pain from the injured. I was uplifted from what otherwise would have been a very boring life and transposed into a more flexible realm with much greater possibilities. I was hungry for the tales of its great past. I felt the Mansion spoke to me in a secret language that only I understood. The Mansion and its aura stayed with me wherever my travels took me. I believe that in some unfathomable way, it influenced me, my future and my fate.

Some weekends I spent nearly every daylight hour there as a Caddy Boy. At various times throughout the year important professional golf tournaments were held there. Unfortunately these always started on a Thursday or Friday. When I say unfortunately, it didn't interfere with our plans, because we all played truant during those tournaments. I was constantly there in the company of a group of local lads who became lifelong friends. We all attended the same school, but school didn't count when the golf was on. One memorable time our truancy caused the Headmaster to deliver the following comments to the whole school at morning assembly:

"The Silver King golf tournament must be on at Moor Park, because the usual suspects are missing". A cough and a pause, "however, they will all be suitably punished."

And we were. We accepted the canings and considered it a fair exchange. I suppose today that would inspire misguided parents to protest at such harsh corporal punishment blah, blah, blah. Personally I think it was a better way of life. None of us became masochists, sadists or the like, nor were we adversely affected by it. The school preserved good order and discipline and those of us with enough daring had our freedom and an early lesson in bending the rules. Unlike my friends I went on to make an art form out of that.

A character-forming incident that took place at that time concerning the Silver King Golf Tournament deserves telling at this stage of the story. Strangely though and most interestingly, the story's final act was played out some forty-two years later. Caddying at Moor Park for us local boys wasn't just work for which we were well paid; it was a way of life and an education. We mixed with older caddies, who spent their time on the road travelling from tournament to tournament and living rough. They were legends in their own right in golfing circles; they were kings of the road and great characters and we boys were exposed to them and their ways. They lived in that style because they chose to. They were scruffy and smelly and wore the same clothes all year round, but they were highly prized as skilful caddies. The great golfer and now world renowned TV commentator, Peter Allis, often talks of them and includes little anecdotes about them in his commentaries. He often speaks of Riley. I knew Riley and we learnt at an early age never to stand downwind of him and his friend Trumper. Then there were Jud, Ice cream Jock, Maurice, who was Harry Bradshaw's caddy and Gardener Jock. They were from a bygone age. They were all rebels against the system, but they never posed any harm to us boys.

Now, back to the incident. If my memory serves me right I would have been fourteen, maybe less, at the time. Gordon Cooper, Dave Phelps and me, all caddies, boyhood friends then and still friends today. We had all played truant to caddy in the Silver King. All the above-mentioned adult caddies had turned up at the course and were booked out caddying for their regular professionals. We however were needed for the lesser pros. This was one of the main southern tournaments with good prize money for those days. Consequently there was a full field, so lots of caddies were needed. The Caddy Master had control of the appointments. The method of allocating appointments was barbaric. However, that was the way of things. There is a pecking order at every level of life, no matter how basic and this was basic. The Caddy Master's name was Middie. His office was the front section of the Caddy Shack, a dilapidated ramshackle, wooden ex-army hut. The door was in two sections, like a stable door. At the chosen moment Middie would have us all crowd around his office door. Full of importance, he would come to the door and pick somebody from the murmuring, agitated crowd of scruffy adult caddies and young schoolboys, all eager to make some money. The system suited those with the least pride, or the pushiest, biggest, or most servile amongst us. I was none of those. There was no evidence of loyalty or fairness. And this from the land that allegedly introduced the notion of "women and children first" and had fought great battles for trade union recognition. This country was world famous for its culture of queuing. What happened here, however, was a mini demonstration of the law of the jungle and what happens in a life without the benefit of order and the rule of law. I often found myself standing forlornly on my own, or with another couple of unfortunates in life's lottery, who had suffered under Middie's favouritism. I realised that fairness was a rare commodity and whoever dished out luck didn't manage to do it evenly. Bad luck and good luck were realities and your life could be mightily influenced by how and which of those two rascals was in dominance. At that stage of my life I was probably a bit too sensitive to be exposed to the rough and tumble of Middie's selection process. I felt real pain and bitterness over the exclusions I experienced there and I've never been much good at waiting patiently in queues ever since.

Golf in those days was very much the preserve of the upper classes, an expression of the obnoxious British class system. In support of that contention consider this as an example. As late as the fifties, the golf club professionals were not allowed in the clubhouse, unless invited for a specific purpose by a member. With that attitude applying to the professionals, you can see where we caddies were in the pecking order, stone cold last. I was in the crowd outside Middie's door. Plenty of jobs had been allocated and I was still there and the crowd was thinning. My expectation of a job and hopes of money in my pocket were fading. I surprised myself.

"Middie, what about me?" I heard a frustrated angry shout. Christ! That was me. The worm was turning. Middie was startled; almost confused.

"Err, err … yes, you take Mr John Sheridan, he's off in twenty minutes on the high course."

Mr John Sheridan; I couldn't believe it. He was a local, well known and high-performing pro. This was a bit of a coup. Middie interrupted my state of shock. "He's over on the putting green, get over there now." I sprinted off, fearful that Middie might change his mind. I was calculating what this might be worth to me - three days if he qualified, at possibly a pound a day and maybe more if he did well. So this is how you have to act in this world to get on. My involuntary shout had caused Middie to notice me; it was an early lesson in the squeaky hinge syndrome.

"Mr Sheridan, Sir, I'm your caddy."

He regarded me with an uncertain look on his face. I recognised it as doubt. I was fourteen and still spindly so I had to get in first.

"I know the course, Mr Sheridan, I'm here every weekend and I play with the other caddies down at the Municipal course," I said to try to impress him.

He weighed that up. I could see that I was winning.

"Okay," he said "grab my clubs, that's them over there."

He pointed to a fine, big rust-coloured golf bag with his name on it leaning against the wall at the entrance to the spike bar.

It was a gorgeous, late spring day, probably made better by my promising new circumstances. We made our way past the tennis courts to the tree-lined path leading us up the hill and to the first tee of the famous Moor Park High Course. John was a tallish, slimly built man, with a deep tan from his life on the golf course. He must have been in his early thirties. It was 1953 and professional golf was building again after the lull caused by the Second World War, which had finished just eight years previously. We were joined on the tee by two other pros; one had a caddy, the other a young player in his first season who probably couldn't afford one. The starter called them forward. John had the honour and hit a screamer of a drive, well up the right hand side of the fairway, leaving him a six or seven iron to the green. The tees were well back, so it was a good shot, a good start, a good omen. The other two played reasonable drives, but they were well short of John's ball. They all made standard par fours on the first hole. The round was a good one and I gave John a couple of good putting lines on the greens. I watched every shot intently. I always had his ball well spotted when he missed a fairway and it went into the rough. As a result of that we didn't lose any, which is probably the most important job in the caddies role.

So all in all I had done a pretty good job. At the end of the round John told me he was pleased with me and confirmed me for the next day. He paid me my pound, which was the rate at the time in a pro tournament. I was very happy with that.

"Okay, Len, that was good, you did very well."

He had played well and was pleased with himself. He was like all golfers who had played well. The world becomes so much a better place, the course superb and the greens fabulous. You the victor are the proud possessor of a natural talent. You don't intend to be patronising about the efforts of others, but for a little while it becomes your right. This first round score of John's, two over par, had placed him in the top ten, a good start in the competition. On the other hand you always have the golfer who has played badly. He is the one who has been unjustly treated, who must have been in a parallel universe. He had found the same course and greens just the opposite, in fact very poor. Bloody unfair to be truthful and he had also suffered extraordinary bad luck. It's a universal syndrome in golf. There may not be such a rigorous test of character in any other sport. We caddies learnt early that golf could make a person the kindly caring king of all he surveys who will happily pay you a bit more than arranged. Or it can make him a foul-mouthed demon who might hold you totally responsible for his lack of form or ability. And then be reluctant to pay you at all.

So with the first round behind us, let's get on with the case of the missing golf balls. I was feeling pretty confident with myself and pleased with my day's efforts. I had money in my pocket. He liked me; he said I had done well. That's when I made the first mistake. We had made our way back to the clubhouse on leaving the eighteenth green. We caddies used to play pitch and putt behind the Caddy shack on a makeshift green. It was really a grassless piece of ground used for parking tractors and implements. Sometimes there was an old club hanging around, or otherwise we used bits of conduit pipe bent to resemble a club. Being the type of lads we were, we used to gamble on the results. We didn't see ourselves as cowboys, or soldier heroes. Our role models were the leading golfers of the day. Panton, Faulkner, Rees, Allis, Locke, Von Nida, Bradshaw, Cotton were our heroes.

The gambling used to get pretty serious, as did the card games in the caddy shed. Mostly pontoon, or seven-card brag. We were raggedy arsed Bugsy Malone's, but this was no game, or a film. This was life in a pretty hard lane. We were out there trying to make some money in all sorts of weather. Unfortunately there was no such luxury as protective clothing for us. In our families we had to get out and get our own money. Pocket money was a concept that didn't get much traction in Mill End; there was precious little of anything to spare. The funny thing is though, we were happy and we achieved not only financial independence, but also more importantly, independence of spirit. The real upside I suppose was that along the way, we learned some of the hard, but valuable lessons in life.

John had gone to his car and retrieved something. He opened the boot and came back to me, saying "Make sure the clubs are clean. Put them in the boot, its open, make sure you slam it tight shut and I'll see you tomorrow," as he disappeared into the scorer's office. I went to his car. I think it was a black Wolsey, they were quite popular then. This responsibility had induced a very strong sense of propriety within me. I carried the heavy bag to the car, glad I was finished carrying it for the day. I leaned it against the bumper and then gave the clubs a final clean. I had noticed that John's bag contained an unusually high number of brand new golf balls. I couldn't resist it. I looked again. There must have been at least a couple of dozen of them, loose, but still in their crinkly shiny black wrappers. These were brand new Dunlop sixty fives, untold riches for us, but mere baubles for the pros. I wrestled, not with my conscience (which was known to be a poor wrestler) but with the odds of getting caught if I snaffled two or three of them. This was like putting Raffles the famous jewel thief in charge of the Kohinoor Diamond. Or more to the point, it was like leaving the rabbit in charge of the lettuce patch. It really was a foregone conclusion. I counted them, there were twenty-two. John must have taken delivery of them from a company rep and the boxes would have taken up too much room in the bag.

I took three; I thought he wouldn't notice that amount missing.

I wandered down to Ricky with my pals. We had played a quick gambling game of ours called 'up the mop', which consisted of flicking coins against a wall. The winner was the thrower who managed to completely cover a previously thrown coin. If he did he scooped all coins on the floor. You know how it is; some days, things just go right. This day was one of those for me. I won two large pots that probably amounted to a couple of shillings in change. We were all in high spirits. We had money in our pockets and the prospect of more. Particularly me, as John's score was the best of the pros we had caddied for between us. With his low score he seemed certain to qualify for the next two days' play. It must have been about four o'clock; the sun was still shining (well it was for me). We stopped off at the Municipal Course at the bottom of the hill. It was known colloquially as "Tricky Ricky". The pro there was Alec Herd, a well thought of club pro in the golfing world. His major claim to fame though was the fact that he was the son of the famous Sandy Herd, who was a winner of "The Open." The ultimate win in the world of golf and maybe of all individual sport at that time.

We were the proud possessors of money, so we hired some clubs and played a few holes. No quarter asked and certainly none given. The winners were, as usual on the golf course, Gordon Cooper and Johnny West. These two went on to become fine golfers who both achieved a handicap of one. That was in the days when your handicap was calculated from rounds played away from your own course! This made your handicap a far truer indicator of ability. The other distinction they achieved was that they both represented the County, which was a real feat for working class guys in those days. Such was the measure of their talent that in a more recent age they would both have had the opportunity and ability to have gone far in the Professional game. Development and subsequent progress in life is so often defined by the relevant opportunities available to you in respect of your occupation. The emphatic rule for success is luck and timing. Talent is a necessary component, but secondary to it. That rule applied to all endeavours, as I was to learn.

Next it was off to the pictures, where, as we were still in funds, it was smoking Senior Service 'ciggies' and eating Kit Kats and Mars Bars. The day would have been finished off with fish and chips and making our way home at about ten o'clock. I went to sleep feeling pleased with myself and not thinking that there was a storm awaiting me in the morning. I was up bright and early; I made my way to the golf course. I was still enjoying a flush of success when Middie spotted me. "Russell you little shit, come over here," he roared. He verbally laid into me for all to hear. It transpired that John Sheridan had checked his equipment thoroughly and knew he was missing three new Dunlop golf balls. I was not only suspect number one; I was the only suspect, suspect not being quite a strong enough word. I was a thieving little bastard. My euphoric world came crashing down; I had gone from King of the Kids to a sad loser in a flash.

Middie carried on with his tirade until at last he ran out of breath. "Sod off, now!" were his last words. He barred me for a month, which he had the power to do. He had demanded the balls back; but I said I didn't have them. There was no point in returning them; it wasn't going to get me off the hook. So there I was walking back down the hill to Ricky on my lonesome, deflated and dejected. I still had some money left even after giving seven shillings and six pence to my mother. That was the rule in those days; everybody had to chip in if you had made some money. Middie's punishment could have been worse. He could have barred me forever, but the Middies of the world were no angels themselves. Thinking about the incident years later as I often did, I realised that only one hundred years or so previously I would probably have been transported to Australia for such a heinous crime. Some forty-two years later after living in New Zealand and Australia and becoming quite a force in the golf equipment-retailing world, amongst other things, I returned to Rickmansworth. I had re-established myself with my old friends who were still serious golfers. I played quite a lot with them at Moor Park, our spiritual home, particularly for me considering my mother's background there. These games and this company took me right back to the times of our youth spent there. In my mind I could see and hear us caddying, roaming, scrapping, playing our card and gambling games. I relived those glorious and sometimes not so glorious days, memories of which had meant so much to me in my travels and my new life down under. I had resolved some years ago that when I returned to England I would seek out John Sheridan and make myself known to him. Not in any mischievous or bad way, but for me it was burying a ghost. I had two or three jobs like that to do!

John, I had found out, was now living on the Denham Golf course, where he had been employed as the professional for many years. I understood he had a house there made available to him in his retirement by the club. I armed myself with three new Dunlop balls. I also took some souvenirs of my golf shops in New Zealand and a New Zealand All Black scarf as a present for him. I thought that incident had benefited me in some way, but I also wanted to put things to right. On my arrival at the Denham Golf Course I made some enquiries and I was told John was in the bar with a couple of friends. I made my way there and even after all those forty-two years I recognised him. I chose my moment and went and introduced myself with the following words. John you don't recognise me, but I owe you these three golf balls.

"Do you?" he said. "When was that from?"

"Forty-two years ago," I said. Then much to the amusement of his friends I related the tale and the circumstances around it.

"My God," he said. "I remember it well. So you're that little bugger."

He looked intensely at me. I think he was reminded of pleasant times; I could see him reaching back in his mind. Then he slowly smiled.

"I was disappointed at the time as that was my best opening round in the Silver King. I felt it took the edge off things a bit."

Anyway we shook hands and had a drink. His friends joshed him unmercifully over the incident and his getting me the sack etc. We chatted about golf down under and my shops and the like. We had a pleasant hour and then it was time to go. I hope it brought back some pleasant memories for him and it put a ghost to bed for me even if it had taken forty-two years. I remember I was smiling as I left John and the clubhouse. It was such a perfect day as I drove through the golf course. I drove down those lovely Buckinghamshire country lanes and back to Rickmansworth. This little event in my life was far from a bank robbery, or financial scam relived and put to rights, but in accomplishing it, I felt a real glow of satisfaction. I couldn't help but wonder what Middie would have thought.

Chapter Eight

I often wondered how very different my life might have turned out, had I followed the normal course upon leaving school and gone into a trade. My father had arranged a plumbing apprenticeship for me with somebody he knew. I had never felt happy with that plan. I had been spending time on weekends working with a mobile greengrocer. It was paying more than the caddying and I was learning the precious skill of selling, or as importantly, communicating and presenting myself. We called on customers at their homes; it was the way of shopping back then. The baker, greengrocer and milkman all did most of their business door-to-door. It was lively and humorous. I loved this job; I became very relaxed dealing with the housewives, joking, chatting and selling them fresh produce. Selling is selling, whatever the product. To do it well you have to be able to relax people and make them want to deal with you. I found that I had that quality in abundance, even at an early age. Dealing with and chatting up those housewives, that was my apprenticeship for the world I would someday enter.

I duly turned up at the plumber's workshop early one cold morning; it was still dark outside and miserable. It was cold inside as well and still miserable. Introductions were made and I was set to work counting screws, washers and things. It was soul destroying. I knew it wasn't for me. I started at seven o'clock in the morning. At ten o'clock I was told to go to the shop close by and buy some sandwiches and other food. I walked out of the door and it felt like breaking out of jail for me. I bought the things they wanted and took them back. I handed their sandwiches and pies around. I was fifteen years old and couldn't bear the thought that this would be my life. This just wasn't for me. I thought: it's now or never, be bold or give in for life. I had to pass the boss's office on the way out. I think he knew what was coming. He looked at me and just said, "Your Dad will be angry." I jumped on my bike and pedalled home as fast as I could. There was much arguing and remonstrating with me. My Dad was particularly upset as he had secured the plumbing opportunity for me. I was told that a dark future awaited me. In that they weren't absolutely wrong, but I wasn't going back. I said I knew what I wanted to do. I didn't really. I just knew it wasn't in that plumber's workshop. I was always very headstrong, so there wasn't much more to be said. A few more dire warnings and that was it.

I was free again. I was euphoric and I felt I had won an important battle. I had escaped shackles that would have bound me to a life and future I was never meant for. Straightaway I got a full time job with the greengrocer, carried on chatting up the housewives and carried on with my journey. The job with the greengrocer was perfect for me. It was an extension of my weekend job. This time however there were major advantages. Fred Graves, the boss, was a bit of a local legend. He had a shop that one of his daughters ran and it was very successful. One of the reasons for that success was the fact that Shirley, his daughter, was a beautiful film star-looking girl. She also sported a magnificent bust, which always seemed to be bursting out of her smock. It was an early lesson to me in good marketing. All the local lads and men found all sorts of reasons to call in for more fruit, salads, or turnips; whatever the season dictated. She was a cracker and knew how to use it. Thanks Shirley, you were much appreciated in those austere times. However, let's go back to my job. Fred had worked up four rounds, which involved house calls to regular customers. They bought what they needed and generally booked it up and paid for it on the following weekend. Well I was lucky, Fred had decided to split his four rounds into five and I was to get the new one. What a start for me. I was fifteen just going on sixteen and I was independent and largely my own boss as long as I kept the sales up. Luckily for me that wasn't a problem. I was good at it and I was happy in the job. I loved to chat up the bored ladies. I was always singing on my round; the women liked me. I learnt that people respond to happiness. Consequently they looked forward to my calls and always bought from me. It was a recipe for success. After about a month Fred had noticed the increase in takings, due to new customers I was bringing on.

"Young Russell," he called out one morning in the yard before we all set off on our rounds. "I'm putting you up to the man's wage."

That was great news for me; it was an extra two pounds a week. On top of that I was on the fiddle for another two pounds a week. I covered it by short weighing and adding on a shilling here and a shilling there on the accounts for weekend payment. We were all at it and Fred still became rich. Anyway there it is; I was a kid and earning more than the local tradesmen and enjoying every bit of it.

I am now sixteen-and-a-half, more mature, still singing and happy on my rounds. The inevitable happens. A certain lady had started to take more than the usual interest in me. She was on my Tuesday round and it became a red-letter day for me. I found myself hurrying to get to her street and house. She was an attractive woman in her late thirties. It happened slowly, so slowly that at first I didn't realise the deliberateness of it. Sometimes the women would come out to the cart. Other times I would go to the house, knock and take the order, fill it and then walk it back to the house. This particular woman used to come out to the cart, have a chat, get her order from me and linger. I noticed that it only happened if there were no other customers around. Whilst lingering I wasn't sure, but felt she stood very close to me, so much so that I would feel my knee fleetingly contacting her leg. Then there would be a hand on my shoulder, or a gentle playful push. She had a wonderful smile and laughed at my little jokes.

"Who's your girlfriend, Len, I bet you have more than one you naughty boy."

"No, not me," I croaked, "none at the moment."

Eagerly, too eagerly from me, "I'm looking for one."

I hoped that I was being adult and playing out this little game properly.

At sixteen these encounters had a very obvious physical effect on me. When I moved on to the next street, walking wasn't easy. I suffered a painful condition we young males referred to as the "Devils Clutch". Believe me, it's painful. I was like a puppy dog around her. This pleasant torment went on for about three weeks. In this time from red-letter day to red-letter day, I was in a state of permanent sexual arousal. The frustration building up caused me sleepless nights. I lay there planning how to make my move. I would form a plan to bring this to fruition and then discard it. In the end nature took its course. It was a Tuesday and I was high with anticipation. I had bathed the night before. I put on my smartest working clothes. I slipped a bottle of Aqua Velva into my pocket. The scene was set. I nearly ran to work that morning.

My eagerness to take this three-week tease to its magnificent conclusion knew no bounds. Why had I ever doubted it? She definitely wanted me and at last I was ready. My usual time spent with my customers was drastically shortened. So much so that two of them noticed and commented on it. Nothing mattered; sod the takings for today. I was a man on a mission. At last I got there. I was in a lather of expectation. I showered myself with Aqua Velva; that should impress her I thought. I walked up the path lined with high hedges that had recently been trimmed. I thought the garden looked very tidy and well groomed. I walked around to the back door as usual and knocked. I adopting a practised pose, sharpened in the saloon bar of the Cart and Horses. This is it I was thinking. Nirvana is just on the other side of that door.

Well it was, but not for me. The door opened and the object of my desires, who definitely fancied me stood there smiling. I accentuated my pose. I was prepared to be swept in to fulfil any demands that might be made of me.

"Hello Len, you're early today," she said with a smile. I was paralysed and stammered something about changing my round. But wanted to shout 'here I am, let's do it.' I started to slowly realise all wasn't well. She handed me a list of fruit and potatoes.

"Len would you be a doll and get these for me?" That's it I thought, she wants me to get them, bring them back and then she will ravish me. Of course that's it.

"Okay" I said, about to turn and run down the path. As I did that I could see behind her into the Kitchen. I almost turned to stone, for there sitting at the table with a smile that creased his face was a local chap I knew. He was a jobbing gardener. She didn't come out to the cart that day, or any other day again. That bloody gardener was always there, every Tuesday no matter what.

One of the most painful things I ever had to do was to take those veggies back up that manicured path. However, I did so and took my punishment as well as I could. Which as it happened, wasn't very well at all. But as they say, there's a moral or a lesson in every story. This one was quite simple and it was never lost on me again. It's so very obvious really. It doesn't matter how clever you are. It doesn't matter how deserving you are. Success or failure in all things is generally down to one thing and that's timing. I sure didn't time that unbelievable opportunity correctly. That low down gardener surely did. Life can be so unfair to a naïve, keen young chap.

Chapter Nine

The Grand Union Canal runs through the town of Rickmansworth. It was and still is, though on a smaller scale, home to a major barge and boat building service. In those days the canals played an important role in the transport of goods from country to town and town to country and all stops along the way. The canal meandered peacefully through many hamlets and towns. It terminates in the London docks. A sign of the importance of Rickmansworth in the canal and barge trade was testified to, not only by the fact of the barge building and repair service, but also that an early school for barge children was established there. A much needed delousing station was also situated there. One can easily imagine the need for that facility. Whole families lived their entire lives in those cramped conditions. That was the norm; it had been their lot for generations and what was still accepted then. Overnight stabling for the towing horses, which were still being used in about 1930, also stood there. All in all, my hometown was very important to the barge community and its attendant industry.

At that time my grandfather, John Russell, an ex-bargee having come ashore, was living with his family in the Canal Cottages. At this point the Grand Union Canal formed a natural barrier between the town of Rickmansworth and Moor Park. The canal was crossed by Batchworth Bridge, which provided the only link to Ricky from Moor Park. All the staff from the Mansion had to cross this bridge on their forays into and out of Ricky. A natural trap if ever I saw one.

John Russell and his brother Albert were marrying the sisters Lydia and Elizabeth, from another bargee family, the Faulkner's. This double union justified a celebration the likes of which had not been witnessed before by the clannish bargee community. One Sunday lunchtime, prior to my going away to sea, I was sitting in the garden of the Cart and Horses. I was with my older brother John and we were enjoying a quiet Sunday lunchtime drink, when riding down the side road on his old upright bike came a great-uncle of ours. This was my Dad's cousin, Bill Faulkner, a legend in Ricky. He was still a tall and lean man. He had huge, strong hands and his skin was leathery and brown from a lifetime of outdoor labour and barge work. In life I was to discover, there are certain men that you meet who are men to be reckoned with and I was to meet and cross swords with many of them in the days to come. Uncle Bill Faulkner, ex-bargee and canal labourer, was certainly one of those. As a younger man Bill had enjoyed a reputation far and wide, as a formidable street fighting man. Even on that Sunday, when he must have been closing on to sixty, he was still a man who was respected by the people of his type in the area and there were still many of those. Fighting was a favourite pastime for some locals. In fact Mill End proudly bore the nickname Tiger Bay and still does to this day. Bill had parked up his bike. Hooked over the handlebars were two huge sugar bags of fresh vegetables. He stood there looking very impressive. He was wearing an old-fashioned tweed jacket, over a corduroy waistcoat. His trousers were thick brown corduroy, tucked into shiny leather calf gaiters. This was all topped off by an old, but comfortable cap. Looking at him, I realised I was seeing maybe the end of his era and type. A whole way of life was disappearing. I feel very privileged and certainly enriched by having known him.

"Okay you bloody Russell's, what are you having?" It was almost a command, not a question.
"No, no Uncle Bill, let me get them," I said.
Being the youngest, I was in awe of him and felt it was my duty to do the honours. I went to the bar and got them in. Bill had a foaming pint of a local bitter. John, as usual, had a pint of mild. I had started to order my lager and lime when I thought better of it. Seeing me drinking would not impress Uncle Bill one bit. Although I didn't see a lot of him, his approval was important to me. I settled for a pint of Brown Ale shandy. Bill asked how our parents were and said how much he had always thought of our mother and what a nice chap our

Dad was. I think he commented that Dad was too bloody nice. A couple more drinks went down and we encouraged Bill to open up on the old bargee days that he knew so much about. It didn't take long and off went Bill. He took delight in regaling us with tales of the great wedding party. It allegedly went on for two days and ended with the local police being called to break up a mass brawl between the two families, fought out by the Batchworth Lock. I suppose if you reflect on the fact that this was a bargee wedding party, the fact that the main protagonists were the mother of the brides verses the mother of the grooms wasn't that surprising. Apparently the police wisely came to the conclusion that arresting anybody would only further inflame the situation and anyway Ricky at that time boasted only one cell in its Police Station house in Talbot Road. In any event discretion prevailed. The Sergeant, a well-known local man, persuaded all concerned to shake hands. A peace formula was agreed. The brawl was declared a draw, pride was salvaged all round and everybody then went home and slept it off. Some party. I clearly remember an earlier occasion, sitting on the floor in our new council house with my sisters and mother; we were making rugs out of cut up old clothes for the floor. That was the way of things for most families in those tough times. I was about nine; my father had related that same story of the great bargee wedding while we were making the rugs. It remained deep in my psyche and to hear

Bill's telling of it reinforced a sense of belonging and history in me that may have been very timely considering where my life was going.

"It was a big do. Barges were ramped up against each other, three deep and fifteen long, way back down to the canal bend," said Bill, taking another mighty swig of his fourth pint of bitter. He continued, "family and friends came from Northampton and all over for the celebrations". Another mighty swig; he was getting excited now. "They knew there would be a scrap." He looked at John, then his glass. John jumped up obediently and went to the bar, faster than was usual for him, much faster. "There was never any love lost between the two families," he said laughing. I was dreading the landlord ringing the closing bell. Bill was excited and shadow boxing by now and demonstrating throwing punches. I think the sound of the bell on top of the pints, could have spelt trouble for anyone in the vicinity! I also think the Russells' may have been mighty lucky that Bill was not a participant in the brawl, but in a way definitely a product of it. That was the last time that I saw Uncle Bill. I was pleased that John and I had shared that time with him. He had enjoyed recounting the tale, as much as we had enjoyed hearing it. I had heard other versions of it before, but this was confirmation from the closest of sources there could be, Bill being the son of Albert and Elizabeth. As I said, it was a privilege, thanks

Bill.

I wondered whether my grandparents had lived happily ever after. Apparently not, according to my Mum.

"Lydia was a tyrant," she exclaimed, "she gave me a hell of a life."

My mother and I were sitting having a cuppa and chatting one afternoon.

"She didn't like me. I was never good enough for her, Len," she said bitterly. "And I was a northerner and she didn't mind telling me that she didn't like us."

Be that as it may, my grandparents' marriage did lead to them leaving the barge life and settling down in Rickmansworth, initially, by the canal. The purpose of relaying that story of course, relates to my Dad, Len Russell and his snaring of the lovely young Sarah on the bridge over the canal. Not quite the Bridge of Sighs in Venice one might conclude. It was however, certainly a good substitute for a young man of Rickmansworth, intent on furthering his intentions with Sarah. In which task, luckily for me and my brothers and sisters and all who followed, he succeeded. Len and Sarah married in 1931, Len being twenty-seven and Sarah, then eighteen. Len at this time was a dragline crane driver employed locally digging out gravel ballast, which was a plentiful and valuable resource in the area. One of the main outlets for the ballast being dug at that time was its use in the construction of Wembley Stadium and the road leading into it. A fact often boasted about, by football mad locals.

Chapter Ten

Looking back I was always aware of and troubled by, the prevailing class system in England. I like to think I fought it in my own way, whenever I could, or whenever I felt oppressed by it. I rebelled against it then as I continued to do through my later years. Fortunately though, there wasn't a lot of it around down under. I didn't let it dominate me and I was never going to be a servant to it. I had watched how my mother and father had reacted to it. We were a typical council house family and saw no way of things changing. At times, like many other locals, my parents took on second jobs to supplement the family income. Money was always in very short supply. My father, who was an excellent tradesman, gardened on weekends. My mother, well known as a bit of a firebrand, cleaned the houses of some of the local middle and upper classes, as they were deemed. I knew that in all the years they worked those secondary jobs they gave good work for their money, but they never gave subservience. Mum in particular was very sensitive and very proud. She never gave an inch to a slight, be it intended or otherwise. Luckily, even though young, I recognised that strength and determination in them. Maybe that's why in later years I was so comfortable in New Zealand and Australia. After all, being bred from bargees and a Geordie was a pretty good pedigree for anywhere down under. Not quite Ned Kelly, but everything has to start somewhere.

It was June 1955 and my life was about to take a whole new path. I was seventeen and restless. I had been starting to get into the usual juvenile delinquency. A favourite was legging it from taxis without paying. Then there was the odd skirmish with the Teds from other areas who came into our territory. It was one in, all in, whether you liked it or not if you came from Mill End or Ricky. Looking back I was probably getting too big for my boots. Well that's what my Dad said and he was probably right. The trouble was I really felt driven. I wanted something else, something more, but I didn't know what. Maybe I felt I had outgrown our small town. I didn't really know the answer; I wasn't much given to deduction, or thinking of actions and their consequences. I was more into reacting to what was happening around me.

I followed the usual pattern of my peers. It was wages on Thursday, out on Friday nights. We all used to congregate at the Cart and Horses. It was the same pub that our parents had congregated in and no doubt they had done the same things we did. Our first priority of course was chasing the girls who were brave enough to enter the Cart and Horses. We local lads considered the pub our territory. The girls were usually Geordie Girls employed as domestics locally in a private Mason's school. They were lively and mostly pretty. They certainly played a part in lifting the local social life. There were the usual scuffles with other lads from out of the area who had the cheek to invade our territory. Fortunately, that was mostly left to tougher ones amongst us, who seemed to enjoy it. I always prided myself on being more of a lover and a dresser.

Saturday rolled around and the entertainment was usually a trip to a local dance hall. It was the chance to preen, to dress up as best as we could afford. We wore our four button suits and string ties, posing to show of our Tony Curtis haircuts. We revelled in the clothing fashion of the time, the great Edwardian Style. Yes, you got it, we were Teddy Boys. It was exciting to feel part of the rebellious youth of the day. The clothing was our proud badge of belonging. I was very attracted to the stylish clothing and the Jive and Rock and Roll music that went with that era. We jived to Bill Haley and the Comets. We were serenaded by the Platters and Fats Domino. We drank lager and limes and bought Babychams for the girls. Jesus! It was Saturday night. Who cares about tomorrow? For just one night a week the dream was almost lived. Remember life was still pretty austere. We were still recovering from the Second World War. But never mind the austerity, there was an impossible dream to chase.

There were times when trouble flared. When it did, we were well served. We had lads who were very capable in the scrappers department. There were many occasions when those, the more 'agro' amongst us, saved the day. I am reminded of a Saturday night sojourn to a dance hall in Chesham, a pretty Buckinghamshire market town. The hall was the old Military Hall in the High Street. It was located on the first floor, up a steep flight of stairs. We had arrived, 'en-masse', some on the back of Freddie Graves' lorry, others by train.

We hit the hall, we were jiving away and chatting up the Chesham girls, when the knife-edge tension, that was in the air, just exploded. A scuffle started near the stairs. A whole team of local lads had martialled themselves in the courtyard downstairs. This was a planned by them; there had been a couple of incidents on previous Saturday nights. They were intent upon taking back their territory, as it were. Our lads, nearest the stairs, were Ken Cooper and Bernard Beckley. They quickly realised what was happening and put up a good scrap and resisted the surge of the Chesham boys up the stairs. They were quickly joined by the likes of Dodger Beaumont and Charlie Shipway, two real heavies. They carried the day, as others fought and squeezed to get in. I hold my hand up, I carried on dancing, just like in a Western bar brawl, the music never stopped. I suppose the upside was, there were no knives or bottles, no one was badly injured or killed, such was the way of a scrap between young men then. And that story reflects our Saturday nights.

Chapter Eleven

"You won't last new boy." It was a chant I would be hearing a lot during the next ten weeks of sea school. We were propelled through the gated entrance of the training ship TS Vindicatrix, an old sailing ship taken from the Germans as war reparations after the First World War. She was moored in a cutting alongside the River Severn, within sight of the old Severn Bridge, in the West Country county of Gloucestershire.

Street-wise tough looking lads, in dark blue serge uniforms, lined the main entrance road to the characterless, unwelcoming induction centre. From the more outrageous of these lads came the shout in a singsong Liverpool accent. "She won't wait for you." As that was the first Liverpool voice I had heard, I was more taken by the accent than the intended unsettling jibe. Glaswegian, Taffy, Geordie and London accents joined in the hail of abuse. Our few weak attempts to return the flow of insults failed. We new boys didn't have the required togetherness and confidence needed to retaliate; but that would change as we shared our training, our hardship and became a unit. It follows an old law of nature that we all gravitate to our own tribal groups for acceptance and security. It took only a couple of weeks and we were bonding and looking out for each other.

I had ended up here as a consequence of my growing waywardness and the resulting problems I was causing at home. I had decided I wanted to go into the Merchant Navy. Strangely there were no objections from my family. Dad couldn't get me to the shipping office fast enough. My decision had been heavily influenced by a chance meeting with an older boy I had grown up with. He was two years older than me and had been a bit of a local hero in our road. He was what I came to know down under as 'the leader of the push' - a self-explanatory title if you think about it. This was Bill Horwood. One day I was in our High Street doing nothing in particular. Looking further down the road I saw a youngish, confident looking guy. He was just ambling along, looking like he didn't have a care in the world. He was looking in the shop windows and appeared to be killing time. By now we had drawn closer together and I was struck by his cool appearance. He was tanned and smiling. It was what he was wearing that had really caught my eye. He was wearing what I came to know as a denim Wrangler jacket and what I later found out to be a pair of Levi Jeans. Wow these were untold riches in the UK at the time. In fact they were almost unheard of in our little outpost. I couldn't help staring and feeling and probably looking very jealous. I thought he had stepped out of an advertisement. I thought Hollywood had come to town; he looked so out of place. Then imagine my shock when he looked over the road to me and smiling called out "Watcha, Len. Wanna have a drink?" I realised it was Bill, whom I hadn't seen for a couple of years.

What a change. I knew he'd joined the Merchant Navy. Here he was a walking advert for cool. I'd never put the Merchant Navy and cool in the same breath before. This was for me. I wanted to be tanned and cool. I wanted to stand out among my peers. I wanted to walk down the street and have people notice me. I immediately saw that as the way ahead for me. I determined right then that nothing would stop me. I wanted those clothes that tan, that confidence. And that was how I came to find myself at the TS Vindicatrix, a Merchant Navy training ship, on that late June afternoon in 1955. I was mixed in with a crowd of seventeen-year-old boys from all parts of the UK, queuing for an Induction Medical. We were all looking with great interest and sniggering at the venereal disease posters that plastered the walls. I found out that the Teddy Boy battles, that I had expected to follow me here, were left at the gate by an unwritten law. We were in this together, no matter what our origins, or how our accents defined us. We were all a long way from home, often for the first time, so I think that in a way we knew we had to support each other. Our shared battle would be to get through the course. There were very few fights apart from the organized boxing night, which was the highlight of the week. We had now finished our induction. The doctor had checked us over; a brief examination, then cough.

"Okay, pull up your trousers, you'll do."

I followed the line over to the next desk.

"Name please?" the orderly called out.

"Russell," I barked out, without knowing why.

"Okay, sign here."

We were herded out again.

"Follow me," from a senior boy, who wore an anchor badge on his sleeve signifying that he was a Bosun and had nearly, finished his course.

"Right, we're going to the stores for your uniforms."

More abuse was hurled at us. There would be plenty of that in the testing, rough and challenging weeks ahead. Somehow it felt right. We were kitted out, not a lot of attention given to size. Things generally fitted; if not, you could swap with the other boys to get it near enough, if you were lucky. Later events showed this to be an important part of my journey from Mill End. I found myself driven to a new and adventurous life in New Zealand. At this time air travel was beyond the reach of most and still very novel. Getting to this new life was to cause me many frights and many difficulties. I was on a necessary learning curve and on it I found a comradeship not often available in civilian life. It was a time that has stayed so clearly in my memory, a time that I loved. I was seventeen and driven to go in search of a new life.

"Righto, boys, let's have you," piped up a miserable looking, ruddy-faced, middle aged man. He was dressed in a well-worn naval uniform and a naval officer's cap. He's an officer, be careful, I thought to myself. Don't blow it now. We had been herded into a large room. It was bleak, with a few faded ship prints and medical bulletins mainly connected with venereal diseases displayed on the walls. They really hammered us at every opportunity on the perils of contracting one of them. They made Interesting reading, but we were seventeen and lusty and about to be turned loose on the world and its opportunities. Those posters and lectures would be faded memories that would not be able to compete with the temptations that would come our way. Well that's what we fervently hoped. A bare, but highly polished, cold floor gave a clue that we were about to enter a disciplined world. One that wouldn't be impressed by our Teddy Boy suits, our haircuts and black square-toed fashion shoes. We postured; trying to feign indifference and a tough, I've seen it all before, attitude. We had quickly adopted the manner of the boys who'd jeered at us on the way in. Lessons are best learnt quickly in these harsh environments. It was all part of the preparation for the future that awaited us, provided we stuck it out. That meant eating food previously sampled by cockroaches, drinking bromide laced cocoa and sleeping under a threadbare blanket on a mattress that had long since lost any comfort factor. All these obstacles, though not an official part of a screening process, helped to weed out the unsuitable. For them it was probably better sooner rather than later. Every intake had some members who struggled, with this massive lifestyle change. They took the way out known as going over the fence. Generally these lads were from more affluent homes. Like us though, they had been seduced by the thought of sunshine, freedom and travel. Unfortunately for them, they found the entry price too high. There is however another more positive side to the tale. The Vindicatrix, during its productive life, turned out and trained 70,000 boys. Some went for catering and some, like me, for the deck department. Unfortunately a large number of these young lads lost their lives in the Second World War, particularly on the notorious Atlantic and Russian convoys. Many of these boys progressed and became experienced seamen. Often they rose to senior positions. Some as high as chief stewards and pursers in the catering department. Others in the seamen's department became deck officers, with many rising to become captains and senior harbour pilots. Whatever the progress or position achieved, I think It very fair to say the Vindi and its boys, contributed a good deal to the great British Merchant Navy. And as importantly, it gave most of us a foothold in life. We were enriched by the knowledge, travel and opportunities it provided. The Vindi experience developed in me a sense of pride. I felt a sense of belonging. I think we all did. A feeling I doubt we had experienced so intensely, prior to throwing our lot in with the old red duster brigade. For me and countless others it was a life-changing time. A time I would never forget, nor want to change. So that's how it was, ten weeks of hard discipline and training, for a group of adventurous young working class guys, drawn from all over the UK. We were thrown together in what often descended into survival of the fittest encounters. All this, coupled with the bad food, uncomfortable beds, learning seamanship, knots and lifeboat procedures. I learnt all these things, which really did help when I joined my early ships. Above all though, it gave me a sense of confidence and an improved physical condition. That was so very important in the life and work, I was now judged to be able to do.

I now had my precious Maritime Board Seaman's Discharge book. I was very proud of this book, which prominently displayed my name and number and photograph. These books were issued to every British merchant seaman. They were used to identify and document particulars of the voyages undertaken by the bearer. They recorded details such as the name of the ship, length of voyage, rank and most importantly, ability and behaviour. On applying to join a ship, the discharge book had to be produced for the first mate's approval. That was always required prior to his accepting you as a crewmember for the voyage. The discharge book gave him instant information regarding the bearer's character and ability. It was a good incentive to stay on the straight and narrow and perform well. More than one bad report and woe betide the bearer. He would soon find himself restricted to either notorious trouble ships or maybe worse still, the tanker trade. Or if you were a real bad boy it was 'Hello Sergeant Major' and the Army got you.

To me and countless others, this discharge book was a real man of the world possession. It was the passport and membership badge into what seemed to be an exclusive club. With it I could travel the globe, be accepted by my peers and with a bit of luck fulfil my destiny. I was to learn so much more in the voyages to come. Voyages to countries I may only have heard of in geography lessons at school. Maybe I had seen them on weekly trips to the pictures and perhaps seen them on the Gaumont British News; the pictures that in those days were a major part of our limited entertainment opportunities. I felt the main thing was that life now seemed to have a purpose. I was needed and a part of what seemed a special, formidable, elite group of lads and men. I felt we occupied a special place in life's pecking order. I felt that I now counted.

Chapter Twelve

Is my letter here Mum? Her face told me the answer; it had been the same question every night and the same sad shrug in response. I knew she shared my growing disappointment. I had just come home from the casual job I was doing in the waiting time between leaving the sea school and joining my first ship. I was working for a family friend in his little groundwork company. Little being the right word as I recall it. The company had three workers, Ernie the boss, me and another Bill Horwood, a cousin of the one who had influenced my decision to join the Merchant Navy. Bill was a nice quiet guy. Ernie, a Geordie, was married to Joyce a lovely girl and local beauty from another respected family the Cadmores.

In those days most families in Mill End knew one another. Our parents were often friends of long standing. Our little outpost was small and strangers coming there stood out. Many of the local families were connected by blood and marriage. It was safe and secure, but for some it could get a bit stifling. I was one of those who found it stifling. Bill was a young married man with young children. He, like many others, had completed his term of National Service fighting communists in the jungle during the Malayan emergency. Fortunately he had returned safely.

After a lot of prompting from me he would regale us with stories of his times on jungle patrols and ambushes he was involved in. We listened with bated breath. Bill painted very lurid tales of life in the jungle.   We munched on thick cheese sandwiches and drank mugs of hot sweet tea, while we sat on boxes and bags of cement.

"Bill, did you kill anyone?" I asked while pouring another cuppa. I couldn't stop myself from blurting it out. A luxury allowed only to the young.

I was seventeen going on eighteen. Bill I think was twenty-four. Our boss Ernie was in his mid-thirties. He had served in the Navy during the war and had seen action.   I think my imminent departure for places unknown and Bill's stirring tales of action in the jungle had awakened a dormant need for excitement that was lurking in Ernie. Was it a hangover from his Second World War days? That was probably a situation faced by many ex-servicemen and women.   A vexatious product of those post war years, maybe. It must have taken a lot of courage of a different sort to settle down to the eight to five just survive mantra. Something I was not then and never would be able to do. Good luck Ernie, I thought to myself, I'm off.

I had a rather more acute interest in Bill's army tales. National Service was still a compulsory part of life for all lads of eighteen years of age. It was a fact that joining the Merchant Navy, then more importantly serving till you were twenty-six, exempted you from having to do this much feared stint in the services. It was an added incentive to answering the call of the romance and lure of the sea. So, off to foreign ports and not least of all to the welcoming ladies who, I had been absolutely assured would be excitedly waiting for me. As the Vindi legend had it they preferred English boys above all others. I had no reason to question that. After all I knew from school, that everything coloured red on the geography maps was ours. Funny but not much of that red trickled down to where we were.

So there it is, I don't really care if you call me an army dodger, the popular title that we heroic volunteer young seamen had to live with. Call me what you like but just let me get to my first ship. Had the shipping office forgotten me? Had they lost my papers? My frustration was building; the waiting was making me irritable. These were the thoughts filling my mind, whilst down in Ernie's trenches. I was furiously digging while I waited for that letter from the shipping office. Where was that letter that would send me on my way? Where was that letter that would to set me free from digging? Sod the army was a thought that figured largely in my mind. They would have to manage without me. This letter would take me to my first ship. This letter was the most important letter of my life up to then and may still be so now, considering the way things have turned out.

"Bill, come on tell us Bill," I almost pleaded. Did you kill any commies?"
Bill shuffled his feet, looked down, then looked up and said, "I was in some fire fights and some ambushes. I did my share of the shooting. Sometimes there were casualties and we would find some bodies." His face looking grimmer, "But the jungle, the stress and excitement of the fire fight, made it very hard to be sure who actually made the hits." Thinking about his answer now causes me to reassess Bill. Not only was he a very nice guy, but also his answer showed him to be a thoughtful and considerate man. It was the answer of a wise man, one who had been shaped by his experience. Over the years I reflected on Bill's answer a lot. Mainly, when thinking of similar types of life threatening situations I was called on to face. My dangerous times though not being of a military kind, were nevertheless, very testing. There were many very dangerous, scary and life-threatening incidents that somehow, unfortunately, I seemed to attract in my life.

Three weeks had gone by and I still hadn't heard from the shipping office. I was moping and miserable as I walked up the road to our house. It was Friday and Ernie had knocked us off early. I was feeling disappointed. Then it happened; life changed.

"It's here, the letter's here," Mum called out with a broad smile on her face. She must have been watching for me coming home and was walking down the path to meet me. She was triumphantly waving a brown, official looking envelope.

My little town of Rickmansworth was connected to London by the Metropolitan railway line. In those days it was a good thirty minutes train ride to Baker Street. It was such a contrast leaving Ricky and the rolling countryside and the foothills of the gorgeous Chilterns. It was a world apart from my destination, the bustling London docks. Rickmansworth station has always held fond memories for me. It was the hub of local activity and it was and still is, a classic example of early railway station design. It featured graceful curved overhanging roofs and lovely, cast-iron, filigreed arches and beams. A ladies only waiting room, a small tearoom, trolleys and handbarrows. Old fashioned metal advertising boards, featuring Capstan Plain cigarettes, the unfiltered one with the sailor on the packet. Colourful Gold flake and John Player cigarette boards featured as well. There was always a porter or two present. Presiding over all this was the very important Station Master. He was the type of man that exuded authority. This particular gentleman ruled his domain with a rod of iron. In those days stations were safe, peaceful havens.

It was early September 1955, about eight o'clock on a Monday morning. A van driver friend Les had picked me up from home and dropped me off at the station. Les had departed with a few ribald comments about painful hospital treatments that would await me should I be a naughty boy. Dad had given me a similar lecture the night before. Ernie and Bill had previously taken great delight in providing very graphic details of embarrassing situations suffered by friends who had found they needed treatment for "that sort of problem". Funny that it was always their friends they spoke of!   These stories were accompanied by lurid descriptions and warnings. Apparently I could lose a prized part of my anatomy if I was not very careful. They had a lot of fun with this banter, as I did, but I don't think Dad found it quite such an entertaining topic.

I find myself waiting on the platform for the train to Baker St. My feeling of importance is heightened as I check again, the inside pocket that holds my so very important Discharge Book. Also the letter commanding my presence in the shipping office at the King George V Dock in London, known to us as "the Pool" is attached to it. Dad's huge old khaki army holdall is at my feet. It is filled fit to burst. It just holds the kit that I was instructed to bring with me. I have squeezed in a few favourite shirts and trousers. Later on the train, a thought struck me about Dad's holdall. It had gone with him through the Egyptian, the Libyan and Italian campaigns of the Second World War. Fortunately he had returned safely, with the, by then rather battered, holdall. I hoped it would be a good talisman and companion for me, as it had been for him. And so it proved to be.

I stood there on the platform. I was proudly wearing my prized blue diagonal three-piece, four-button suit with its velvet collar. That was the badge of young rebellion at the time. I felt no fear, just excitement; my new life was now definitely beginning. The Station Master strode out of his office, studying a large pocket watch in his hand. An air of expectancy enveloped the platform. A shrill whistle blew in the distance. Then around the bend, spitting steam, chugged the big black engine, towing its brown carriages which looked for all the world like a line of ducklings dutifully following their mother. Belching and hissing the train came noisily to a stop. The waiting passengers surged forward. I picked up my holdall and was almost propelled aboard and into a carriage. I heaved my holdall up into the luggage rack. I bumped another passenger as I swung it up. "Sorry, very sorry," I said as I turned to take a seat. I was startled to find that I was surrounded by city toffs on the way to their offices. There had been a bit of a scramble to get on the train, the station was always very busy at that time of day. In my rush, I had parked myself in the first class section. A couple of the toffs looked at me with something bordering on disdain in their eyes. It's the velvet collar, I decided. What to do? I decided to stay put, so without being belligerent, I returned the look and then smiled. They know and I know; it's an unspoken thing. I have thrown it into their lap. I carry on looking. They get behind their copies of the Times and it's over! About then I notice that they also all wear their badge. There they are for all to see. Just as mine is a velvet collar, theirs is a bowler hat. It's a funny thing about life; we're all in one tribe or another.

The first stop along the way is Moor Park. It had lovely wide tree lined roads. Its wide pavements had large grassy areas dotted with plants and bushes and the big houses with beautifully manicured gardens stood back on large plots of land. It was as pretty as any residential spot as you could find anywhere in the wealthy southeast. Moor Park was at that time and is still today, a desirable upmarket snooty haven. In case you are thinking I am too biased in these matters, I firmly believe, that there is always room for a bit of snobbery in life. I think it adds a bit of spice. I have found it exists in all societies. In fact I think it's a good thing. It allows people to express themselves and their chosen lifestyle. I also think there's nothing wrong with a working class lad like me picking a few holes in it from time to time. And anyway, I think a system where a chosen few hog most of the perks in life created a great incentive for the more rebellious types amongst us to emigrate to far off British Commonwealth countries. Whilst on that particular subject, I still wonder where the wealth in Commonwealth went. Not to the commoners, I would suggest.

The Moor Park Mansion House has been the home to many famous and infamous characters. The one whose star shines the brightest in local folk law is Cardinal Wolsey. The Cardinal acquired the Tenancy in 1524. At the time he was a close confidante, advisor and Chancellor to King Henry VIII. The King was the source of Wolsey's wealth and power. It was here in the Mansion, often visited by Henry and Anne Boleyn, that the King declared his love of the beautiful Anne. It transpired that the King asked Wolsey for his assistance in persuading Queen Catherine to give him a divorce, making a marriage to Anne possible. Wolsey's efforts were to no avail; in fact the King suspected Wolsey efforts had hindered his case. Wolsey, who had enjoyed many years of patronage from the King, then found himself rather on the outer - a dangerous position in the Tudor court. The King eventually persuaded Catherine to give him his divorce. This put old Wolsey in a bit of a tight spot, because as Cardinal, he found it necessary to refuse to sanction the divorce. This rather upset good old King Henry, which was not a clever thing to do. The King responded by stripping the now forlorn Wolsey of his titles, money and properties. There must be a lesson, to be learnt in there somewhere.

Of the succeeding owners, the one that interests me most is a certain gentleman named Benjamin Styles. Mr Styles purchased the Mansion in 1720. He purchased it, with his ill-gotten gains from the South Sea Bubble. The South Sea Bubble is considered to be the first recorded insider-trading rip off. A body called the South Sea Trading Company was formed by various luminaries of the day. This company was granted a monopoly to trade in the South Pacific, in return for bailing out the government debt. With much hoo-ha the company started trading and promoting itself and extolling the potential riches of the South Seas. Come in suckers, may just as well have been their logo. As is the way of business, there are winners and losers; some later tales will bear this out. Mr Styles was definitely a winner. It transpired that the main success of the company and its business was its ability to talk up its shares (sound familiar?) Mr Styles was very well positioned to make a fortune from this venture. Conveniently his brother-in-law, a certain gentleman and I use the term loosely, Sir John Eyles was the Sub-Governor of the company. Sir John with his inside knowledge was in a position to know the game would shortly be up. By now the shares had been artificially pushed higher and higher. Fortuitously Mr. Styles was advised by his brother-in-law to sell up before the bubble burst. Styles, following his brother-in law's advice, carefully arranged to sell his shares slowly, so as not to cause alarm. With perfect timing he managed to sell his shares at very inflated prices giving him a huge profit. Sometime later the company collapsed. Our old friend Styles had made his money and lots of it. And he didn't even have to climb in a window or do an honest day's work with a hacksaw. The good Sir John, well looked after no doubt, would have been smiling too. Meanwhile back at street level there were thousands of smaller investors left destitute. They were now seriously regretting their unwise dabble in the share market and following the advice of their 'betters'. It does sound a rather familiar story, don't you think. That little episode took place three hundred years ago. Will we ever learn?

Chapter Thirteen

"Russell, Sidney Leonard, deck boy," shouts the hassled looking man behind the counter. It has protective metal bars running up almost to the ceiling. I am in the shipping office in the Port of London, situated at the beginning of the King George V dock. There are lines of ships moored as far as the eye can see. Huge cranes, looking like a swarm of praying mantises, were swinging their arms out over the ships. Tractors pulling rows of trolleys were busily hauling to and fro along the wharves. They vanished into the giant warehouses. Their open doors were like the gaping mouths of monsters demanding constant feeding. Dockers were shouting and sweating as they manhandled frozen carcasses out of the cargo lifting nets and onto the jitney trolleys. It was Bedlam but organized Bedlam, if there could be such a thing.

"Russell," the call echoed again. I was still standing by the window and was fascinated by what I was seeing and lost in thought. I came back to life with a startled, "Here, here, I'm here sir."
"Over here, boy," he replied. I picked up my holdall and scrambled over to him. I handed over my precious discharge book. He already had my letter, which I'd supplied when I'd come in.
"Right, Russell, here's a job for you. Deck Boy on the Highland Monarch and you're off to Argentina.

You'll be away for eleven weeks. The shore supervisor will be signing the crew in the first class dining room at ten o'clock in the morning," he barked. "The first mate will be there to check the deck crowd."

"Where do I go?" I managed to stammer. I felt that all eyes were upon me and knew I was a first tripper.

"You go straight down the KG V dock on this side. You'll find her down there. She's on berth nine."

He handed me a shipping office appointment docket.

"Give this to the First Mate or the Bosun. You'll be okay, now get along."

So I joined the madding crowd. I was very pleased to have left the shipping office; the atmosphere in there had been pungent. Smoke had hung heavily in the air, competing with other unpleasant odours. Most of the seamen who were hanging around in there looking for jobs appeared to be suffering from hangovers and looked much the worse for wear and very unkempt. A few of them, mainly the younger ones, were smart and well dressed. Like me they appeared to want to get a ship and get out of there as soon as possible. I set off down KG V looking for my first ship. I felt pleased with myself and assumed a swagger as I walked. In my ignorance I expected a short stroll, how wrong I was. Dad's holdall soon started to feel heavy. I dodged trolleys; I dodged dockers. I avoided great swinging hooks gouging into big bales of wool. It was go, go, go, on the London Docks. The holdall was cutting into my palm and I had to keep changing it from hand to hand and keep moving in this maelstrom of activity. I felt like I had tumbled into a mad, noisy and strange world that probably couldn't exist in the same universe as Mill End. My nostrils were picking up strange new smells from the oily water splashing against the wharf pilings. This mixed in with the aroma of various foodstuffs and spicy products being unloaded by the swearing, sweating dockers. They were a breed of men completely alien to me. They were the real East Enders and proud of it. They were tough men doing a tough job. Remember this was all prior to the containerisation system introduced in the mid-sixties. A system that completely changed the way goods were shipped and cargoes were handled. I struggled on. I must have looked a bit strange in this environment. There I was, decked out in my full Teddy Boy regalia and humping a huge ex-army holdall. The spectacle drew plenty of good-natured comments from the dockers and stevedores as I passed. The ribald cockney humour followed me down the dock, from shed to shed, from crane to crane. Some of it very original, alluding to other heavy ugly bags I must have carried the night before! I managed to muster a smile in return, but any vestige of the original swagger I had assumed when starting this walk, was now completely gone. Then

I was saved from further torment. I saw a great big 'NINE' painted on the sidewall of a massive warehouse. With huge relief I dropped the holdall like a hot brick. By now I was gulping air like a drowning man. I turned and looked up and there, towering above me, was the great black iron plated hull of a moored ship. At last and very tired I had found her, my first ship. Painted in large gold letters on that great black hull I read the words that were a harbinger of a new life - *Highland Monarch*.

"You look like the new Deck Boy," were the words that greeted me as I struggled to the top of the gangway. Dad's old army holdall felt twice as heavy now, but I tried not to let that show. From now on it was imperative that I hid any weakness.
"First trip?" he asked.
"Yes, the man at the Pool office sent me, here's the letter he gave me."
I was talking to a smart, handsome, youngish man of about twenty-four or so. He was dressed in a crisp, white sailor's uniform. He was sun-tanned and confident. Unlike me who was pale, skinny and nervous. I needed to change that. I discovered later that he was a Quartermaster who regularly sailed on the Royal Mail Line ships. The QM's as they were known were a part of the Deck Department, enjoying a slightly exalted position above the rest of the deck crowd. They had special duties some of which required them and only them, to wear the traditional sailor's uniform, even

though we were Merchant Navy. Ah well, I was used to weird rituals; I'd been a caddie at Moor Park. The QM's were always to be found on ships that carried passengers. They manned the gangways, generally did most of the steering and bridge duties, particularly if a pilot was on board. Often, they were also used as window dressing in functions to do with passengers, posing in their crisp white uniforms and sailor hats. And yes, we were a bit jealous of them. Maybe that's where the saying 'all the nice girls love a sailor' comes from; they say it's all in the uniform.

"Right," said the QM, "go along to the Deckies Mess Room for'd."
This was sailor speak for 'forward' as opposed to 'aft'. I had picked this abbreviation up from my time at the Vindi and I had been addressed in sailor speak for the first time and understood it. It felt like that was a good start. He pointed, along the working alleyway.
"Keep going along to the fo'csle. The mess room is in there, you should find the Bosun then, or just ask; he won't be far away. And good luck," he added.
Maybe he remembered his own first trip and the trepidation that went with it.

"Watch yourself, look out, look out," a docker was shouting as he struggled through the throng. The starboard, working alley was a hive of activity with people hurrying and scurrying. Dockers pushing through, no beg your pardons here; everybody in a hurry. I was to learn that this was always the way of things in the days prior to a ship sailing; the tempo building up the closer it got to cast-off time. 'Let go forward, let go aft.' This was the shout we all anxiously waited to hear, some with more reason than others to put England and the laws of the land behind them. I still had to find the Bosun. I had to get signed on and be assigned to my shared cabin. However, we were sailing and those matters were just procedural. I was leaving the shores of my homeland for the first time. Somewhere in the shadow world that accompanies me, an umbilical cord had been cut.

This Bosun, whom I hadn't yet met, was to become a great influence on me during the next twelve months. The Bosun was the main man on-board as far as the deck crowd was concerned. He was the law, the Sergeant, he who must be obeyed. Even the officers deferred to him. Imagine a company Sergeant Major in the army; our Bosuns enjoyed roughly the same status and respect. I was to find that he could make the trip good and exciting, or if you foolishly crossed him, he could make the trip a nightmare. I was lucky; the Bosun on Highland Monarch at that time was a good one. I was to do three trips down to Argentina on this Royal Mail passenger cargo liner with him. Unfortunately during the last one we suffered a major accident in which the Bosun lost his life. The longer I was on ships, the more I realised that accidents at sea carried far more danger than the equivalent on dry land with their nearby hospitals. In this one the Bosun paid the highest possible price with two more of the able bodied seamen very badly injured; in fact one was crippled for life. We treated them on-board, as we carried a doctor and a nurse and headed for Buenos Aires, the nearest place with adequate hospital facilities, but we had to transfer them ashore and leave them there. I was very lucky to escape the accident. The Bosun had sent me up on deck to help out there. I had been working in the 'tween decks with the Bosun's gang, where the accident occurred. I was eighteen at the time and I can only assume it wasn't meant for me to be one of the injured or dead. Fate, or just dumb luck? I believe it's fate, but of course we can't prove it either way.

As my confidence at sea grew I really started to enjoy the South American run. In all, I did five trips down there. Apart from the one in which we had the accident, they were great fun. I made friends in Buenos Aires and Rio de Janeiro. They were very hospitable people. I was shown their great cities away from just the dock areas. I got very close to one family, but they suddenly disappeared. I was given to understand that the father had been arrested on some political charge. Argentina was a politically turbulent place at the time. The Peron problems were still fresh and the Police and the Army were an intrusive and ever-present aspect of Argentinean life. I called again to try to see my friends, but their neighbours advised me to stay away. I often wondered how they fared. I hope they were okay, they were very nice people, but the country was littered with the victims of political abuse from a repressive regime.

Our first port of call was always Vigo, one of the harbours on the west coast of Spain, to pick up hordes of Spanish immigrants bound for Argentina. They were looking for a better life, the driving force that feeds all emigration everywhere. We usually took them on board in the Spanish port of Vigo. This was no luxury liner for them. They were crammed into dormitory type accommodation. The men and boys separated from the women and children. Some parts of their accommodation were situated under the waterline in the stern of the ship. I saw the hope for the future written on the faces of the adults as they streamed excitedly on board. I hoped that it was enough to overcome the disappointment of the cramped, difficult conditions they were being herded into. I was to learn that this had been the fate of all assisted migrants since these great population shifts started. They didn't' really care how they got to their new worlds; the thing was to get there. I realised that like me, they had dreams of a better life awaiting them. And if you think about it, this was probably exactly the same impulse that got our distant ancestors out of Africa all those hundreds of thousands of years ago and out into Europe and eventually the whole world.

The ship's siren was starting to sound. This was the first of the warning calls that we should soon be sailing. The next siren blast was repeated a bit louder and longer. This was the last call for the crewmembers not on duty, who had gone ashore to slake their thirst. It was the last opportunity for about eighteen days to do so on dry land and perhaps to spend a little time with one of the senoritas who were readily available in the waterfront bars. Many a young British sailor enjoyed and supported these bars. Remember that the average age of the deck crew was only twenty-one, at most twenty-two. Remember how you, the male readers behaved at that age; but probably without the temptations and opportunities that presented themselves to us. One more blast on the siren. It's getting urgent now, so the second officer has been sent ashore with a couple of QM's and the Bosun to round up the stragglers. Most of them were very much the worse the wear from drink. Once they were rounded up and led on board and the new stores taken on and the cargo loading finished we were ready to depart. The deck crew were battening down everything and making ready for sea. The Bosun and First Officer took their supervisory positions on the foredeck.

The last minute shrill calls on the ship's siren were blasted out and we were going. We Deckies would take our positions to release the great thick ropes and wire hawsers that bound us to the quay. The engines came to life with a thunderous roar. The ship vibrated, the tugs had taken up positions fore and aft and the gangway was up now. "Let go for'd," came the cry; the bow starts to swing out. "Let go aft," called to the second mate in charge at the stern. We drifted out into the stream, the tugs fussing around us, carefully heading us towards the open sea. Outside of the harbour we turned and set course into the Atlantic. We steamed onwards, down to the warm climes of the equatorial Atlantic Ocean.

That first trip was an experience that has stayed with me all my life. I was to go on and make many trips to a multitude of countries and locations, but during my first trip, full of innocence, I was hypnotised and captured by the balmy days, sunshine, blue skies and the clear green ocean. I remember it now as if it were yesterday, standing in the bow and watching the stem of the Monarch cutting through the water. I was captivated by the porpoises as they played their seemingly choreographed game. They were cutting dangerously close across the bow of the ship in unison. Then diving and leaping as if in a dance. I could feel their joy. It was as if they knew they were performing for a very appreciative audience and perhaps they did. I can still feel the sunshine on my body and hear the seagulls wheeling above the ship as if to music. Every waking moment, in every day, was a new experience that I couldn't wait to savour. I would get up early in the mornings and join my shipmates in holystoning and washing down the decks. My naivety and enthusiasm for this new life knew no bounds and made it into something so very special. So much so, that now, fifty-three years on, the impressions it made were so strongly etched that I can relive those wonderful days. Perhaps joyous memories are life's greatest riches.

We were heading for the east coast of South America. There we would visit exotic countries such as Brazil and Uruguay and then head for our final destination, the great city of Buenos Aries and the capital city of Argentina. What a magnificent experience for seasoned travellers, let alone a seventeen-year-old boy from the lovely, but hick, town of Rickmansworth. We started on what was called the deep-sea dive down the east coast of South America. We were calling into such fabulous ports as Rio de Janeiro and Santos, in Brazil, then Montevideo in Uruguay. I was to sail into many ports on my future trips, but few had the same majesty as Rio de Janeiro. I was woken by the Charley the Senior Ordinary Seaman of the four to eight watch. "Come on," he said, "We'll be in Rio in an hour and the Bosun wants you on deck." It was about five o'clock. I scrambled, bleary eyed, out of my bunk, grabbed my shorts and a tee shirt. Charley was still trying to wake the other two lads, both Junior Ordinary Seamen. If it were a competition they could have slept for England. I made my way up to the foredeck and reported to the Bosun.

"Okay, young Russell," he said, "I want you to stay with me and be my runner." He broke off the conversation to give an instruction to one of the AB's. Turning back to me he said, "Just don't get in the way when we start to go alongside in Rio. Stay behind Steve and do what he tells you."

Steve was the lamp trimmer, a hangover name from earlier days of sailing ships.

"Steve's on the main winch. Stand behind him and help coil the heavy rope as it comes off the main drum."

The Bosun, whose name was Allen, was a man of about fifty, he was an impressive figure. He was slim and tanned from a lifetime at sea. He had, like most seaman of his age; served through the war years and he had been torpedoed twice, one time having spent six days in a lifeboat on the open ocean before being rescued. Allen was a hard man, but a fair one. He was a classical music fan and well read, as the bookshelves in his cabin attested. He enjoyed the respect of all. He knew his job and an air of confidence surrounded him. He and his type were the sort who held everything together, particularly when under pressure. They were the cement that held together a great nation and empire. They contributed as much as the great generals, governors and explorers who were the ones who enjoyed all the acknowledgement and fame. I believe that their achievements, however great, were built on the backs of people like Allen, the Bosun on the Highland Monarch.

By now it was about six o'clock in the morning. We were steaming for Guanabara Bay and it was like an inland sea. The capital city, Rio de Janeiro, as it was then, was built around a river that flowed into that huge bay. The city took its name from it, the River of January. As we were reaching for the city, the amazing Sugar Loaf Mountain came into view. What a spectacle it was. This was Rio's calling card; you could compare it to The Statue of Liberty in New York, or The Golden Gate in San Francisco, or as I was later to find out, Rangitoto Island in Auckland Harbour. These iconic features, which are so recognisable, serve as inviting butlers for those great cities. After that spellbinding sight, towering above the city, one sees the Corcovado Mountain rising two thousand three hundred feet high. It is topped by the magnificent statue of Jesus with outstretched arms, one-hundred-and-thirty feet tall overlooking the city and harbour. What a statement it made. The sight of it was mighty impressive, but the intended message was probably more so. In 2007 that monument, the

'Christ Redentor', was named as one of the new Seven Wonders of the World. It gave me a secret pleasure to know that I had been privileged to see it as a very young man and recognise its grandeur then and know that I was seeing something so very special.

I had run a couple of messages for the Bosun and I'd got back in time to support Steve on the big forecastle winch. We had picked up the pilot and he guided us into the port and to our berth. Steve, who was very experienced, handled that heavy rope on the winch drum with great expertise. He had to hold the tension when instructed, holding it steady on the big winch drum, or else be prepared to feed it out quickly if called upon. This was a technique that only came with experience. Steve had plenty of that and I felt safe behind him. There have been accidents during that manoeuvre of coming alongside. The man on the main winch had to be alert for a sudden swing of the ship. A swing could easily be caused by a current. Sometimes it could be an offshore wind shift. Or even possibly a sudden pressure from the tugs. If that first main hawser wasn't released quickly enough and snapped, it cracked like a gunshot and snaked across the deck with tremendous force. That happened on a later ship I was on. Luckily the result wasn't fatal, but the AB had his leg very badly fractured. We had to pay him off and leave him behind in a local hospital. Such is the way with accidents on ships.

Later that day, when we had some time off, a few of us went ashore together. Some of the guys had been there before and knew where to go. I was very surprised not to be led to one of the red light districts. We all piled into a couple of taxis, happy and enjoying some time on land after the sixteen-day dive to Rio. We had a rattle of a ride seeing parts of the city and then we were dropped off at the famous Copacabana Beach. I hadn't heard of it and maybe in 1955 not too many others had either. We settled into a waterfront bar and were served with icy cold local lagers. We sat outside in a comfortable seating area. The beer was so different from the warmish English ale we were used to. It was so cold that it made me feel like I had a steel band tightening around my forehead. We sat there in the balmy late afternoon sunshine. Lovely bikini-clad girls with their boyfriends walked the gorgeous beach. Family groups were casually strolling together. Some were enjoying games of football. Some a hand tennis game, rather like deck tennis. It seemed a very sophisticated and comfortable lifestyle. I almost wondered if I had died and gone to heaven. I sat there and sipped my lager and knew that I had been transported into a different world. This first look at Rio was however balanced out more evenly on subsequent trips. Like most great cities it also suffered from extreme poverty, which was not to be seen around the upmarket Copacabana district. We were urged to be very careful where we spent our time ashore. It was dangerous to wander in certain districts on your own. We always travelled in groups and there were always a couple of guys in the crowd who knew the ropes from previous trips.

I think we only spent two quiet nights in Rio. This was acting to a pre-prepared plan, whereby we had all agreed to be good boys and save our money for a magic time in Montevideo. This plan had been instigated by a seaman called Ginger, who claimed to have amazing contacts there from his last trip. His graphic descriptions of the pleasures that awaited us had fanned us young guys into a lather of sexual expectation. We stuck rigorously to the plan while in Rio and saved our pennies. We withstood some intense provocation and pressure from very beautiful Brazilian working girls, which was remarkable given we had been at sea for three weeks. We didn't have the normal restraints that would have applied in our hometowns.

We cast off from Rio and I think it is fair to say that we four young seamen carried out our duties with even more enthusiasm than usual. As we cleared the port and turned into the river we slapped each other on the back laughing and joking about our planned debauchery, which was now close to hand. A quick trip into Santos, a day's steaming down the coast; berth there for one day and then on to our Latin American 'Nirvana' where Ginger's girls awaited us.

We had just steamed down the river and were about to turn into the Bay. We four were leaning over the rails having a cup of tea and boasting about our (mostly illusory) prowess with the ladies and past conquests. I remember turning to Ginger and saying that when his girl saw me she would probably ditch him and I doubted that I would have to pay either. This boasting young man's talk all came to a shuddering halt, literally. We had run aground. The whole ship shuddered, the rails we had been leaning on shook. Allen, the Bosun, reacted very quickly. Without instruction from the bridge, he quickly marshalled the deck crowd. He detailed us to return to our berthing stations and await further instructions. There wasn't much we could do at that point, but his action made sure that we were spread around the ship evenly and were available for a quick response if needed. All thoughts of "Monte" and the girls disappeared; this was serious business. We were taught very early and continually, that a condition known as 'safety of the ship' took precedence over all other concerns. While this turned out not to be a major incident, it could well have been. The main danger to a ship, which runs aground, is the very strong possibility of significant holing below the water line. While there was no panic, an air of determination and resolution involving all hands could be felt. Nothing is left to chance in safety of the ship situations. Fortunately this grounding was to prove a minor one damage wise. Groundings though are considered a very serious business and an official enquiry will always follow.

The bridge immediately ran up warning flags. We were in a busy shipping lane and our plight had to be signalled as clearly as possible. The decks shook as the powerful engines were thrust into reverse, in the first attempt to free ourselves. The slow build up of power from the engines could be felt vibrating through the soles of your feet. The roar of the engines, the shaking of the sturdy steel handrails, the reverberation of the steel bulkheads. All this left us in no doubt that we were well and truly aground and could not be shifted under our own steam.

The girls in Monte would have to contain themselves for an extra couple of days. We were eventually freed by a battery of heavy tugs and commenced our journey down the coast. We kept to our planned itinerary and stopped overnight in the port of Santos. We went ashore that night for a look around and a couple of drinks. Eventually we found ourselves in a street called General Camara Street in the red light district and we settled into the Midnight Sun Bar. We were instantly surrounded by giggling girls wanting us to buy drinks for them. They were offering every sexual practice ever heard of. They were very skilled in the art of persuading sailors upstairs. They positioned themselves erotically, sitting on the edge of the tables. It was as though they were on a perch, with their feet on the chairs, blatantly crossing and uncrossing their legs. They mesmerized us, flashing tantalizing glimpses of their inside thighs and more. I had never seen the like of this in the Cart and Horses in Ricky. (On the other hand, although not done so artfully, the basics of it were probably practised often enough in Liverpool.) However, they were very pretty girls and it's hard to blame them for their scornful abuse of us. They couldn't really be blamed for calling us Senorita Boys. Still, we stuck determinedly to our plan of saving ourselves and our money for Monte. "This better be worth it," Ginger was told, "otherwise you're in the barrel." This threat is well known to all as the sailor's greatest fear since time immemorial. Beware Ginger.

We cast off early in the morning and headed south again. We were well down in the South Atlantic Ocean now. It was balmy weather. Everybody was in high spirits; Monte and Buenos Aries were ports that all the crew enjoyed. Not just for the women and the bars. The restaurants were a great attraction, along with the markets, theatres and generally laid back atmosphere. A good time could be had here, regardless of your persuasion. We cruised on for two more days eventually arriving at and then entering, the estuary of the mighty River Plate. We steamed into Montevideo, in Uruguay; where the famous 'Battle of the River Plate' was fought. When British ships called in to Monte there was always great excitement. The older hands were happy to air their knowledge, pointing out where the badly damaged German Pocket Battleship, Admiral Graf Spee, lay. She was scuttled by her Captain, Hans Lansdoff. Apparently he preferred that fate, rather than facing the waiting British ships stationed just outside Uruguayan waters. These ships included the New Zealand light cruiser Achilles, which although badly damaged, had acquitted herself so well alongside the Royal Navy Heavy Cruisers Ajax and Exeter. The Royal Navy ships and the Achilles were all heavily damaged from the ferocious exchanges. Although badly outgunned, they had managed to inflict enough damage on the German ship that she was then forced to run for shelter in Montevideo, a neutral port. The Battle of The River Plate was the stuff of legend amongst all Brits and Kiwis, particularly for a seafarer. Being there and feeling the moment gave me a great surge of national pride. This opened huge possibilities for me. Having been there and actually seen the scuttle site first hand I had a tale to regale my friends with back in Rickmansworth and later in New Zealand. I certainly did that and I used it to bolster my growing reputation as a man of the world.

The tugs nursed us alongside. Heaving lines were thrown ashore. We busily tied off our ends to the heavy hawsers. The guys on the docks took up the strain and pulled in the heavy securing lines as we fed them out. They were grunting under the strain as they pulled in the heavy waterlogged ropes. They heaved them up onto the dock then placed the spliced holding eyes onto the bollards. We were secure and the pleasures of Monte awaited us. We finished our tying up tasks and made ready the ships derricks and lifting gear for the Dockers. All was ready and we were free for a few hours. There was always a day or two stay here in Monte.

"C'mon, let's go boys, the steaks and girls are waiting for us," urged Ginger, the cockney lad, who had been on a previous trip and was busily and excitedly organising us. There was no inkling then of what lay in store. We were off to enjoy a real steak meal. Something that we hadn't had a lot of in post-war England. It sounded a great idea to me. A steak that really did cover the huge plate, with a couple of eggs on top, yes please. This gastronomic adventure was then washed down with large jugs of icy cold 'cerveza' the local lager. To me and my colleagues, this represented fine dining at that stage in our young lives. How things would change. I recall that this was the famous 'bife de lomo' (a dish so beloved by us, we ate it on every trip ashore). We ate it in both Monte and Buenos Aries. Looking back I think the bife de lomo was almost, I say almost, enjoyed as much as our happy times with the ever available ladies who haunted the bars and dance halls around the dock areas. Remember, I had it on good authority that these ladies would be waiting and they certainly were. We four made our way ashore. Ginger, having assumed complete control, led us. We wandered around a market and brought a few souvenirs. "There it is," cried Ginger. It was a garishly decorated, run down bar close to the Docks. Ginger assured us we would be royally entertained by the ladies of the house for most of the afternoon. Thanks Ginger, we were. As we departed, the ladies waved 'Good-bye'; I secretly hoped I had not purchased an, 'unwanted souvenir'.

The plastic covered tables, the wooden benches we sat on, not particularly designed for comfort or appearance said everything about the dockside café come restaurant we had stumbled into. We were served by a pretty waitress with long black hair and deep black eyes. I secretly hoped that she was only interested in me. Unfortunately the other three each thought they were the chosen one. As you can well imagine this was starting to cause a bit of friction between us. She flirted with us all so cleverly as she glided around the table, constantly smiling. Her long black lacy skirt creating a tempting, swishing sound. As she brushed against us Isabella often found the need to lean over us and across the table, given the way we positioned and moved the egg yolk and blood stained plates left over from our meals. She was quite alert to what we thought so clever and humorous a trick and just smiled as she stretched across us well aware of the impression she made with her breasts so easily visible in their entirety inside her low cut lacy top. "More drinks?" she asked, with a knowing smile on her face. How could we possibly refuse her anything? At this point she owned us. Four tipsy eighteen-year-olds panting for her. "Yes, yes, more drinks, Isabella," we called in unison each of us vying for her sole attention.

'Tarpaulin muster', was shouted. This was a seafaring custom calling on all present to turn out their pockets and pool their money for the greater good. How easy it must have been for Isabella. This was a game she would regularly have played with naive young sailors of all nationalities. The cruzeiros were scattered on the table along with some English pounds. Whatever currency you had, it all went into the muster. The money was counted out. We had enough left to pay our bill and have another round of beers, plus some to spare. Isabella had been closely watching proceedings and made it plain that she would happily take one of us upstairs for the balance of the money. Now we had a problem. "She's mine, I put in more than the rest of you," seemed to be the uniform position. In our youthful naivety none of us was able to mount a better argument than the monetary one and since we couldn't be sure who had put in what in our tipsy state, we reverted to the age-old practice of drawing lots. The drawer of the short straw was to get this much-desired prize. The great draw had captured the attention of other customers and Isabella's boss. They were now all crowding around our table. Carlos, the owner, who was obviously in on everything, magnanimously offered to conduct the draw. Meanwhile a couple of drunken gay stewards off our ship had minced into the bar, tsk tsking disdainfully at the scene confronting them. They soon changed their attitudes and joining in the spirit of things offered to act as umpires. One of them called himself Grace, the other was known to one and all on board as Beulah Peach. Beulah was really getting into the swing. So much so that after downing some very large rum and cokes he was loudly offering to go upstairs with anybody who wanted him, for free. He was also loudly claiming that he was better in bed than any 'Dago whore'. There were no takers for Beulah; we had different fish to fry. The contestants were getting into a right excitable state, like boxers about to enter the ring, or matadors about to enter the bullring. I don't know about the others, but I swear I could clearly hear the trumpet's call to the matadors, ringing loudly in my ears. Belatedly, the ship's siren, which had probably been sounding for some time, now found some receptors in my brain. A sensible seaman would have answered the call, but we were seamen under the spell of Isabella. It's like that old Greek myth of Odysseus stuck on Circe's Island - I really should be sailing home, but fuck me, look at her breasts. Sailors had been delayed by this sort of things for thousands of years before us.

Carlos had now cut the straws under the watchful eyes of Beulah and Grace. The great casting of lots was about to take place. The contestants were highly and visibly excited. Carlos was caught up in the moment. "Ladies and Gentlemen," he announced as if compere of a boxing match (which he nearly was). Then an elegant pause; the showman inherent in all Latin males coming to the fore. "For Christ's sake get on with it, cut the bullshit," yelled out Scouser in a frenzy of excitement. Crash, right at that moment the doors to the bar were thrust open and there stood the second mate surrounded by QM's, the Bosun, the Lamp Trimmer and the Boson's mate. Talk about an anti-climax.

"Okay boys, that's it, back now or we're going without you and that's straight from the Captain," he said, marching purposely forward.

"Fuck me," yells the disappointed Scouser, "we're about to have the big draw for Isabella." Ever the gentleman in the tradition of his hometown, he turned and looked at her as he said this. She caught the drift of things and quickly exited. Carlos, never one to miss an opportunity, grabbed the money off the table. He then turned to the Second Mate and demanded he got us out of the bar. Further he decided he wanted to lay a complaint against us and wanted damages for breakages. Scouser was incensed at this turn of events and rushed at Carlos swinging wild punches. A melee started. It was quite a scrap, but the combined force of the Second Mate's team, ably supported by Carlos and his bouncer, was too much for our band of brothers. We ended up outside on the street bruised and battered. Our money gone, but our pride not diminished. We were well led by Scouser and we'd left a few bruises of our own on the bodies of the combined and much more experienced opposition. And Isabella? Well her name is an old Hebrew one that means "a promise from God". I'm not sure how accurate that is, but the name cropped up again in my life some years later.

The second mate and his team herded us back down to the docks. We were accompanied by the gay stewards, one of whom had honourably obtained a black eye joining in on our side. We were by now feeling not too bad. Scouser once again took the lead and started bellowing out the ribald version of the old Liverpool anthem, *Maggie May*, the lyrics of which had a certain appropriateness to the evening. The song tells the story of a well-known Liverpool prostitute who specialised in robbing young sailors she'd enticed onto her Lime Street patch. It's a song that every Scouser I ever sailed with would sing sooner or later, depending on his state of inebriation; and to this day I'm a bit prone to hum it quietly myself if I've had a couple of drinks and there's an Isobel, or a Jezebel, or just about any belle in sight.

Back on board arguments raged about whose fault it was and who she really would have fancied. We had received a dressing down from the First Mate and a warning as to future behaviour. It was to his credit, however, that he gave it to us with a twinkle of good will in his eye. We later heard that the Second Mate had given a good account of us, largely blaming Carlos and Isabella. The story had done the rounds with the first class passengers and the Captain's table and had filtered down to the rest of the deck crowd. They mostly expressed regret at not having been there for what became known by all as the Second Battle of the River Plate. Many of them later claimed to have been there and taken part.

An amusing side to the story was how the skirmish grew and got exaggerated in the telling. On a subsequent trip to Argentina, the following conversation took place. I was on the twelve-to-four watch, acting as lookout up in the bow and I was waiting to be relieved by Eddie, the senior ordinary seaman of the next watch. It was going to be a lovely morning; it was just starting to get light.

It was already warm and the sea was as flat as the proverbial millpond. I was looking down watching the bow cutting smoothly through the water, which can be almost hypnotic. Sometimes it's just too nice to turn in and I often used to find a secluded spot and watch the dawn breaking. I really appreciated my good fortune and the freedom of the life I was living. I would never have experienced any dawns as fine as this in good old Mill End. Eddie, a nice guy and a regular on the Highland Boats, joined me. He had developed a little habit of taking a mug of tea on watch and sometimes one for me if he was running a bit late in starting. It was an opportunity to have a chat and a smoke, before trying to get a few hours' sleep in. We were enjoying the balmy conditions and talking about what we would do and where we would be going ashore when we made port. The conversation turned to Montevideo.

"Don't talk to me about Monte," said Eddie, "that's a crap place; you have to be very careful there, they really don't like the English."

"Is that right, Eddie," I said, "why is that?"

"Don't you know about the Highland Monarch Four," he asked incredulously. I said I'd vaguely heard about them and invited him to tell me more.

"Well they were four ordinary seamen on a shore run; one of them was a mate of mine."

"Really, which one?"

"Ginger," he said, "Ginger from Tottenham."

Well I had to give him that one. He carried on.

"They were in this bar minding their own business, when one of them went to help some woman called Isabella who was getting hassled by some drunken German tanker men who were tossing up coins for her. Anyway a massive brawl started and they wrecked the bar and put two of the Germans in hospital."

"Did they really?" I said.

"Yep, the trouble was everybody knows that they like the Germans in Monte, but don't like the English; something to do with the war. Bloody unfair really," said Eddie rather philosophically. "Anyway they got arrested after another scrap with the Police. They were held in the local jail for a couple of days where they got a really rough deal from the police who were in the fight."

Eddie embellished a bit further and told me he was in Monte on the MV Desiado, a Royal Mail ship, at the same time.

"I was lucky," he said, "I was supposed to meet the boys that afternoon. Ginger being a good friend." He carried on with the story. "Yes, I visited them in jail when I heard about the strife they were in and I took them some ciggies and made sure they were all right."

I told him I thought that was top deck of him.

He said "Well you have to help out your mates when they are in trouble, don't you?"

I guess so Eddie and what better way to help than by pushing our little escapade up into a full-blown South Atlantic legend. Seaman's scuttlebutt just keeps growing so I suppose at some point we ended up taking policemen hostage and breaking out of jail in Monte, looping back to the bar and spiriting Isabella away with us on the ship.

But among the real participants the story didn't so much grow as fester. Whenever the incident was brought up and the issues and combatants discussed, poor old Scouser would completely lose his rag. Scouser would only ever refer to Carlos, as Carlos the Bastard, as if that were his full name. Like say, John the Baptist. Not a lot of logic to it, but Scouser pretty much blamed anything bad that happened to him after that on Carlos the Bastard. And I can't say we ever reached agreement about Isabella's preferences, although Isabella, wherever you are – thanks for the insight into how bars and the ancillary industries that feed off them operate. I put what you showed me to good use a few years later.

Chapter Fourteen

The siren boomed out and we took our sailing positions; let go for'd, we swung out, let go aft. Another toot on the siren and then we were steaming up the glorious River Plate. Next stop was Buenos Aries where the passengers would disembark and the general cargo would be unloaded. We spent a couple of nights there and then steamed further upstream to enter the Paraná River and on to the huge abattoirs.

The subsequent trips down to Argentina threw up a few more Carlos's and any number of Isabella's, but I have to say that my most abiding memory of the place is the huge abattoir in Rosario. Here we went alongside and loaded frozen beef and sheep carcasses directly from this massive killing and freezing works. I was amazed at the frenzied activity of the Argentinean Dockers; the loading went on from dawn till late at night. The noise and bustle was continuous. Above the pandemonium could be heard the panicking sounds of the cattle being driven into the killing chains. The smell was intolerable; it hung over Rosario like a cloud that never went away. The slaughter continued twenty-four hours a day, three-hundred-and-sixty-five days a year. This organised slaughter was the lifeblood of Argentina, catering for the insatiable British market. Our cargo was needed for that most British of things "'the Sunday roast dinner'. Again the reader must remember this was 1956 and our roast had not yet been overshadowed by our latter-day obsession, the curry.

We were now in Rosario, Argentina's third largest city. It was inland and three hundred kilometres northwest of Buenos Aires Here we would go alongside and load frozen beef and sheep carcasses. Going ashore in the port area of Rosario was quite an experience and not an advisable thing to do on your own. Wherever I have been in the world, the towns in which the great abattoir freezing works are sited are without exception tough hard towns. They are populated by the tough hard men and women who are employed in them. The job is such that sensitivity is not high on the skills required to be employed in such environments. In my observation this job is not for the faint hearted or those with a delicate constitution. These people have to constantly perform the gruesome requirements, which are required of the men in the killing rooms or on the chains and the other associated, gruesome, smelly and dirty tasks surrounding this work. They all require an aptitude either natural, or acquired, to continually work in this arena. It breeds tough people; there is no other sort that can mentally or physically handle that environment. I am aware that in New Zealand many students became temporary workers in their holidays, as a way of funding themselves through university. In practice that's not nearly the same as the daily grind, year in and year out faced by the permanent workers of the slaughterhouse.

The industrial dockside area of the city of Rosario, remembering that this was in 1956, was a dusty run down area containing the abattoir and cattle holding areas. The port and surrounding district were reminiscent of an old Wild West frontier town complete with cowboys, although here they were called 'Gauchos'. Luckily they didn't wear six shooters, but probably just as deadly were the long knives called 'facons' which they all carried tucked into the back of their waist bands, which held up the baggy trousers they tucked into knee high leather boots. This with a big voluminous coloured neck scarf and a hat was their attire for all seasons and reasons. I was lucky to see real Gauchos who by now no longer wandered the Pampas, but had become ranch hands on the huge ranches that had developed as soon as methods of keeping meat fresh and exportable had become possible. This development had caused them to become highly prized and in demand commodities, valued for their cattle herding and horse riding skills. They were no longer seen as only vagabonds and orphans, the true translation of Gaucho, who had wandered the Pampas living an itinerant lifestyle, shunning the law and creeping civilization. It seemed the sidewalks and the bars readily welcomed the few Gauchos we saw. I think the Argentineans saw in them, the independence and the spirit, with which they had fought the Spanish to achieve their country's freedom. They confined their drinking, celebrating and womanising to the dockside bars and bordellos. I remember that the local armed police made no bones about it, as they didn't want them carousing in the city proper. I think that arrangement suited the Gauchos as well. They got away with a lot more hell-raising than they might otherwise have. It was probably a part of the deal. To the casual observer they appeared very frightening, but in truth they were just letting their hair down as we did. They reminded me of seamen enjoying themselves while in port after a long voyage, but with a huge touch of Latin gusto thrown in. The difference wasn't in lifestyle; we both earned our livings in sometimes harsh and sometimes dangerous conditions, away from home and loved ones. The difference was that their sea was the vast Pampas, which gave them their livelihood, as the sea in turn did so for us. They had the weather-beaten look of men who worked in all weathers. Their calling was hard and as a consequence, like us, they played hard. I suppose my bargee breeding, which stretched way back to 1826, has always caused me to see similarities with our ethnic groups and to view them with great interest. Since that time my family had continually lived, worked, bred and died on or around the barges on the Grand Union Canal. For those reasons, the Gauchos of Argentina aroused my considerable interest. As in them, I sensed a strange similarity of past lives.

I was struck by the magnitude of the foreboding abattoirs of Rosario; the continuous loading of the frozen carcasses was amazing. It operated like a huge conveyer belt. Live cows being herded in from the holding paddocks to the slaughter men. Viewing this kaleidoscopic scene from high up on the wing of the bridge, it was a moving tapestry, a huge killing machine that never seemed to slow down or stop. It appeared that simultaneously a matching number of beasts were entering the killing area as were spewing out from the dark, cavernous bowels of this slaughterhouse, as carcasses. Death does have a stench, not just the blood and guts, there was something deeper, something necessary, but sad hung in the air and it must invade the very soul of the habitué's of the slaughter house. Many years later, I was relating this experience to a friend of mine in Auckland. So before leaving this part of the tale, I feel it may be appropriate to repeat this conversation between me and an old hand Auckland Westfield freezing company worker. I was talking to a great Maori mate of mine, Tommy Abrahams, who at the time had become a wharfie. Over a drink one afternoon I naively questioned Tommy about life in the works and the disposal and use of various body parts, some of which I assumed were wasted. Surely the hoofs must get thrown out, I argued. He roundly dismissed any suggestions I made.

"Look Len," he said getting a fed up look on his face, "it's like this, the cow goes in one end, it gets killed, it gets processed and everything gets used."

"Everything?"

"Yes Len, for the last time, everything, the only thing we don't use is the MOO".

It transpired that like most Argentinean cities, towns and villages, there were always well-equipped boxing clubs at hand. It seemed that there was one operating on every street corner. To take this story further I have to introduce a character known as 'Slinky Inky'. As his name suggests he was the ship's printer. I also have to move us forward to the Highland Monarch's next trip, which I had happily signed on for again. I was to complete three trips on her before I eventually spread my wings and then it was to her sister ships, Highland Brigade and later, Highland Chieftain. 'Slinky Inky' or, just 'Inky', as he was also called, was an old boxing type, the sort who hangs around gyms hoping to find a meal ticket and a champion. Then on the side they wheel and deal to squeeze a meagre living from the sport, though sometimes that's barely available in professional boxing. In later years, in my boxing promoting period, I was to meet and be plagued by many Inkys. However, let's go back to Rosario. Inky had made contact with one of the small time promoters who spend their lives around the gyms waiting for the big opportunity. When he met up with our Inky he knew he had just found one. It was later disclosed that they had made a plan to promote a boxing tournament in Rosario from which they would split the profits on a fifty/fifty basis. It was to feature boxers from the Highland Monarch versus local amateurs; I stress local amateurs, novices like us, well that's what good old Inky told us!

Inky had got a few of us training in the evenings; we would use the deck space surrounding the for'd hatch. We had been at it for about three weeks since we had left Vigo in Spain. I have to give it to Inky, he knew his stuff. He had punch bags, medicine balls, oversize sparring gloves and even speedball gloves. He knew when to encourage and when to complain. He was lucky in that one of the new catering crew was a successful amateur boxer. He had just completed his national service in the army, where he had achieved real celebrity status as a top army boxer. Now he was more than happy to join Inky and his eager, but misguided, band of innocents. The army boxer was just twenty-two; and as I recall, his name was Terry. He had been and still was a top class amateur and a London boy and had fought for and won, Amateur Boxing Association titles. This was a godsend for Inky, but as it happened, a nightmare for us other willing mugs. In an effort to make things clear, I had better explain the circumstances surrounding the pending promotion. We, that is, the volunteer boxers, were rather enjoying the shipboard interest in the upcoming event. Our training evenings were watched with greater and greater attention and we, the heroes of the hour, were milking it and enjoying the little bit of celebrity status. But as in all things, there is a price to pay. When we arrived in Rosario we were staggered to find that the promotion was not just the talk of the downtown area, it was dominating things in Rosario proper. The local promoter had papered the city with posters. While that in itself was good; it was a tad disquieting to find out that we were billed as 'The British Merchant Navy Representative Team'. We were 'the Marinaros'. The penny took a long while to drop and we still thought that we were just going to a local gym or hall, for three two minute rounder's each.   There might be a few people there, opposition trainers and the like and it would be a bit of an outing for the crew. Anyway no need to worry, we would be up against pretty much novices like ourselves, apart from Terry of course. Good old Inky charmed us again, with a clever play on our eager egos.

"Leave it to me; don't you boys worry," cajoled Inky. "You boys are good; I can't believe how much you have improved."

After arriving in Rosario Inky took us down to a

local Gym, for acclimatisation as he called it. We all thought that great, as he had negotiated time off for us until after the great event. Whilst there was still a degree of nervousness and a 'what have we got ourselves into' suppressed communal thought; confusingly we were also starting to feel very important. Old Slinky Inky was a past master in tickling egos; a valuable life lesson was going begging here. It was two days before fight night; we were in a local boxing club working on the bags and trying to look at home. Terry of course was. In all endeavours in life, particularly ones that have a degree of underhandedness about them, a mistake is usually made; this is often to do with pride and or ego. Slinky Inky had made a great play with us about what to do in the gym in front of the opposition trainers. He had come round to us individually with little bits of advice. I was working on the medium bag, I must have been showing off a bit as his advice to me was, don't let them see you can punch hard. I was flattered, I didn't know I could; anyway it's easy because the bag doesn't punch back. These little titbits made us feel even more important. He had conned us into believing a nudge, nudge, we're pretty good wink, wink scenario. The only real trouble with that build up of confidence on the one hand and subterfuge on the other was the fact that Terry was obviously so good. So much so and so natural and honest and proud of his ability, honed over a lifetime's hard training, that he looked, moved and obviously was, the real thing. He had jumped up into the ring to shadow box and working the ring, he was so proficient looking that all the local trainers had gathered around and were hugely impressed. We should have realised the ramifications; they were excitedly talking amongst themselves. Calamity reigned; they were gesticulating and pointing at Slinky Inky who was in the corner talking to his co-promoter. What had happened of course was that they had seen old Inky talking slyly to us out of the corner of his mouth and convinced themselves that we were like Terry, but were disguising it. Well there was a fat chance of that; but they were convinced Slinky had tried to put one over them. We and Inky were in trouble, but mainly us. The upshot, although we didn't know it at the time, was that they upgraded our opponents.

A hard lesson was ahead; boxing being what it is and it's the same all over the world. The exaggerated word had spread like wildfire among the local fans. The word apparently was of a treat in store, as the Marinaros were all champion amateurs. You get what you deserve in this life and we were about to pay for the milking and preening we had so readily slipped into. The big night arrived. By now old Inky had us three novices believing we were really good. It was a case of just go in there, make it look good and get your photo taken; simple really, what's all the fuss about. You may recall that I previously noted that we thought this was to be a quiet affair in a local gym. It turned out that our two venerable promoters had a smash hit on their hands. It turned out that the event was to be held in a large YMCA-type arena, which was sold out; in fact they were hanging from the rafters. We three still didn't twig, though Terry was in his element. The place was alive; it was jumping with Latin enthusiasm; there was Latin music blaring; half the ship's crew had brought tickets from Inky, at a discounted price of course. We couldn't believe it. They played the national anthems of Argentina and Britain; some old geezer got up and made a speech, everybody cheered and we felt quite important. We started milking it again. What was it old Inky had said? Oh yes, that's it, 'just go in there, make it look good and get your photo taken'.

We arrived at our dressing room and found they had pinned a faded Union Jack on the door. Inky had got an old pug laundryman from the ship to help him in the changing room. It's time to go, first up was one of the junior cooks. He went out looking rather nervous. Terry, who was totally relaxed, offered some words of encouragement, in between shadow boxing. I didn't know what to do so I started to copy Terry. We could hear the crowd noises. We heard them announcing the cook's fight. The bell went, there was muffled cheering, then a big cheer. We weren't sure what had happened until Inky came rushing in and said, "are you ready?" pointing at me. The poor old cookie had been knocked out almost immediately in the first round. As I was going down the corridor we had to stop and take the blood splattered dressing gown off the cook, who was being helped back and give it to me; we only had the one. I suppose it was lucky for me that it was all happening so fast. Alan the cook looked glazed and just shook his head at me. Inky was propelling me forward by the arm. He was talking to me, but I didn't have a clue about what he was saying. In retrospect I must have been like a Christian being led in to fight a lion in the Coliseum, with about as much chance as it turned out. I climbed up into the ring, by now I was feeling like a condemned man. I looked across to the other corner and I swear my opponent was like a welterweight, ten stone seven pounds, version of 'Rocky Balboa'. He was bull necked heavily muscled, at least thirty and by the look of him had a lot of fights behind him.

The formalities were observed the bell went and Inky the bastard pushed me out with the advice of "hold your hands high, he looks like a hooker". Unfortunately not the type of hooker that I would have greatly preferred at that given moment. He sauntered out slowly. Despite Cookie's demise, they still thought we were top amateurs and he had obviously been told to be careful with the cunning Marinaros who had held back in the gym. We circled each other, he feinted with a couple of punches and I nearly fainted when they whistled past my ears. They missed, but he could really punch. I knew I had to keep my right hand up or it was curtains. I managed a couple of good straight lefts, which sort of puzzled him and temporarily held him off. We danced around as if Victor Sylvester was playing in the background. A couple more left jabs and the round was over, thank Christ, as they say down that way. I think Inky had to drag my right hand down from the side of my head even now I was sitting on the stool; it was like it was 'perma-glued' to the side of my head.

"Christ, Len you did well."

"Did I?"

"Yes. Now go out and double up on that left jab and then follow it up with your right. He shouldn't have said that. He shouldn't have said I did well. I wish he'd kept his mouth shut. I immediately respond to praise, what a dope. The bell went, I skipped out a lot faster and we clashed together in the middle of the ring. Double up on the left jab; that worked. It didn't slow the Argie down though. Try it again and throw the right. It hit him, but it didn't show. Still, at least I was landing punches. I could hear Inky.

"Again, Len, again."

All this time a barrage of vicious hooks were coming my way. In desperation to hold him off, I panicked and threw a right-hander. Bam! Crash! The lights went out; hello dressing room. That was the next thing I was aware off. As soon as I

155

dropped my right hand he just left hooked me, rather unfair really, but I wasn't hurt long term. Our next lad was a second trip, gangly steward from Aylesbury, but what a surprise, he was the original 'sleepy fox'. He put on a good show and went the distance in an exciting scrap, he lost on points, but impressed. The guy he fought was the guy I was supposed to fight, but for some reason they changed it and I got Rocky Balboa, shame that.

Anyway it was time for the big one and our Terry was up for it. They fought a tremendous fight, they did four three minute rounds and they were good rounds. Even if the paying punters had been disappointed with our early efforts, they got their money's worth from Terry and his opponent. Terry won it, but it could have gone either way, the main thing was our pride was saved and the punters went home happy. And old Inky was saved from a lynching; it could easily have been by us. Thinking back on these things as you do, I suppose there could have been a bad accident, us three novices was something like Mill End Sports and Social FC playing Manchester United; maybe not that bad. The point is though, that in the end everybody gained and life is made up as much by mistakes and bad decisions, as it is by considered actions. Old Inky conjured up a bit of skulduggery, which went further than he planned. It was probably the highlight of his scheming, ducking and diving career and good luck to him. We ended up with a bit of a highlight and short-lived status as boxers, but importantly we had something to remember. The Argies had a good night and through the skill and experience of Terry, we kept some respect. And all that came about by someone showing a bit of initiative to make a few bob by doing what he knew. I take my hat off to Inky and battlers like him. They make life interesting. It was a close one, but what a memory, I wouldn't change a thing.

Chapter Fifteen

Joining a new ship was always an exciting event, but sailing wasn't all a matter of battling the locals in foreign ports. There was also the music. Most of the ships I sailed on had a guitarist or two in the crew. Skiffle bands were soon formed, generally using a converted tea chest as the bass. We improvised using soap cans for drums. A great fun instrument we made was called a boomps-a-diddly. The contraption was made with a broom handle. It had nails driven into it. Each nail had been loosely driven through some metal bottle tops. The effect it produced was quite a loud clinking, shaky sound similar to a tambourine, when bounced up and down to the rhythm. There was always a singer or two on board; remember this was the age of Lonnie Donegan and Tommy Steele. We had some great nights often taking a turn to play our home made instruments and singing the pop songs of the day.

There were many and varied stories told of our Tommy Steele. He was a steward at sea for a while. Tommy often performed for the crew in the Pig and Whistle, as the ships bar was known. Legend has it that Tommy was always quite happy to perform a few numbers in the dockside bars while carousing ashore with his shipmates. In any event this proud Bermondsey boy was well thought of by his shipmates. And that is the premium accolade that can be bestowed on you as a seaman. Tommy left the sea and went on to pursue a show business career. He became an international success as a professional entertainer. We were all proud to claim him as one of us.

Other entertainment at sea was often provided by gay stewards. They seemed to have a knack of forming concert parties or duo's and performing various little comedy and dance routines. They really came into their own on what was known as Channel Night. That was the term used to describe the time when a voyage was nearly completed by a British ship and we were safely home and back in, or closing on, the English Channel.

On the bigger ships with larger crews this night was celebrated with a party. There was always one for the crew members who had the good fortune not to be on watch and a separate one for the passengers. They were generally uproarious affairs. A happy spirit born of soon being home, seeing loved ones, family and friends after a long and sometimes arduous voyage pervaded the air. A newfound enthusiasm seemed to invade everyone, even the hardest cases on board. The celebration was usually held in the crew bar, the Pig and Whistle. The most famous one that I recall was on the Highland Brigade, a sister ship to the Highland Monarch. There were the usual early starters waiting for the bar to open and when it did a great cheer went up. Pints of McEwen's Strong Scottish Ale were flowing. Laughter was beginning to burst out; enmities from the voyage were forgotten. Promises to meet up together for further voyages were solemnly declared. The Chief Officer and the Bosun weren't such bad blokes after all. The ship's cook had done his best. A popular Irish AB, his name really was Pat, was persuaded to sing and didn't take too much persuading. He sang a medley of Irish songs, all the usual ones, with most of the gathering joining in. Pat had a warm voice and sang with pride and a tear in his eye. The challenge was set and there was a clamour to sing. The "Me next, me next," call was echoing round the bar. It brought back to me a distant, but warm, memory of the classroom uproar of my childhood.

Next up by common consent was a humorous rendition of that famous Liverpool song I've mentioned, *Maggie May*. Not to be confused with the popular Rod Stewart version of today. It was led by a Scouser fireman who sang it as if he owned it, which to be fair, was how Scousers always did. As that finished the London boys immediately commanded the floor with *Maybe it's because I'm a Londoner,* which was always a favourite with everybody. Again all joined in. It seemed a singsong was the cure all for all ills in those days. Things were going well and Ginger, a real genuine

Cockney boy by birth and by nature, jumped up on the hatch and sang the old Cockney classic, '*My Old Man*'. I think it was a song made famous by Flanagan and Allen, a wartime London duo. In any event Ginger sang it with great gusto and feeling. His performance wasn't that great from a singing point of view, but it showed his pride in his heritage. That night I came to realise how important town and national identity songs are and why we cling to them. Some real pride became evident as they were sung and it was enjoyed right across the age groups. For me it was one of life's important lessons learnt. As the singing began to subside a flurry of activity started on the back of the hatch.

A steward placed a Grundig tape recorder and player by a screen he had erected. With a fine stage presence he then quieted down the throng and introduced 'The Swinging Sisters'. The music started and from behind the screen out danced three fully made up gay stewards in drag. They all had blonde wigs on, bras, flimsy skirts, stockings and suspenders. A great roar went up as they went into a dance routine. They danced and mimed to an old Andrews Sisters' song. They were terrific. They were high-kicking and stepping. I'm sure they enjoyed it as much as we did. The catcalls and lewd shouts didn't affect them, they just danced on. The electric atmosphere, the dance and the music built up to a crescendo. It finalised with them dropping off their skirts and then flipping backwards from bending over. Their pants or knickers now exposed were made from a Union Jack. The dance climaxed to a sign hoisted behind them that boldly proclaimed 'Many a battle has been fought under this flag'. It would have been a showstopper in any venue, but here it was special. The cheers, clapping, whistling and laughter would have graced the Palladium. It was a Channel Night to stay in the memory of all who were there. The Swinging Sisters stopped for a drink and mingle. They were then herded up to the passenger's party to perform again. Their act was received uproariously there as well. The Swinging Sisters efforts had provided a treat for all. They must have put long hours into the rehearsals. I think their routines did more to overcome the anti-gay prejudice of the time than any amount of politically correct ranting does these days.

I had many reasons to remember that particular Channel Night; apart from the Swinging Sisters and the singsong. That trip on the Highland Brigade was particularly memorable because on board with me was my friend, Bill Horwood, the Mill End boy whose clothing, confidence and appearance had so fortunately inspired me to join the Merchant Navy. There was another Mill End Boy sharing this trip with us. We had all by chance been paid off our last ships at about the same time and found ourselves at home in Mill End on shore leave together. We had gone out to a pub called The Fox and Hounds in Croxley Green. We had heard it was jumping and it really was. Bill Haley records were pumping away on a record player; one of the Croxley boys, Doug Joiner, used to take it there with his record collection. Doug was a steward, so we wouldn't have run across him much at sea; however he was a good bloke, so the fact that he was a steward couldn't be held against him. Fifty years later Doug and I met up again and become firm friends. We had both become members of the same golf club, West Herts, a fine members club in Croxley. That however is another story, so we go back to the matter at hand. We three had enjoyed such good times on the leave that we had decided to join our next ship together. The third member of the trio was another local boy and great friend of ours, Dave [Dinger] Singleton, who features significantly later in this tale. He was a guy who had the bottle to jump ship with me in Sydney and ringbolt to New Zealand. We did some tough growing up together. The streets of Sydney were pretty mean when you are a stranger, broke and nineteen. But those times hadn't arrived yet; this was the Fox and Hounds night out. We were having a good time; the music and company were great, but there were no girls there, which didn't suit us. The Croxley boys may well have been able to enjoy themselves without girls; and the fact that they could do that, though a cause for concern, is entirely a matter for them. We three Mill End boys however, had normal attractions for the opposite sex.

"Let's go down to the Cart before it's too late and all the crumpet's been snaffled," said a visibly concerned Bill.

"Yeah good move," replied Dinger, "It'll be swinging down there."

So there was a sense of urgency as we left the Fox. Time, as they say, was of the essence. We were not sure how we would get to the Cart in time to hopefully interest three ladies and attract them to join us for further activities. Then it happened, as if by a miracle; in front of my eyes stood a gleaming Morris Minor with its driver's door slightly ajar, inviting me in with keys in the ignition just waiting to be turned. I jumped into the driver's seat and the lads followed me. I had only just learnt to drive and didn't know the car but that wasn't enough to stop me, so off we went. We careered back towards Ricky like a drunk and horny homing pigeon. The boys were really enjoying the ride. The traffic was so light that it should have been hard to have an accident; however, I managed to. We were having such a good time driving along that we had decided to pass up on the Cart. We had wheels; why not carry on to the Green Dragon in Denham, another honey pot for girls but rather more upmarket and harder to get to without transport. Dinger was very excited at the thought of some upmarket crumpet. He always had ideas above his station, which was probably brought about by his going to a posher school than vagabonds like Bill and me.

Picture the scene, a nice new motor and three healthy young fairly inebriated males. Each with those beautiful old-fashioned white fivers that really felt and looked like money in their pockets. White fivers that would be flashed around in pursuit of upmarket 'totty' in posh Denham. I think it was those thoughts that clouded my judgment. By now we were hurtling along the Main Road, eager to give the posh totty a chance and not be disappointed, by missing out on us. Bill and Dinger unfortunately were singing, both flat as pancakes. Frankie Lane's 'I Believe' was well butchered. I was hunched over the wheel, like I was in the lead at Monza in a Formula One Ferrari, not an eight horsepower Morris Minor. Somewhere about 'above the storm' in Bill and Dinger's rendition, our own storm struck. A Vauxhall car had pulled out of the Halfway House car park. It just shot out onto the road. Even with all my imagined skill, the crash couldn't be avoided. "Hold on!" was all I had time to shout in the pre-seat belt era. Crash! We hit it in the rear driver's side. The impact spun the Vauxhall around to face the other way. We had both stopped by now. The other driver, who was on his own, got out of his car, shouting. He wasn't hurt. Not a word was required on our part; we climbed out of the car and all legged it in different directions. About half-an-hour later we all wandered into the Cart separately. The night was coming to an end and there were no unattached girls waiting for our arrival. We made the decision there and then. We would head up to the pool first thing in the morning and join a Highland boat so we could give those South American girls a treat. As a bonus we would also be out of the way of any repercussions that might arise from our purloining of the car. And that's how we three came to be on the Highland Brigade together.

Anyway back to the cheery Channel Night. Lots of beer was downed, lifelong friendships were sworn and songs were sung. Stories of previous trips were swapped, sometimes, but very rarely, old disputes surfaced due to alcohol. They were never allowed to go on too long before a couple of the older AB's stepped in and broke it up. Unfortunately this night it got a bit more serious. Somehow or other our Bill got into an argument with a belligerent Scottish greaser and in a flash punches were getting thrown. In the scuffle they crashed into a group of greasers. One of them started in on Bill as well from the side. Dinger quick as a flash nailed him; then for a couple of minutes it was on for young and old. Two or three of the deck crowd jumped in to help us as we were outnumbered by other greasers who had joined in. Luckily for all concerned, probably us the most, the Bosun and a couple of QM's and two older AB's broke it up before too much damage was done.

Apart from Bill who had an enormous shiner. We all shook hands and got on with the party, which was a great one and all was forgotten and forgiven.

By now, I had become established as a seaman. I had done a run job over to Hamburg on the Melbourne Star; a run job generally refers to a short Continental trip. It took about three weeks and apart from the crossing, we were in dry dock all of that time. I took myself off to the bars in the Reeperbahn. It was as famous for the music there as it was for the red light houses. It was a pretty lonely time as short run jobs are usually the preserve of the married guys and they used to shun shore trips on run jobs for obvious financial and other, shall we say, more personal reasons. The Beatles played some of their early gigs in the clubs on that notorious street before they made the big time. The most notable thing that happened on that little trip was my meeting a nice German girl. She very kindly took me to her home to meet her mother and family and have a meal. Our brief, sweet little liaison lasted about two weeks and then sadly I had to sail off back to the UK. We had done the usual thing that teenagers do, we exchanged addresses and declared that we would like to see each other again and both promised to cause it to happen. Ich Liebe Dich. It was the first foreign phrase that embedded itself in me. She said it with much feeling. She later wrote to me what it meant. Life however was beckoning me on and as soon as I got back to England my old friend Dinger and I teamed up again.

As a result of some general carousing we decided to ship out again. What wonderful independence our chosen occupation gave us. We were still teenagers, but with this unique opportunity to travel, while fulfilling an important job. It may sound like we were frivolous and just there for the fun, but in fact you can believe me when I say British crews were very good and capable, with a well-disciplined work ethic. I speak for all the guys I sailed with, or went to sea school with, for all merchant seamen, when I declare that we may have been young, we may have played hard, but we knew our jobs and responsibilities at sea. We were well trained and we were proud to belong to that prestigious but now decimated British Merchant Navy. Sadly, it and the type of men it attracted are no longer wanted. Fortunately for us shipping was still in full swing in the late fifties and we were in demand. We could almost pick and choose where we wanted to go. Well, this was the case provided your discharge book was clean and contained no bad reports. The general rule of thumb was that the system allowed us to choose from three offers of ships; if you didn't take one of those, the choice was lost and you had to go where sent.

On a fine early summer morning in July 1956

Dinger and I making our way to the shipping office at the Pool of London. We were both well in funds as we hadn't been home long from previous trips. We treated ourselves to a taxi from Aldgate station down to the docks, but stopping in an East End café for breakfast, somewhere in or near the Commercial Road. With cash in our pockets our independence and appetites knew no bounds. The shipping office had all the usual suspects there. There were the smartly dressed, young 'Teddy' boy types, mainly deck crowd and stewards, probably seeking jobs to take them to New Zealand or South Africa. Then as always an older motley group who seemed the worse for wear from alcohol. They were mainly greasers, engine room staff. Where we were generally around our twenties, the engine room crew were always much older; I never worked out why that was. Our turn came up with the harassed clerk. We handed him our discharge books.

"Two OS's," said Dinger, "what's on offer?"

We were offered a shell tanker; they always tried that one on. No thank you, one down, two to go. "How about this one, an Ellerman line ship to East Africa?" asked the clerk.

We looked at each other, "No thanks".

We were both thinking that things weren't going well. The clerk smiled a quite malicious smile. He has seen it all before. He felt very much in control now. I suppose in his job he saw guys like us picking and choosing where we would go in the world. While at the end of every day he probably hopped on his bike to an old terrace, or rooms, or got the tube home to the same old thing. Who wouldn't be pissed off after arranging fascinating voyages to sun-kissed destinations for young, free guys all day long? He came back to us with a cunning look on his face.

"There is this ship; she usually sails out of Newcastle; she needs two ordinary seamen."

Dinger asked where she was going.

The clerk made a big play of looking at his paperwork, "oh very good," he said, "this is interesting; how do you two fancy a trip to Finland via Newcastle for a load of pit props?" We looked at each other. Not a lot of choice here, we nod; why not, the other two choices were worse, weren't they?

"Okay then, get yourselves down to the Tate and Lyle sugar wharf. You'll find the Sandhoe there. She's due to sail for Newcastle in two days' time and she's already overdue." As we left the office with the appropriate paper work, Dinger turned to me and said, "I think we got the best of a bad lot, besides I couldn't put up with you for two years on a tanker."

He delivered those lines with a worryingly straight face.

"I know what you mean," I responded. "I wasn't looking forward to getting you out of all that shit you would get yourself into in East Africa."

I was hoping that exchange was a draw, but I think he got me. We made our way to the Connaught Arms, a popular seamen's pub. Neither of us was ever a big drinker; but visiting these pubs around the docks was always an experience for us country boys and it was always likely you might run into an old shipmate. We chatted about the unknown Sandhoe. We were in no rush to get around to her, but at the same time we were keen to know more about her. All we knew at that stage was that she had just returned from the West Indies with a cargo of raw sugar, so she was berthed down by the huge Tate and Lyle's processing plant in Canning Town, being unloaded. It slowly dawned on us that she had just carried a cargo of sugar from the West Indies and her next trip was going to Finland for a cargo of pit props. There was no doubt about it; she had to be a jobbing tramp. Let's face it; we had committed ourselves to an old tramp steamer, worse still, out of Newcastle. Christ, that said it all; she would be rough and when we found her, we were right, she was.

The MV Sandhoe was, as we had suspected, an old type tramp steamer; she was only three thousand one hundred and seventy three tons. She plied her trade for her owners, Sharps Shipping Company, wandering the oceans, picking up cargoes wherever they were offered. Before the advent of ships with refrigerated holds and the development of regular food trade routes, the old tramp steamer was in its heyday. They were generally owned and operated by small companies. In our day they were rarely seen in the Royal London Docks. They were struggling to survive in the new world of co-ordinated, regular shipping schedules by much larger and more economic ships. They laboured on for a while until they were dealt the deathblow by the new frontier of shipping - containerisation. The age of the romantic tramp steamer, glorified in old black and white movies featuring 'Humphrey Bogart', 'John Wayne' and co., was dead. More's the pity; something valuable died with them.

I can clearly remember standing on the Tate and Lyle wharf, looking at this rusty, run down ship. Her paint was fading; her decks and bulwarks were shabby. She reminded me of a sweet old working class lady in need of some TLC, trying to bravely face the end of her useful life. Her holds were open and dockers were busy unloading her raw bulk sugar with huge grabs, which swung from the arms of wharf cranes. We stepped aboard and found the Skipper in the officer's mess. He was a gnarled old Tynesider who had spent his life on coasters and tramps and it showed in every line on his face and in every movement he made.

"So they've sent me a couple of cockneys," was his opening gambit. To all Geordies anyone from the south near London was a 'cockney' and not well regarded. He studied our discharge books; we both had a few trips under our belts by then and there were no blemishes on our records.

"I see you've been good lads," he said in his Geordie voice and I was expecting a burst of 'Blaydon Races' to follow. He looked at us, those deep lines on his face almost showing his thoughts.

"Okay, you can sign on now, but you'll find this a bit different from the posh ships I see in your books. We don't stand on ceremony lads, I just want you to do your jobs, is that okay?"

"Yes, that's okay," I said.

"Right then, we sail for Newcastle the day after tomorrow. We're there for a night then we're off to Finland for a load of pit props."

I should perhaps explain here, for the uninitiated, that pit props were lengths of lumber cut to size for use in coal mining tunnels. The Skipper stepped out of the mess and called out for the Bosun, who duly appeared. He must have been loitering nearby.

"Take these two and sort their cabins and watches, they turn to in the morning."

With that the Bosun said "This way, boys." and led us to the sparse bleak accommodation. Oh well, it's only for a few weeks, so why not try something new and take advantage of this rare chance to see Finland? We turned to (started work, in sailor talk) the next morning. Our first jobs were battening down everything to make ready for sea. The discharging of the sugar had been completed late the night before; everybody had worked late to achieve that. We hosed down the decks and bulwarks; they were coated with a sticky film of raw sugar. The speedier unloading allowed us to sail a day early, so that afternoon we slipped the moorings and made our way down the Thames. It was about four o'clock and we had got clear of the Estuary. Southend was well astern of us.

How strange it was for me whenever I passed that iconic landmark while at sea; memories flooded my mind of childhood trips there. They were usually on coaches, but on one memorable occasion we made the trip on the Royal Daffodil from Tower Bridge. That outing was with another Mill End family, another lot of Horwoods; Mill End was full of them. They had a boy of my age we called Binga; he grew up a typical Mill-Ender and was involved in many of the skirmishes we got ourselves into and in true local fashion he never backed down. As I recall it, Dad had bagged a biggish win on the greyhounds. In my mind I saw myself again standing on that long pier on my own, while the other kids' interests were in the rides and excitement of the famous Southend Kursaal. I was captivated watching the ships slowly disappearing from view and fascinated by where they were going. Treasure Island, Mutiny on the Bounty, Horatio Nelson, Captain Bligh, Fletcher Christian and the like had been my staple reading diet. It was at that point that I believe the sea cast its magic spell on me. Now it was my lot to be on those ships that seemed to disappear so mysteriously over the horizon. The smoke from their funnels charting a trail to a destination that presented such a mystery to the observer on land.

The all-important job of allocating the watches had been tasked by the Bosun; fortunately I'd had a bit of luck in pulling the four-to-eight, the favoured watch. I went up to the bridge to relieve the last helmsman from the twelve-to-four, known as the 'graveyard'. The Skipper and Chief Mate were both there; the Pilot had been dropped off. The helmsman I was relieving advised me of the course, which would take us into the North Sea. The Sandhoe operated on the old magnetic compass, not the easier modern 'gyro'.
"Steering North Nor' East," I repeated to him, as was required to be done whenever the helmsman was changed. Another trip was underway, another experience awaited and it was comforting to be sharing it with an old friend from my hometown. Newcastle here we come. I was looking forward to the stop in Newcastle; it was an opportunity to look up some relatives I hadn't seen since I was seven or eight years old. Late in the following day we found ourselves nosing up the Tyne, that river so revered by Geordies. In those days of busy shipping the major shipbuilding yards on the river, which along with coal mining, provided most of the work and financial opportunities in and around Newcastle. It was this mighty Tyne, the 'god of all', that was the vital link, which for centuries had powered the

economy, enabled growth and promoted the prestige of this very northern city.

My knocking on that familiar door reverberated around an old terrace tenement in Byker. I remembered it well as my mother had brought us all there just after the war. We had stayed for quite some time, being boarded around various 'aunties'. My grandfather, 'Sammy Gilchrist', was a bit of a legend in the area, sadly for the wrong reasons. Many of his antics are recorded in a book, *A Shieldfield Childhood,* published by the Newcastle City Libraries and Arts Department and written by Joe Hind, a very distant relative. Grandfather, Sammy Gilchrist, apparently was one of those nuisance drunks whose actions caused discomfort and havoc all around them. The tales about him and his exploits are legendary. They range from pub fighting with only one arm to womanizing and verbal abuse. Old Sam had been badly injured in the First World War while serving in the Northumberland Fusiliers. He had lost an arm, he had a steel plate in his head, he had lost an eye in the, 'Battle of the Somme' and add to all that the fact that he had been gassed, you begin to see him sympathetically. In those days there was no, or very little, support to assist the returned soldiers, wounded or otherwise. So I guess with all that he suffered it's reasonable to excuse his erratic and brawling behaviour. It was popularly held in Byker and in family folk law that he was to be recommended for the VC. It was bitterly unfortunate that the senior officer, whom he had rescued in combat, where he had received his multiple wounds, was later killed in a subsequent battle before his recommendation and report could be posted and actioned. Such is life, though one wonders what changes and benefits that fateful death of the officer destroyed for Sammy and his direct family.

Sammy appeared at the door. He was wearing an old grey collarless heavy shirt that was tucked into a pair of blue serge trousers, held up by a pair of stout old khaki army braces. The whole attire topped off with a flat cap, the type that was the Geordie badge of office. I thought it was probably the same one he had worn nine or ten years previously. I went to speak, but before I could he said, "Bonnie lad, you're Sarah's boy."
His loss of an eye and the addition of a steel plate hadn't interfered with his memory; I was both impressed and flattered. Dinger and I followed him inside. It was dark and gloomy, as it always had been, but childhood innocence shields you from such unpleasantness. As a young man my vivid memory of this place, with its outside shared toilet, was now matched by its gloomy reality. My grandmother, who had been chair bound, had spent agonising years here. In my mind's eye I could see her sat in that great chair, often given to crying. Then I realised it must have been with

frustration at the stunted life she was forced to live. I sensed immediately the reason behind my mother's early flight to the south, for release from what must have been such a miserable situation. Not just brought about by the primitive living conditions, but also by the depressing penury that surrounded this abode. I gave old Sammy a few quid and left, not sadder, but definitely wiser. In a way it was like burying a ghost and I never returned there. The visit had explained a lot of unsaid things that had sullied our lives as children. But now as a seaman I had created the opportunity to move on and not be bound by the ramifications of the past, in the same way as my mother had done before me.

On the trip up through the North Sea, we discovered that the Sandhoe was the very worst sea ship we had ever had the dubious pleasure of sailing on. Her steering response was slow, she yawed very badly to starboard and so to keep her steady you had to hold a permanent half turn on the wheel. In a way it was lucky we had that early opportunity to learn how to steer her, before we had to navigate across the North Sea, then up through the Skagerrak and then turn down the Kattegat, a testing stretch of water. Fortunately it was in the northern summer and storms were less frequent. The next hurdle was the big one though; we had to negotiate the very difficult island studded waters of the channel separating

Denmark's Copenhagen, from Sweden's Malmo. It's as tricky a stretch of water to pass through as any in the world. The old Geordie skipper never left the wheelhouse while we were manoeuvring through that difficult channel. As we steamed through it sometimes appeared that we were heading to beach on one of the Islands, a gap would then appear where we had to take on that hazardous pass to the Baltic Sea. Once through we then had to beat our way north up to the 'Gulf of Bothnia' and on again, sailing up Finland's west coast and to a welcome sanctuary in the bay close to where the town of Jakobstad was situated. Tranquillity and almost permanent day time; these were the pleasures in being so far north in the summertime. We were enjoying something like twenty-two hours of daylight. It was very strange, but as a consequence of that the night times were gloriously light and peaceful. Jakobstad was set in a beautiful picturesque area of Finland. Perhaps the whole country's like that. The town in those days was small and most folk seemed to know each other and they were friendly and happy. Over the course of the few days we were in that small town, we became quite well known. The bar we frequented was always pleased to see us; we spent our money and were no trouble. Well actually Finnish beer at the time was so weak you'd have had to drink an awful lot to get yourself ready for trouble. We worked all day helping the local stevedores load the pit props and our main job was to assist the Second Mate with making sure they were stowed securely.

Everything was going along smoothly; we spent our time in the same bar most nights. Then out of the blue, completely from left field, trouble struck us. It was entirely unprovoked by us and did not involve any of the locals. The troublemakers were a group of Finnish lumberjacks who had come into town for some sort of celebration. Apparently they had been out in the forest for quite some time working and for them it was party time. The only problem was that the local girls preferred us, more gentle young foreign souls. And there weren't enough of them to go around for us, let alone them. One of the age-old causes of war was about to be launched and it was no place for the faint hearted. This didn't go down too well with the bar owner who could see what was coming and was exceedingly concerned about what might happen to his bar. His sensible move was to immediately try to close up for the evening. The lumberjacks, however, who had brought their own drink with them, (it was some sort of firewater), were well liquored up by now and were not about to go anywhere. I don't know if it was fortunate, or unfortunate, but there was a wild redhead engineer with us (I think he was Irish). He was also very boozed up from drinking on the ship, prior to coming ashore. He was actually a very aggressive character, who had been pushing for a fight with us a couple of times; but none of us wanted to take him on. Not so the lumberjacks. It didn't take long and off it went; the engineer was embroiled with a couple of the Finns. He was doing okay, but they started to get at him. We didn't like him and didn't really want to get in this; we were severely outgunned, by weight, age and numbers.

Our girls were trying to get us out of there and we were all for going when it spilt over as one of the Fins threw a bottle and hit one of our lads on the head with a glancing blow. The die was cast; there was no choice now. It completely erupted; tables and chairs were smashed and thrown. It was more like a gigantic wrestling match involving everybody and it was going badly for us until, believe it or not, the girls joined in. Now the Finns really are very nice people and there was no way that they could hit or hurt the girls, who were shouting abuse at them and attacking them alongside of us and were probably doing more damage, I'm embarrassed to say. In any event their actions stopped us getting a severe thrashing; of that I'm sure. Unfortunately, although in hindsight it might have been fortunate, the riot police arrived just about then. They sailed into the Finns with their battens and they didn't hold back; it was brutal. They had obviously had trouble with this group before. They started throwing the lumberjacks into the 'paddy wagon' and they quickly got them all locked up. We thought, that's it, we're okay; let's carry on with the girls. Oh no, life isn't as easy as that; there is always a surprise around the corner. The police were standing in the road and seemed to be having a conference and they appeared to reach some sort of agreement. With that they turned around and grabbed the red headed Irishman and put him in the back of a car. As they did that two of them collared me and put me in the car with him. It was a case of they had to have transgressors from either side and for some reason I had been picked on as the support act to the redhead Irishman.

So that's how life is, you have to take the good with the bad, only this time the bad was very bad. The Finnish police must have had training in 'corrective treatment', or maybe this crew suffered from a twisted sense of humour. In their wisdom, complete with stifled chuckles, they put me in a cell with another drunken Finnish lumberjack, luckily not one of the group who had been in the bar brawl. However, notwithstanding that, it still didn't make for a very comfortable night. This guy was right off his tree with whatever this local firewater was that they seemed to get hammered on. He spent half the night crashing around the cell yelling, then singing and kicking the door. He would then turn his attention to me, glaring at me and spouting unintelligible words. He was huge, well over six feet, very burly and a nutter. I can't say it was the best free nights' lodging I ever enjoyed;

but I can say this, if it was meant as a deterrent, it worked. I am not saying I went in there as a lion, far from it, but I certainly came out next morning like a lamb, to the huge mirth of the station police. There again so did the redheaded Irishman. He was very subdued for the rest of the trip, which almost made the night in the station worthwhile; actually, on reflection, it didn't.

The remainder of that trip was uneventful, which really suited me. The old Sandhoe was completely loaded out with the pit props, the holds were full and we had secured them as deck cargo as well. They were stacked and belted up to and above the ship's side rails. We had to walk across them, to get the fo'csle head and also the poop deck astern. We must have looked like a floating timber yard. I must hand it to the Skipper; he knew his job and had carefully planned the loading, particularly the deck cargo stacking. The thing was he also worked at it himself, he left nothing to chance. Even though she was a scruffy little tramp, she had the benefit of a top-flight skipper. Luckily the return trip was blessed with glorious weather, so apart from the cranky steering, we enjoyed the trip back to Newcastle. We tied up in one of the Tyne docks and were paid off in North Shields. We could have stayed on for another trip and we were asked to, which wasn't bad for a couple of southerners. So there it was, another voyage completed, another country visited and a completely new experience of ships, so life's learning curve was being attended to.

We didn't hang around in Newcastle; we had plans which included a couple of local girls back in Ricky and our home town in summer was a really nice place to be. Even more so if, like us, you had some leisure time available and money in your pocket. At that time the ship owners paid us off with those big old fashioned white fivers. They really felt and looked like money and possession of them increased the feeling of wellbeing. Significantly at that time, I came to realise that I had achieved what I set out to do. I remembered the time that with envy I had seen Billy Horwood, strolling through Ricky High Street looking tanned, confident and without a care in the world. My envy had caused me to pledge myself to follow Bill and aspire to that same situation. I felt a glow of real accomplishment inside. I had done it and in the process improved my life and sense of worth. This new life had bought me great options, which had not been thought of or available to me before that fateful meeting with Bill. I think that meeting was an early and very timely crossroad in my life.

Chapter Sixteen

Oh, Oh, I woke up one morning with that dreaded feeling which comes with running out of money. I had enjoyed nearly a month of larging it up around Ricky that had included a few long, slow, sunny days around the Aquadrome with 'Dinger' and the girls who could wangle time of work by swapping shifts and that sort of thing. Dinger, who was more money conscious than me, had left a week earlier; I think he had gone off on a 'New Zealand and Aussie' trip for about four months. I was so enjoying my comfortable, lordly type life and new girlfriend that I was reluctant to leave, but the shortage of cash had the same effect on me that it has worldwide. It was time to ship out and earn some more freedom, or money; it amounts to the same thing. "Time flies when you are enjoying yourself." Add to that, "All good things do come to an end", another of those correct but faintly annoying sayings. Unfortunately, banal or not, they proved true. It was now late September 1956 and those summer days of late August had disappeared about the same time as my money and strangely the girl as well. Coincidence you might say, but I think old Dinger knew something.

The 'Desiado' needed a senior ordinary seaman and unlike a lot of the lads, I was comfortable on Royal Mail Ships, the Highland Boats of course falling into that category. This would be my fourth trip with the company and as a result of that I was getting known amongst the crews who frequented them, which was good for the old esteem. As you get known and get the time in, you learn a few tricks. You start to get the perk jobs and the best watches. In fact I received a telegram from Royal Mail offering me the job with an SOS rating. They must have been desperate. It was a quiet, well-run trip. She was a refrigerated-hold ship, designed and built especially for the South American meat run. The crew accommodation was superb and she was what we call a good 'feeder' and that always makes for a happy ship, which she was.

We, that is, the deck crew, spent most the outward-bound voyage steam cleaning the holds and bull bars, which the frozen carcasses would hang from. I had pulled the day shift, which came with almost unlimited overtime available; things were starting to happen for me. The AB's were mainly married guys who were regulars on the 'Desi' as she was known. It made sense for them, as she was regular as clockwork, eight to nine weeks away and good money with the overtime. Anyway it all added up to a quiet, well behaved trip. Sitting out on the deck in the evenings chatting, I heard stories again about the boys from the Monarch and the brawl in the bar in Monte. And the boxing night in Rosario, which wasn't something I could brag about. I hadn't told anyone of my involvement in either of those two incidents, but like most sneaky things, it surfaced from a strange source. As I recall it on that trip to Argentina on the 'Desi' our first port of call was 'La Plata' on the southern shore of the Rio de la Plata Estuary. We had been at sea for two and a half weeks, possibly a bit more. That was about as much as was comfortable, before things started to get a bit niggly. We were keen to get ashore and do the usual things that attracted seaman to that part of the world. No prizes for guessing that one and it wasn't going straight to the library, sorry you got that wrong.

However it was a drink, usually a few cold lagers, then the famous meal, the 'bife de lomo' with some Latin music and probably a late visit to a girlie bar. Well it so happened that in our trawl around the bars, we invariably bumped into guys we had previously sailed with on other ships. We were doing the rounds and enjoying rum and cokes which were a popular drink at the time. We ended up in a well-known seamen's bar called the First and Last, obviously called that as it was close to the dock gates. We made a noisy but happy entrance, bellied up to the bar and ordered drinks and then I was shocked rigid. A scream came across the bar.
"Lenny, Lenny."
Two, girlie, high-pitched and excited voices. I froze in horror. Yes, you've probably guessed it; Mesdames Beulah Peach and Grace, the two gay

stewards of the Monarch' and as usual they were absolutely hammered. They minced their way across the bar, trilling and grinning, rum and cokes in hand. "Look, Lenny, the wild 'ordinary seaman' is here."

Well that was insult number one. I was now a proud SOS; the pecking order was all-important to the deck crowd. We saw ourselves as the royalty of the crew. It turned out they also knew the boys on the Desi. Most Royal Mail crews knew each other; they often swapped ships to suit certain times when they were needed at home for weddings, or christenings, or such. Beulah and Grace started chatting to Mike and couple of the AB's they knew. I was busy signalling in a stage whisper. "Don't mention Monte."

I should have kept quiet. Grace piped up, "Did you say Monte, Len?"

"Nothing, forget it, nothing,"

"Monte? Fucking Monte," said Grace; then very bitchily, "I got a fucking black eye and I was only minding my own business; it was you and your mates' fucking fault, fighting over that fucking Dago tart."

Beulah chipped in, "Shut up you drunken bitch, it wasn't Lenny's fault, it was yours, you were throwing yourself at that Dago bastard Carlos and you got shitty because he ignored you."

Stand back now, if you have never witnessed a catfight, you probably don't understand what's going on here, but any reader who has been at sea will. They were hilarious and the flow of insults was deadly.

"You deserved that black eye, you fucking tramp and you laughed when Lenny got knocked out in Rosario."

"I did not."

"Yes you did, you lying bitch."

"Well so did you, you treacherous cow." A pause for breath. "And you went off with that Dago who knocked Lenny out."

"No I didn't, you lying cow. Anyway you were jealous again, you're always jealous of me." By this time the 'Desi' boys were in stitches and the whole bar was crowding round. The insults carried on; then they both turned around to me and started screaming, "It's your fucking fault, it was nice and happy till you got here. You start trouble wherever you go. It was you and that Scouser bastard who started it in Monte. Grace is right, it was all over a Dago tart."

By this time Grace was crying, Beulah put her arm around her and the Bar was in an uproar. I had hardly opened my mouth. I hadn't even drunk my drink and then the attack swung away from me. Beulah turned on Mike, one of the AB's with me, saying "And I don't know why you're laughing. You're a useless bastard too. I remember you on the Chieftain, you pissed everybody off then."

Mike was in hysterics by now; he couldn't stop laughing, which made poor old Beulah worse,

"Fuck off all of you. You deck crowd think you're so special."

That was it; now it's gone from humour to danger. That was what it always came down to in an argument, at sea or ashore. Whether it came from the catering or the engine room staff; it was always the keenest insult. We didn't mind that; it was true. It was the pecking order stuff again and we were top of the heap. It got very noisy now and was looking like it could all go off. We would have been five against a big crowd of stewards and a few firemen who would have joined in with them. Then the boss came over and ordered us out. We went, but resisted enough to save face, trading insults as we went through the doors.

We went off to find another bar, looking for some girls, which wasn't hard to do in La Plata, though often there were police sweeps clearing them off and sometimes locking some of us up. It was all part of the game as far as we were concerned; you win some you lose some. This night we were lucky and met some girls who weren't really professionals, more like good time girls. We were sitting with the girls, having the odd dance and could they dance; it was great. I was teamed up with Maria a petite pretty Brazilian girl who worked in a shipping office in the town. I had just come off the dance floor and sat down, when Mike and the other two wanted to know all about the Monte story and the Rosario boxing night. They also were keen to know why I hadn't said anything in the previous discussion about it. I fobbed them off and said I would talk about it in the morning. I had more important things to attend to with Maria. We left at about two o'clock and I took her home. She had two rooms in a pretty run down district, about two miles from the docks. As it happened, the high hopes I was holding in my mind concerning staying the night were dashed, something about work in the morning, but she did get me a taxi and we made arrangements to meet again that night. She turned up which surprised me. It was really nice being with her and she took me into the town, where we went to a restaurant with live music. She laughingly made me get up and join the dancing throng and guided me in a tango, which I stumbled through; it seemed to be the only dance they were doing. It was quite fortunate that when I was fourteen my mother used to insist that I went to the old time dances with her. They were held in the Guides hut, the same one that Gorgy and I used to hide our loot under. Anyway, one of the dances we did at the old time dances was the 'Square Tango'. Nowhere near the same; but it was a help. Incidentally old Gorgy used to love the old time dances! I was dragged along by my mother, so I had an excuse. Getting back to the story, Maria and I had a wonderful time. As the evening progressed the band played some Bill Hayley classics, which enabled me to slip into Jive, rock and roll mode and regain some ground and show off a bit. The night was so good; we travelled on the rattly old buses, which were great. After the wonderful meal and fun time dancing I was holding exceedingly high hopes regarding staying the night; that tango can give you funny ideas. Unfortunately I was sent on my way again, suffering from that most annoying of young male conditions, the 'devils clutch', but with a promise of a date the next night, with great things to come.

I nearly ran off the ship and to our meeting place the following evening and she was waiting there; I don't know why I doubted her. She looked so pretty in a light coloured blouse and a black flared skirt with huge red flower patterns on it. She really was beautiful. We went to a bar and sat outside having a cold drink and chatting. Her English was very good. She had made arrangements for us to visit friends of hers she worked with. They were a nice couple of about twenty-three or four who lived on the outskirts of the city and we had fun going there on the rattler, as I jokingly called their buses. We stopped on the way for some wine to take with us as we had been invited to have dinner with them. The evening and the dinner were simple and friendly. They were very nice sophisticated people; it was a superb experience for me. The night eventually came to an end and our host generously offered to drive us back to Maria's place in his car. He dropped us off at the door. I stood there wondering if it was going to be another see you tomorrow job, when she smiled, took out her key, unlocked the door and invited me in. I must have passed a three-day test. I saw her and stayed every night from then on until we sailed. We exchanged addresses and endearing assurances. Mine was that I would return, hers was that she would welcome it. We had shared a delightful time and I didn't want to let it go, but the Desiado siren would soon be blowing to signal our departure and two days later it did. Maria came down and waved us off; the boys were impressed, but I didn't see it like that; it had been very special.

As soon as we were underway and everything was shipshape and we were sitting in the sailors mess it started. They hounded me about my not admitting to my role in the Monte incident and the boxing night. For absolutely no good reason I was on the spot. I just told it like it was; the boxing night was easy as I hadn't covered myself in glory and at that age my pride was a bit dented, not just from the fight, but also for falling to old Inky's blandishments. As I got older, I saw the humour of the situation, plus the invaluable lesson, which came with it. In regard to the Monte incident, I had found it amusing to listen to the blown up versions, which would always arise in conversations about exploits of ships crews. After listening to some of the exaggerated stories, allegedly from the horse's mouth, as they were invariably touted, it would have been difficult for all concerned, including me, if I'd blown the gaff. Fortunately my explanation was accepted, but I had to tell and retell the story all the way home. I think I made Isabella an in demand star of the Monte dockside bars and that couldn't be a bad thing for her.

We docked at the King George the Fifth dock about three weeks later; I was paid off and went straight up to the shipping office, looking for a ship going back to BA. Lo and behold, there was an SOS job available on the Cortona, a refrigerated cargo carrier belonging to a good company, Donaldson's of Glasgow. She was sailing in two weeks' time for Buenos Aires from this same dock. I took the job without a second thought. I wrote a couple of letters advising Maria of my arrival date. I went home for two days and saw the folks and then I was gone again. I found myself with a mainly Jock crowd; they were what we referred to as company men. They didn't get their jobs through the shipping office; they dealt with and were contracted directly to the company. The New Zealand shipping company which, to avoid confusion I should point out, was a British company, ran a similar scheme. It had financial benefits, but on the other hand it was restrictive as to choice of ships and time spent ashore.

This was the second Cortona. The first had met an untimely end, sometime in 1942. She had been on passage from Liverpool to Buenos Aires when she was attacked by two German submarines, the U 116 and the U 201. She was hit by two torpedoes. She remained afloat for some time until U 201 administered the *coup de grace*. Thirty members of her crew and two RN attached gunners were lost. As with most shipping companies, the losses in ships and men in the Second World War were huge. They must have been very brave men to continually man those ships, particularly during the Battle of the Atlantic, which was largely to feed the population as well as transport war supplies. Even though there were huge early losses, the Royal Navy eventually got on top and decisively won this battle for command of the sea and safety for our ships. So much so, that Admiral Dönitz, the German Commander of the submarine operations, was forced to withdraw his fleet from the battle, as their losses were so great. He also experienced the cost of warfare at sea losing both his sons, one a U boat watch officer in one of the Atlantic attacks and the other in a torpedo boat attack on HMS Selsey.

This Cortona was relatively new having been built in 1947. The crew accommodation was the best I had experienced; mine was a two berth cabin I shared with a J.O.S. on the same watch. This was luxury compared to all the previous ships, I had sailed on. There was a further treat, the food was outstanding; Donaldson's did it right, though I have to qualify that a bit. I believe the Captain Cook, a Donaldson's liner chartered to the New Zealand government for immigration services, did not cater for its emigrating passengers on such a lavish scale. The Cortona was a bit over nine thousand ton displacement, but quite nippy with her twin engine, single screw set up. Again I was lucky, she was a happy ship. We set off from King George V one day in late November; it was a typical grey, late afternoon sailing. The dismal weather was not having any effect on me; my mind was elsewhere in that cosy two-room dwelling of Maria's. The voyage to BA was uneventful. We had called into Las Palmas for bunkers. Then as I recall it, we had that long hot slide down across the equator to BA. We did all the usual jobs, steam cleaning the empty refrigerated holds and blacking down the rigging. The latter was always an interesting job. It entailed having a Bosun's chair shackled to the rigging and sliding down it, blacking down as you were lowered, from a big pail of mixture usually made up by the Lamp Trimmer. It was a good crew; no shirkers and they all knew their stuff. Nobody swung the lead. I met an interesting character on board; he was an older AB we called Wattie. He had been around a bit and he had this huge flat broken nose. I often thought that I wouldn't have liked to face the guy who gave it to him. Wattie was a real tough Gorbals man and he took a shine to me, so we shared a few McEwan's Strong Ales from time to time. Wattie told me about the hard life in the Gorbals, the notorious tough, crime-ridden area of Glasgow. The population lived in bleak overcrowded tenements and extortionate criminal moneylenders preyed on the folk there. By going to sea Wattie had earned enough regular money to get his family out of the Gorbals and into a more liveable area. He had been the sole breadwinner from the age of thirteen for his mother and two younger sisters, when his father, unable to face that hard, deprived life any longer, had committed suicide. Wattie had been involved in all types of criminal activity gravitating from shop lifting at an early age to armed hold ups as a member of a notorious gang. This had resulted in a five-year stretch in prison, which he admitted had been light and much less than he had expected. He had decided that on his release from prison, he would try to go to sea. He had got his start with commercial fishing and then graduated to a couple of years on coasters and managed to get his AB's ticket. Life at sea had given him stability. He was of the opinion that his life would have been one of criminal activity and being in and out of jail, or worse, had he not become a seaman. He was a modern day version of the guys who were press-ganged so successfully into Nelsons' navy as 'privateers', or in reality, pirates serving the crown. He would have been a fearsome sight, swinging aboard with a cutlass in hand and a couple of pistols in his belt. He was using his spare time at sea to study navigation, with a view to officer training under an adult training scheme, if he could find one to take him. I hope he made it.

I was continually amazed at the diverse backgrounds and types I met at sea. While many were balanced and happy there were a lot of unsettled souls who were running from something, maybe domestic, maybe something more sinister. There was one man of about fifty; he claimed to be Hungarian who had fought against the Nazis. One of our older AB's, who had been on Atlantic convoys in the war, suspected him of being a Nazi from one of those 'satellite' countries, who sympathized with the Nazis and served as prison guards etc. The AB may well have been right, as on a later trip on a Royal Mail boat the guy disappeared in Uruguay, a well-known haven for Nazis on the run.

It seemed no time at all and I was back in BA. We unloaded our general cargo and headed back to La Plata to load beef and lamb. I realised that I was behaving like the married AB's I had noticed, who took those short regular trips and didn't go ashore. I wondered how long that could last. I don't know why, but again I was surprised that she was there waiting in our usual meeting place. She looked great; she was wearing three quarter length white slacks, with a red patterned top, also to complete the outfit she had an Indian style red bandana round her forehead. I couldn't believe my luck, she was stunning. It was less than nine weeks since we had waved good-bye and here I was back again looking forward to round two.

Our meetings followed the same enjoyable pattern, but I sensed a slight change in her. It was as if sometimes she was somewhere else and she would look a little lost and sad. She would then realise I had detected this and snap herself back, to us and the now. We had such times together, I got two days off and she managed to do the same. The couple I had met on the previous trip lent her their car for the final day. She delighted in zipping around and taking me on a fabulous sightseeing trip. Towards the end of a near perfect day we strolled across the sand to a really nice beachside bar she knew. As we sat down she was warmly greeted by male and female waiters. In their excited, inimitable Latin way they crowded around her kissing and cuddling. She gave a little giggle, as she often did and explained that she worked there on the weekends and some evenings. She must have decided that now was the best time and place to tell me what was troubling her. I had been worrying that she was pregnant and that was a distinct possibility. But no, that wasn't her problem; it was more irresolvable than that.

Maria was from Brazil. She hailed from a city called Goiania near the planned new capital Brasilia, which unfortunately was hundreds of miles from the sea and a port. She was the oldest child in her family; from the resulting discussions I found she was four years older than me. That wasn't the problem either; it was a two edged one. First her mother was very ill and it was her obligation to return home, to look after the family, which she felt she had to do. Secondly there was a fairly long-term boyfriend waiting in the wings up there and their respective families expected them to marry. Maria explained all this with great dignity and sensitivity. Though I was hurt by the disclosure, no matter how delicately put, I knew deep down that with us it could only be infatuation. I wasn't thinking marriage. I wasn't looking that far ahead really, my thinking stopped at living the moment and enjoying the good fortune that had brought us together. To be honest I saw it as a romantic interlude, as Maria must have. We hardly knew each other really. But as often happens with the confidence and promise of youth, we were embracing and living a dream. Perhaps it was like being in a romantic movie. We had shared a wonderful opportunity to enjoy the times together. It had certainly made the idea of my staying on the BA run appealing for both of us, but now that was just a dream, there were other ships and other places to see.

We decided to make the most of the time we had left. We took the car back to her friends and enjoyed an amazing huge steak and salad meal with them. I was astonished at the amount of meat that was served and eaten with so much relish. Again Maria and I brought the wine. It was really nice sitting in their tiny garden on a warm evening, taking a long time to eat and drink as they did. Eating for them seemed like a celebration, not just a necessary fuelling function. I was seeing and learning another way of life. We left their house in time to catch the last bus back in to the city. We sat there on that huge back seat being bumped around and snuggling into each other for comfort, both lost in our thoughts of what might have been. We reached our stop and from there we had a ten-minute walk to Maria's. It was still warm and although she lived in a pretty poor district, walking along there felt very safe. The terraced type houses butted right up to the pavement. Looking through the windows as we passed, we could see families sitting in the crowded lounges, talking and laughing. It was very peaceful; unlike a few years previously when the anti-Peron demonstrations had been taking place. At that time BA and La Plata could be very dangerous places to be. Maria told me how repressive things had been. She told me of people's homes being invaded in the middle of the night and sons and fathers disappearing, sometimes never to be heard of again. The detainees were mostly writers, artists and politicians. Coming from a poor working class background as she did, it was no surprise to witness her love of Eva Peron. At her friends' dinner parties I had noted the reverence, in their manner, when Eva's name came into the conversation. Eva, who may have had many faults according to the revolutionaries, was to them a true champion of the poor and oppressed. Though now dead, she lived on in the hearts of Argentina's women. They were desperate times for the Argentineans, but all seemed well now, even though heavily armed police and soldiers were never far away.

We arrived at Maria's humble little abode. She unlocked the door and motioned me to follow her in and up the creaky stairs to her rooms, which I was quite familiar with now. Without further ado, she pulled out the extension on her couch/bed, motioned me to her and sat down with me. She smiled and then disappeared for a few minutes returning in a very skimpy nylon top. The only light was from the open windows and a small candle. We spent a passionate night together. She wasn't in anyway shy about her nudity and she quite rightly knew she was flawless. I probably wasn't old or experienced enough to fully appreciate that night and her, but I knew it was special and I knew this was a special good bye. I certainly had no regrets about returning as quickly as I had done. We said our goodbyes in the morning and I found my way back to the ship. There were no tears. I knew I had experienced something quite special and was happy. I think Maria felt that too. In reality we had only spent ten nights together so it was more of a 'ships that pass in the night' affair than something akin to *Gone with the Wind*. We sailed later that day, bound for the good old KG V docks and home. I did go back to BA again on the Highland Chieftain three months later. I couldn't resist trying to see if she was still there. I wasn't sure if I was checking her story or not. However she was not at the old address, or in the same job, so I assumed she had been truthful with me, which was very satisfying to my inflated ego.

Chapter Seventeen

By this time I had completed eight trips so I felt a pretty old hand. I had been fast tracked through the ranks to the dizzy heights of a Senior Ordinary Seaman. The ranks ran from, Deck Boy, to JOS (Junior Ordinary Seaman) then to SOS. After reaching this rank and having eighteen months sea experience we had the option to attend a two-week training course held on a decommissioned ship moored in the West India dock. This course was to attain a certificate of competence as an EDH (Efficient Deck Hand) or AB (Able Seaman). It was a crash course which led to being examined and if you passed, being certified in lifeboat skills and procedures. This certificate confirmed that you had successfully completed the extra training required to undertake and be called upon to perform the more responsible and sometimes dangerous tasks in life at sea. These included working aloft. There was also a very dangerous appointment nobody wanted or looked forward to. It was taking a senior role in a fire emergency and in fire drills. This role involved training for and practicing entering fires in an asbestos suit with a breathing helmet attached. Then what we considered the big one – life boat drills and being appointed in charge of a lifeboat in an emergency. This involved passenger and crew control and being conversant with and skilled in launching procedures and assuming coxswain duties and command when launched. It may sound a bit romantic, but it would be critical in an emergency. This training and certification was required under strict Board of Trade regulations, governing safety at sea procedures.

All of life is an education. Different situations, circumstances and experiences add to the ever changing, but unfinishable product that is oneself. My first romantic education (as opposed to a purely sexual one) took place on the MV Athenic of the Shaw Savill Line. She was about eleven thousand-ton displacement and had been built for the New Zealand refrigeration trade. As was common practice then, these cargo ships were built with a limited amount of passenger accommodation. They weren't for the ten-pounder immigration brigade. These passengers were generally the more affluent type, looking to travel in a relaxed manner. I need to make this point clear, as something quite wonderful happened for me. A situation developed concerning one of these passengers, a very elegant, attractive lady, probably in her early fifties; it mattered not at all as I discovered that real class is ageless. Her age was something we never discussed, well you don't do you? Even at eighteen I knew that.

The trip had been an outstanding one. The deck crew were a good bunch, of which most had previously been to New Zealand. They relayed story upon story of the good times available in all the ports we were to visit. These were Auckland, Wellington and Napier, all in the North Island. Apparently the Kiwi girls had a liking for us well-dressed English boys. We enjoyed a position with them, which was similar to the one that American service men enjoyed with the English girls. It was rather ironic really; as to a man we all got pissed off at home with the success the Yanks enjoyed with our girls. Another reason for our very welcome popularity and I was told this on numerous occasions, stemmed from our willingness at parties and gatherings to dance with and entertain the girls.

New Zealand was and is a very macho society. Generally the Kiwi boys never got round to dancing and chasing the girls till the night was almost over. They were always in the kitchen together, or another room, drinking heavily and replaying their day's rugby match. Well I ask you, what was a young guy to do? That was a pretty big door to leave open for us. It caused a few problems that often finished in a fight. Those Kiwi boys, all rugby players, more so in those days, as that was the main thing in their lives, were tough and didn't mind a decent scrap. We were pretty fit and after being at sea for a couple of years, we were battle hardened. Things always seemed to level out, we won some and we lost some, but usually we got the girl.

When you think about it, the girls were on a winner as they could go out with us, have a good time, which they did and then we were gone. There were no ties asked or given; when does the next ship get in? They suffered a lot of unfair criticism for mixing with us, but why? They were good girls, confident and a lot of fun and they just wanted to enjoy life, as we did. It became a unique situation for me, as I was to know a lot of the girls from my two trips there as a seaman and then continued to know some of them in the years ahead when I lived there. I was able to observe them change their lives, as you do. I saw them as they settled down, met the right blokes and got married, mostly to those Kiwi rugby boys. They bought their group homes, raised good families and lived a good life. So those Kiwi boys generally got them in the end!

I have to take the story back now to that romantic interlude, which really influenced my life. Helen, as I shall call this elegant lady, was travelling to New Zealand with the idea of settling there. There had been an upset in her life, which she hinted about, but never disclosed. She was a member of an influential British family, who were a household name in the film business. She was travelling with her companion, a middle-aged gay chap I shall call Tony. We crew members were under very strict orders when it came to mixing with or being familiar with passengers; for us it was an absolute no-no. Not so for the officers though. That old pecking order thing again. My meeting with Helen came about through an extraordinary and frightening experience.

It was a bleak, miserable, overcast afternoon. This was not a good afternoon, weather-wise, to do the task that I would shortly be called on to accomplish. We had cleared the Thames Estuary, passing South End on our port side. We were turning to head for the Channel; there was a gentle swell running. At this stage we still had the Pilot on board, but he would soon disembark. Readers may be aware that in certain circumstances ships have to fly flags indicating their status and intent. This was particularly so if they were steaming in busy shipping lanes. The English Channel is one of the busiest shipping lanes in the world. The flags all had specific meanings. They advised other ships in close proximity what movements to expect. Some of these flags flew from the top yardarm of the foremast; a very difficult area to access and deal with should there be a problem.

I was feeling very pleased with myself. I had been working with the First Mate and Bosun on the foredeck in casting off and clearing the dock. As the twelve-to-four crew we were still out on the foredeck with the Bosun battening things down. I felt I had performed well; the Mate had left us and gone to the bridge. The Bosun was signalled to take down a flag, which was jammed at the out-board end of the yardarm. Disaster had struck; the flag wouldn't release. The Bosun tried to jerk it free by pulling on the halyard, which is the rope used for raising or lowering the flag. Try as he might he couldn't budge it. It was an embarrassing situation for the Skipper. It had to be cleared. Shit! I thought; this will be down to me to sort out. The job of going aloft to clear it could only be undertaken by a certified seaman (certified being a very appropriate word in this circumstance). Only AB's or EDH's could be called upon to risk it. They would have had the right training, experience and certificate. It was a dangerous and nerve wracking job, especially if it had to be carried out at sea. It was one you didn't volunteer for.

Talk about sod's law, this was my first trip as an EDH. I was quite chuffed about it as it had a certain prestige and you were taken seriously by the rest of the crew. You were the senior man on your watch. I knew it was a pretty serious issue when the First Mate came back down from the bridge to supervise the action. He spoke to the Bosun who called me over to join them. The First Mate asked me how I felt about doing the job. What could I say? It was down to me; it was my job.

"Yes, Mr Mate. I can do it," I said with as much confidence as I could muster. I was more scared of looking scared; I couldn't allow that to happen. To digress, I think that's why they liked us young guys for those types of situations, or for combat in the Army. The worst thing for us was to let fear show. It's all about pride in front of your peers I suppose. In this exercise it's important to remember that this was a new crew on its first day out. There wasn't any established teamwork to help out. It was down to training and experience.

I need to the make the procedure clear for the non-seamen amongst the readers. This job was not without its perils. The mast was about seventy-feet tall to the truck, the highest point. The yardarm crossed the mast about twenty-feet from the truck. That in itself was about twenty-four-feet across from point-to-point. The yardarm was braced by two heavy wire stays that ran out and down from just below the truck to each outboard end of the yardarm. The only way to access the blocks that held the flags was to slide down those wire stays. Unfortunately, there was no other way.

To achieve this I had to follow the standard procedure, which was scary as going aloft, in this situation involved the use of a Bosun's chair. In those days this contraption was made from a solid piece of oak about two feet long by nine inches wide and two inches thick. This formed the seat, which had two holes drilled into either end. Through these holes were passed two sturdy rope slings which were spliced together, forming an eye. This eye was for attaching a halyard to. That was the long rope which ran up and down the mast. It was my job to attach the Bosun's chair to the mast halyard. You always tied off your own chair. Once the tie off was complete and the Bosun had inspected the knot it was time to get the job done. I then had to climb up the mast ladder to the crow's nest. In the meantime the Bosun had wound his end of the mast halyard around the winch drum, which he would use to haul me aloft. I looked down and signalled him to send up the chair. I entered the chair at the crow's nest and then he hauled me up to the mast end of the starboard stay, just under the truck. I was now about sixty feet above the deck, sitting on a small piece of wood. The swell was causing the ship to roll a bit, but it hadn't caused me too much trouble as at that point I still had the mast to hang on to.

This is where it got tricky. To get out to the end of the yardarm where the problem was I had to shackle the chair to the wire stay running down to it. I would then signal the Bosun on the winch to lower me down. However, because I was shackled to the stay, instead of going down, I now would go out to the end of the yardarm. In all my life after this incident, there were times that I got myself into some tricky and dangerous places. I swear none of them came close to the feeling that started in the soles of my feet and swept up my body as I swung out, swaying and down that wire stay. When I looked down the only thing below me was the sea. The gentle roll of the ship was exaggerated up there. What an experience. I was scared, but in a funny way I was enjoying it. So there I was stuck out between the sea and the sky. I was very pleased to reach the end of the yardarm. The flag had tangled up quite badly, so much so that I had to cut it free; but I had to try not to damage the halyard or someone would have to go up again and it would probably be me. I was very careful even though I was desperate to get down. Once the block was running free I slowly let myself back to the mast using the light line I had doubled around the stay. The loose end coming back to me to allow me to control my drift back in. I looked down again and hey presto the ship was back below me. I signalled 'lower away' and slowly down I came. On the way down I started to enjoy it. I was feeling really pleased with myself and my performance under pressure. I had a good look around and saw her.

A large group of the passengers had positioned themselves below the bridge and had watched the show with great interest. Helen was in the front row, enthralled by the performance judging from the look on her face. I climbed down from the crow's nest; I tried to make it look like it was all in a day's work. In truth it was. As I was reaching the deck, the passengers started to clap. The Mate gave me a quick 'well done lad'. He then said something like, "you've done that a few times."

I said, "yes sir, a couple of times twelve feet high on the training ship in the West India dock, two weeks ago."

He chuckled and turned to the Bosun and said:

"Okay, the shows over; get everybody on with their work." He turned to me again and said "well-done again lad, what was your name?"

"Russell, Sir."

"Two weeks ago eh?" He turned and walked off with a quizzical smile on his face. He knew how badly it could have gone. Guys have lost their nerve and frozen out there.

The passengers had all watched this exchange and I had been taking a sly look at them. Helen was glowing, I could tell. The next afternoon I was up on the boat deck, checking the lashings on the lifeboat canvas covers. I was going about the job, when from behind me came, "Hello, how are you after yesterday?" It was Helen and Tony. They started chatting, asking me what it felt like swinging out on the yardarm. We joked and laughed about it. That little visit gave me the chance to really have a look at her. She was attractive in a haughty sort of way. The thing that really got to me however was her beautiful, educated and warm way of speaking. After my dalliance with Helen, it became an important part of the ingredients that would attract me to a woman.   Though strangely, the most loyal and genuine lady of my life, came from a different background completely; showing that a lady is a lady, whatever her background or education. For me those qualities could make quite plain women attractive.   As I said, she influenced me in many ways.   After all I was only nineteen and eager to please. Helen was a mature, experienced woman of perhaps fifty and she gently showed me how to please and treat a woman.

Our affair took a few days to get started. I had told her how the watch system worked, so she knew when I might be around and we could have a few words. I wasn't quite sure that this treat was happening for me, so I decided to test her before making a move. The next time she approached me I took my chances and said if she really wanted to talk to me, we would have to meet in secret. She readily agreed and in that instant I knew this was going to be a sexual affair. We carried it on very clandestinely. I would meet her before I went on watch at midnight. I had organized a private spot near the funnel housing that we used for our meetings. It was actually very romantic, under the stars in the middle of the ocean.

At Helen's request, we moved our liaisons to her cabin. It was accessible for me at night or early mornings, when nobody was around. We spent many happy hours there. I was absolutely taken by the way she would arrange things. She would make so much effort to create a romantic ambience. Nothing was too much trouble it seemed; she left no stone unturned in making our trysts something wonderful. There would be wine, some snacks and soft romantic music. I was mesmerised. For me it was the stuff of Hollywood legends. The excitement was heightened by the risk of getting caught. In my mind I was the pauper and she was the princess in a romantic play. I was in dreamland as I worked and I lived for those surreptitious visits. I was captivated by her elegance and style and everything she did. She was excitingly adventurous as well. There was one afternoon when we were having a brief conversation on the boat deck. As she left, I told Helen I would see her tomorrow. She turned smiled and said, "Yes you will and I have a surprise for you."

I was called at eleven thirty that night to take my place on lookout in the bow, which I duly did at midnight. I had been at my post for about five minutes when my surprise eventuated. Lovely, adventurous Helen had crept up to the bow of the ship, to spend a secretive romantic time with me. She had brought a blanket with her from her cabin. We lay together for a little under an hour and enjoyed an amazing sexual encounter in that most unusual of situations. As I said, style and elegance, coupled with such an adventurous streak. How lucky I was.

I had previously enjoyed lusty relationships with two girlfriends and other encounters in various ports and I considered myself quite the lover man; I suppose that was youthful optimism. Well, the fact is that any previous efforts and encounters paled into insignificance. Helen guided and encouraged me to a sexual maturity that took me from a willing, eager young guy, to a mature unselfish lover. At first, as I saw it, I couldn't believe my luck and then the affair slowly transcended those sorts of youthful thoughts. I developed a real respect and admiring condition for her, which I still hold to this day. I was a willing pupil, she was a delectable teacher. She introduced and guided me to unselfish ways of making love. The whole of the experience changed me forever.

So there you have it, the affair carried on till we made Wellington, where she disembarked. There wasn't a tear or anything like that when we parted. This was a mature practical woman who was very much in charge of herself. She understood better than me that this could only ever have been an enjoyable ship affair. I had greatly enjoyed it and felt enriched and more mature in many ways. To sum it up, I can only say I would swing off the yardarm any time again for such a woman. Thanks Helen for such a gift. The education was greatly appreciated and I hope, put to good use. And I have never mentioned this story to anyone until now.

Chapter Eighteen

The trip on the Athenic was memorable to me for another reason. It was one that stood apart from my wonderful experience with Helen and the start of my love affair with New Zealand. It was another unique experience not available to the general public in 1957. However, with the passing of time it has become a more accessible location to visit today, particularly for devotees of The Mutiny on the Bounty incident. For me it was the fulfilment of a dream and one that I had never thought possible. I anchored at Pitcairn Island.

I remember as a child being enthralled by tales and film of Captain Bligh and Mutiny on the Bounty. What an adventure and it was made even more compelling and interesting in its appeal because it was a true story. It wasn't a product of a novelist, or a Hollywood film director's extravagant imagination. This was a real life test of bravery and endurance that could and should stir the blood of every admirer of courage and resourcefulness. These were qualities that were demonstrated in vast quantities by all the parties concerned. They were shown In particular by the two protagonists, the formidable Captain Bligh and the equally determined First Mate, Fletcher Christian. No matter which side has captured your sympathies, one can only admire their resolve and commitment. And amazingly here and now, the fate that I believed in had decreed that I was to visit the Island of Pitcairn. Furthermore I would see the actual descendants of the mutineers. This was a pretty rare occurrence. The islanders expected only three or four ships visits a year at that time.

Imagine my excitement when it was announced we were to call into the infamous and mysterious Pitcairn Island. The isolated home since 1790 of The Bounty mutineers, their Tahitian wives and followers and their descendants. This was a minute island situated roughly halfway between New Zealand and Panama, on the edge of French Polynesia in the South Pacific Ocean. The tiny community on Pitcairn had been sheltered from the wars, developments, upheavals and the progress of the world. I was anxious to observe how such isolation had shaped them. I didn't see things in those terms then, but I knew I was fortunate and favoured in enjoying and witnessing such a sight.

Pitcairn first came into view as a speck on the horizon. It was a warm Polynesian morning, at about ten o'clock local time. It couldn't have worked out better for me as I had just come off the four-to-eight watch and was, therefore, free for a few hours. I was anxious not to miss any single part of this rare opportunity. Their population in the mid-fifties was declining and I think at that time it was under one hundred souls. We approached the aptly named Bounty Bay and had to drop anchor because there was no wharf to go alongside. The excitement I felt was shared by all. Everybody, crew and passengers, felt the same inquisitive urge. This was a real living throwback to our past, not a visit to a fabricated theme park.

I suppose we were anchored about a quarter-of-a-mile offshore. I don't know what I was expecting to see. Maybe because of my youth I was expecting to see pirates, cutlasses and all. What I did see was like a scene out of a movie. A real wooden longboat had been launched and was coming out to us. It was crewed by a collection of Tahitian-looking men and women. The unique thing about this was the singing. They sang in unison, songs which sounded very much like a west of England dialect. The language was English but barely recognisable. It was happy, with a Polynesian sound woven into it. Well that's how it sounded to me. I was absolutely taken by the moment and it has always stayed with me.

They came alongside us and tied up. We had lowered a gangway down for them. Up the gangway they came with wide beaming smiles. It was obvious that it was a real pleasure and an event for them to have a ship visit and bring them what would be essential supplies. They wandered around freely; one of them asked me for any books or magazines that I might have. I did have some and was glad to give them to him. They helped unload their supplies using the ship's cargo lifting gear. The women worked alongside and as hard as the men. They were aboard for about four hours or so, making two or three trips in the long boat. It was an extraordinary time for me and something I treasured. It was another story to pass on to my friends back home. As they left for the last time they burst into song again; but this time they sang a song that I was to hear a lot of in the years ahead in New Zealand. They sang their version of 'Now is the hour'. It was a haunting, moving moment for all. It surely was the perfect song and perfect way to end the visit. I went on to hear that song sung many times by Maori choirs, in Maori. It was often sung on Princess Wharf; it was known as the Maori Farewell and was sung to family and friends departing overseas on the great passenger liners of the day. They were still the favoured method of travel in those years. I have also seen newsreels of New Zealand troops being farewelled with that song as they left to fight in overseas British wars. It was always a very touching occasion.

Propel yourself forward with me to the late 1960s and early 1970s in New Zealand. Later in this tale I will refer to my experiences and involvement with the game of rugby league in Auckland. This brought me into regular contact with many outstanding New Zealand league players. Amongst these was a certain dedicated and powerful centre three-quarter and wing who went on to be appointed captain of his country. To captain a New Zealand touring team on a tour of England was and still is, a great honour enjoyed by very few. This captain was Roy Fletcher Christian, a great, great, great-grandson of Fletcher Christian, the leader of the mutineers in 1790. What a way for the spirit of his forefather to return to England. It couldn't be more glorious than that.

Chapter Nineteen

It's 1958 and back home in England it looks like I have got myself into some major trouble. I had recently broken off a serious relationship with a local girl. The situation was complicated, as I had got involved in a business with her father. This caused some major problems of a personal and commercial nature involving both families. Things were not looking good for me. After some serious to-and-froing I had made a deal with her father, which hadn't been easy. The outcome left me with five hundred pounds, which was a fair sum in those days. I was nineteen and my wages at sea were about thirty pounds a month, so I felt pretty good about the deal. Unfortunately, the circumstances and arrangement did not suit my parents. Things at home were very uncomfortable for me. The break up with the girl was also a complication. A further problem was looming. I had bought a car with some of the money. This had really elevated me with my peers; as to own a car at that age was unusual. My popularity soared with friends, while continuing to drop even further at home. The problem concerning the car was getting worse. Knowing that I would be going back to sea, I had arranged to sell the car to a local man and had taken a large deposit. I was out with some friends one Friday night. We were in the car, just having left one pub and on the way to another, all well over the top drink wise. The drink drive agenda was not yet in existence. There was a mighty crash and as a result the car was a write-off. Fortunately nobody was hurt in either car, but as we got out of my car all hell broke loose. The guys in the other car were also over the top alcohol wise. They were from a rival firm and one of the guys in my car was a well-known local villain. He and another of his team had recently rumbled with the other firm after a dispute over some stolen lead. They came off pretty badly losing the lead and the ensuing fight. He couldn't believe his luck. As you can imagine tempers just flashed and it was all on.

There was lots of shouting and swearing. Lights in the houses had started going on from the moment of the crash. The other car's horn was still blaring from the impact. It was 'bedlam' and getting very dangerous. I was very relieved when they turned and legged it. And truth be known, we didn't want to chase them, we were all pleased it finished. The car was just drivable, we limped home. The crash and the scrap and the alcohol had kept spirits high but I had a sinking feeling that serious grief lay ahead. In all truth, I knew it was the night's activities that had brought things to a head.

The following day I woke and knew I was in deep trouble all round. I didn't feel that I would get, or deserve, any support at home. There was only one-way ahead for me, get a ship fast. I was dressed and in the hall about to open the door and go out, when through the glass panels I recognized the unmistakable silhouette of a policeman walking up our path. I don't know how they had reacted so quickly but they had. I dealt with him as best as I could. I assured him I wasn't leaving. He knew I was a seaman and would have the opportunity to disappear. In those days the police were local and knew most of what they needed to know. He pressed me for my discharge book, but I gave some excuse about not having it with me.

He left after giving me a severe warning not to leave town. Within twenty minute of his leaving the house I was packed and on my way. My trusty lifesaver, my discharge book, was in my pocket. I had to go. On my way I called at my friend Dinger's house. He'd just been paid off a ship. We had previously discussed getting a ship together again; we were good shipmates as well as good friends and there is a difference. We had sailed together before. We had regaled each other with tales of how good a trip to New Zealand would be. I told him I was in trouble and had to go straightaway. "Okay," said Dinger "let's go." And just like that we were off. Good old Dinger.

We got to the pool. I kept thinking the old Bill was going to tap me on the shoulder at any moment. We were lucky; a big passenger liner, the

Dominion Monarch, was looking for crew and she was on the New Zealand run; and better still, she was sailing in two days' time. She was a 'trouble ship', which was why there were still crew vacancies. I didn't care. I just wanted to get out of here. Dinger was happy; he had been to New Zealand and knew how the girls really welcomed us. I was on tintacks for the next two days. We left the KG V dock and steamed down the Thames to Tilbury. We stayed there overnight for the passengers to board. When we had completed loading them we made our way to Southampton for more passengers. I still didn't feel absolutely safe. Remember what I said about the call, 'let go for'd, let go aft' and I had never been so pleased to hear it as that time in Southampton. I didn't come back to England for thirteen years and then only for ten days. In all I was away for the next thirty-six years.

The 'DM', as she was known, turned out to be a good ship. A lot of the younger crew were signed on her because they had to be, owing to previous misdemeanours. This showed up in the first port we got to, Las Palmas, where there were fights in every bar. The stopover finished with most of the crew being herded back down the wharf by baton-wielding police who really used them. I don't think they had much choice, as these lads were up for the fight. Another fateful pointer to my strange future was evidenced on the DM. Ray Miller, who was to become my business partner and trusted associate in a myriad of activities in New Zealand, was also in the DM crew. In fact, he led a few of those forays ashore, which so upset the local police. Ray was a man to be reckoned with. Next stop was Cape Town and sure enough the boys were ashore and at it again. The difficulty was that those South African police weren't like friendly London Bobbies. These guys didn't mind getting their batons out. In fact they enjoyed it and who could blame them? There were some pretty serious beatings and injuries. Apparently there were a few old scores to settle on both sides from the ship's last visit. This was going to be some trip! I wasn't too worried, as I knew I wasn't coming back.

It was a lovely morning when we left Cape Town bound for Freemantle in Australia. We again experienced that frenzy and particular mood that accompanies a ship preparing to leave port. It's not replicated in any way on trains or flying trips. Any old differences are forgotten or forgiven in that moment of leaving. It really is all hands to the wheel as it were. It certainly is for the deck crowd. Whether you were a first trip Deck Boy or a seasoned Bosun, when the call came, let go for'd, let go aft, that was our task and we relished it. It was a special time for us then and I believe historically it has always been so. The trip across the Indian Ocean was uneventful and any time not on watch was spent on working overtime, or sunbathing in that glorious weather, but I had other things on my mind.

As you've probably realised the DM was a ship of last resort for a lot of the crew, particularly the younger brigade. That wasn't all bad news though as there were some good guys among them. Tommy Adderley, a Brummie who features elsewhere in this story was one of them. Tommy was a steward, so I didn't see a lot of him on board, just now and again in the Pig and Whistle, when I wasn't on watch. He was usually playing his guitar and singing for the lads and generally entertaining them. He was a really nice unassuming, gentle guy.

Tom was a great singer in the rock-and-roll style in those days. He was also a very talented cabaret type who could sing ballads with extraordinary feeling. He often brightened our nights with a performance, on the foredeck or in the Pig and Whistle. He could do a pretty good Elvis routine as well, which was very popular wherever we went; but he was steadily developing a style of his own. There were a couple of nightclubs in Wellington and Auckland that he appeared in when we were in those ports. He was also asked to perform on one or two radio stations as we made stops along the New Zealand coast. I think we all got a vicarious thrill from his fame, although I don't think I realised how good he was. Much later on in

Auckland in the early seventies, when we were both getting plenty of exposure, I would furnish him with VIP tickets for the boxing shows. It was a two-way thing though; I was always welcomed and well looked after at his shows. Sometimes he would introduce me to his audiences, introducing me as an old friend and the President of the South Pacific Boxing Association, which by that time I had become. That always went down well in sports-mad Auckland, particularly as at that time I was getting a lot of TV exposure. Tommy being Tommy always took things a bit further by singing two of my favourite songs. By that time his style of singing had changed and matured a lot. Tommy had carved out a great career in cabaret; performing the classic crooner's numbers I enjoyed so much. There were two great songs I was particularly fond of, *'These Foolish Things'*, followed by *'A Nightingale Sang in Berkley Square'*. Tommy knew how much I liked them, so he would perform and dedicate them to me. He also used to sing another great favourite of mine, that wonderful hit of Gerry Marsden's, *'Girl on a Swing'*. Much later on he had a greater reason for appreciating our friendship. This incident took place in the Mid-seventies almost twenty years on from that balmy trip across the Indian Ocean. Those intervening years had been very much a life-changing time. By then Ray and I had chiselled out a name for ourselves in the night-life business with a sauna parlour called, the 'Pacific' and I had also achieved prominence in the boxing world. Let me take you on a brief diversion twenty years ahead in time to Auckland of the late seventies.

It's a fact of life that both boxing and night clubs bring you into close contact with the criminal underworld. Whether you want it or not, it goes with the territory. This story concerns Tommy and another friend Dave Henderson. They had opened a new club "Grandpas" which was doing exceptionally well. It was a smallish, well-appointed club aiming at the higher spenders. I had been there a few times when he had overseas touring acts performing. Those artists used to come there after their concerts had finished. Tommy really went out of his way to allow them to relax and enjoy themselves. They would then often do a complimentary show, sometimes with Tommy. They were really good nights and admission was selective as the premises were very small. One popular artist I saw there in those days was Chubby Checker, of that great hit *Let's Twist Again* fame. He had achieved international acclaim and was on a sell-out concert tour of Australia and New Zealand. How obliging of him to perform for Tommy and to such a small audience. I think the club only held about one hundred and fifty or so customers. Still it was a quality place and that night was one to remember.

On with the story, it transpired that Tommy was being hassled by a couple of really heavy guys. Tommy and his partner had tried to keep them out of the club for obvious reasons. This hadn't gone down too well with one of those guys who was a definite psycho. They were making heavy threats that they were more than capable of carrying out. Tommy, who was scared out of his wits by it all, came to me to see if I could help. Normally I wouldn't have got involved, but as Tommy and I went back a long way, I felt obliged to try and help. As it happened I knew the two guys rather well, particularly one of them who was involved in the boxing scene as a trainer and had been a Commonwealth Champion. He and the other guy sometimes did some door and security work for Ray and me. Because of this, fortunately, I had some leverage. These were pretty bad hombres and will remain nameless. I really hadn't wanted to get involved, as I knew down the line it could backfire badly on me. Deals with a psycho never stand up. Still, I felt obliged to intervene for Tommy's sake, even though I might eventually be putting myself at very serious risk. I had a sixth sense about these things.

It so happened that I had a big boxing show coming up and I needed quite a few preliminary boys. These two guys were training some of the boys I could use. Also there were some other security jobs Ray and I needed covering that these two were ideal for. So much about life is in the timing and negotiation. I arranged a meeting with the two at the Pacific Sauna Parlour that Ray and I owned, to sort the matter out if I could. I explained that Tommy was an old friend of mine and the difficult position this situation had put me into. It wasn't good to have guys associated with me turning on my friends and in the long run it would be very damaging for all concerned. I was pleasantly surprised and quite amazed at their response; they agreed with me that they would drop the matter, as they wouldn't want to cause me a problem over it, which was good.

I didn't want it coming up again so I made an arrangement with Tommy and his partner Dave. Dave himself was a tough guy, an ex-pro wrestler, a representative rugby league front row prop and a doorman. Think about that and you realise how heavy these other two guys were. Anyway, I arranged to bring the two down to the club with me to have a drink and a shake hands session. The upshot was good; the two would be granted entry on the condition that they behaved and respected the club. All went well and actually they ended up as unofficial security there, which is what I was planning on all along. So there it is, all's well that ends well; a minor victory, but that's what life was made up of then, wins or losses. You just had to make sure you had more wins. But that was a close one and later it did come back to haunt me.

Psychos can't be dealt with that easily. Tommy and Dave were not only relieved, they were extremely grateful and went out of their way to show it. Fortunately, things moved on and there was no more trouble on that front at that time.

My life was really on a winning streak. Everything was rosy; the money was really starting to come in. The Pacific became a huge success. Ray and I decided to reinvest most of the profits back into the Pacific by installing even more exotic facilities. The crowning glory being the outside swimming pool and decking, which was really special and a first in those days. The whole outside area was adorned with soft lighting and had secluded little areas for privacy. 'The extensions', as we grandly called them, took the Pacific to a new level and we were able to increase prices and still we got busier. So much so that we were then able to really take money out for ourselves. Couple this with the other obvious fringe benefits, shall we call them that? It made us very happy bunnies and able to enjoy a lifestyle that one could only have dreamed about. Our friend, Bay Boy Jimmy, stayed with us all the way and was very welcome. His presence with us as a genuine friend was an asset that I am sure helped to keep a lot of jealous predators in check. Whilst on the subject of extensions, it became an in-house joke. It was like this, we had a continuous stream of female customers who wanted to become regulars at the

Pacific. Not as workers, but just wanted to be in on the action. A strategy was soon organized to handle this situation. It followed a pattern something like this: the usual chat-up lines were exchanged and a wine or two was had in the private bar. These ladies were then invited to view 'the extensions'. I was constantly surprised at how many of them did, with an interest that knew no bounds. Maybe they were studying building techniques. Who knows? You will have to be patient and wait for the full story on that one, all is revealed further along in this narrative.

There were other perks associated with my newly established business. We had the money for extravagant holidays and none better in New Zealand than the Christmas break. Christmas time in New Zealand in those days featured a complete shutdown. All offices, factories and warehouses were closed for three weeks. This was the custom allowing everybody to enjoy their holidays at the same time. Excluding the Pacific Sauna of course. This particular public need that we serviced, recognised no seasons or timetables. Glide time, as a concept was still to come. Rainton, a strip club owner, Ray and I, all had boats. Rainton and I had quality cabin cruisers. Ray had a nice sailboat with an auxiliary engine. New Zealand and particularly Auckland have always enjoyed a fine reputation in the sailing and boating world. Auckland's Hauraki Gulf is considered one of the world's finest harbours for cruising or sailing, hence the country's high standing in the field of international yacht racing. Children are encouraged to learn to sail when they are very young, generally in the many yacht clubs that dot the Waitemata and Manakau Harbours. Christmas holidays always found a huge swathe of the population out on their boats, crewing or guesting with friends. They either cruised the gulf with its many islands, or headed up to the beautiful Bay of Islands, one of the world's finest boating and holiday areas. It was a very enjoyable ritual. This particular holiday time we agreed that we would all spend it together. We had decided to take up our own boats to the Bay of Islands. Once there we planned to ramp the boats up together and party. The weather was great, the company was great and we were all doing very nicely thank you. We had all the components needed to enjoy life and we did. It was idyllic.

An extension to the Tommy saga took place up there. Unbeknown to us, Dave Henderson, Tommy's partner in Grandpas, was now living in Russell in the Bay of Islands, where we had moored up. Dave soon found out about us and came aboard with an old friend Les Clark, another English bloke, now living quietly in the Bay of Islands. Les was a fisherman in Russell with Dave. We were already programmed to party, but this new turn of events took it up another notch. Dave could not do enough to show his gratitude for what had taken place back in Auckland. He was amazing; he just loaded the boats with crayfish, a real New Zealand delicacy, champagne and some other requirements to keep the party going. Two other sporting characters from Auckland, Craig Brown and Zach Ratana also turned up with lots of female company. Talk about coals to Newcastle, it became one of those situations of absolute enjoyment that sometimes happen in life. Dave and I rang Tommy and invited him to come up, but he was busy with Christmas gigs so couldn't make it, but appreciated the call. Dave was not a man given to sentiment and it gave me a thrill that he went so much out of his way to show his gratitude for what I'd done. It taught me the value of always standing firm and backing your friends.

Chapter Twenty

Anyway back to 1958 and we called into Freemantle the port town for Perth, the capital of Western Australia, where we disembarked a lot of the passengers. They were mostly assisted immigrants. They were called 'Ten Pounders' as that was what the Australian government charged them for their passage. History showed that many of them were successful in this new world. Most of them adapted well to a life and culture that was very different for them and their young families. They were generally hard working, happy and took the opportunities that this booming country provided and became assets to their new country. In those days, to use the vernacular, they were 'New Australians' but their children grew up as 'Aussies'. They in turn would refer to immigrants as 'New Australians'.

Leaving Freemantle behind us we steamed down the coast to the edge of the Southern Ocean. Skirting the Great Australian Bight we made our way around the coast of South Australia and met the Tasman Sea. Then we made our way via Adelaide and Melbourne, to Sydney with its beautiful harbour. We passed under the famed harbour bridge and berthed in Circular Quay. They had commenced the demolition work that preceded the building of Sydney's then controversial and now world famous Opera House, right on the very edge of the harbour. I was really taken with Sydney. It was busy and friendly, as so many places down under seemed to be. Even at that early age (I was just turning nineteen) I felt a really positive aura surrounding me; maybe subconsciously I was preparing myself for what lay ahead. Dinger and I planned on jumping ship here when the DM returned to Sydney.

I had no idea what an influential part this great city was to play in my later life; but that was all still twenty years ahead. I had the good fortune to travel there a great many times on business and pleasure. Then I was to live for two wonderful years in Sydney's finest marine suburb, a unique place with the interesting name of Double Bay. It was such an upmarket expensive place that it earned the nickname 'Double Pay'. Double Bay and the surrounding area compare very favourably with the finest marine suburbs anywhere in the world.

While in Sydney Dinger and I took the time to acquaint ourselves with the pubs that were used by the Kiwi and Aussie seaman. We established a few contacts to assist us with our plan to jump ship on the DM's return to Sydney. Our plan was to ringbolt back to New Zealand on one of the ships that traded between Aussie and New Zealand. The term ringbolt is used by seamen who are assisting other seamen to travel unknown on their ship.

Usually to their home port, or wherever that ship is going. It's a step above stowing away that is generally reserved for seamen. There is no payment involved. It's an established secret practice amongst seamen of most nationalities and you were bound to help if called on.

Fortunately for Dinger and me this practice was honoured to the letter by merchant seaman down under. I have come to believe it must have had a lot to do with their convict heritage and I do not joke. It is an undeniable fact that most Aussies and Kiwis have a real anti-establishment streak about them. They combine this with a strong ethic of loyalty to mates and a natural dislike of authority. Then they have their great aversion to what is called 'dobbing' or 'grassing' as it is called in the UK.

Along with the aforementioned qualities, I was fascinated by another one that was always observed in New Zealand in the fifties and afterwards. This particular ethic was and hopefully still is, known as the 'Fair Go Clause' and it applied to all who wished to be accepted there. It applied in fights, arguments, in the work place, on the footie field, or even in a queue. It was a call for fairness and restraint. 'Give a man a fair go.' It applied greatly with a new man on a job when he may have made a mistake. I often heard it on wet and cold Saturday or Sunday afternoons at fiercely fought footy matches. It was used and applied in all manner of situations. A famous New Zealand Prime minister, Robert Muldoon used it in a squabble we had with the Australians over a one-day cricket International.

The Aussies had pulled a fast one; a dirty trick which came to be known as 'underarm 81'. And to some extent the row it caused is still festering more than thirty years later. Perhaps it will move into New Zealand folk law like the Tangiwai train disaster and never be forgotten by the Kiwis. It is remembered in every cricket club and in fact, in every sports club. The story passes on from father to son; it is a part of the on-going sporting rivalry between the two countries. Public anger was hot and everybody felt greatly affronted by it, whether you were into sport or not. Rob Muldoon was very vocal about it and the Australian Prime Minister admitted it was 'contrary to the traditions of the game'. Muldoon called the incident 'a most disgusting act of true cowardice' and said it was appropriate that the Australian team's uniforms were yellow and indicated that the Aussie Captain would not understand a fair go if he fell over one.

There were many examples of 'fair go' in my life in New Zealand. At one stage, there was a very popular television show that was called "Fair Go". It identified and publicly whipped any company, official, or organisation that was transgressing that golden rule. Modern life has eroded so many of our core principles, but I hope that down in New Zealand that one still holds true.

And for those of you who don't follow sporting trivia in the Antipodes I should now relate the details of the incident. The cause of this vitriolic exchange lay in the conduct of a certain Australian cricket captain. The miscreant was Greg Chappell, a member of the famous Chappell cricketing family. The incident occurred at the end of a one-day match between New Zealand and Australia at the Melbourne cricket ground in February 1981. The match was the third of a series of five, which constituted the final of the World Series Cup. New Zealand had won the first one and Australia the second. In the third one Australia had batted first and had reached a tidy score. The Kiwis had fought back to the extent that from the last ball of the last over, the Kiwi batsman had the unenviable task of having to hit a six to win. With all credit possible to him, the Kiwi batsman being asked to perform this herculean task was a recognized bowler, not in any way one of the top batsman, who may have had an outside chance of achieving the six required.   In fact Brian McKecknie, the batsman, was better known as an All Black rugby full back. It was almost absurd to think that the six required was in any way possible. That is, to everybody but the cautious Greg Chappell. He instructed the last ball to be delivered underarm along the ground, making it impossible to play a decent stroke and removed even the most outside chance of the game finishing in a semblance of a sporting contest. In support of some of the Aussie team, it has to be said that they didn't all agree with the action. The bowler, Trevor Chappell, his younger brother protested and didn't want to bowl it but had to. Also, the famed Aussie wicket keeper, Rodney Marsh, took his gloves off and threw them on the ground in disgust. The eldest brother of the Chappell family, Ian, who was commentating, was heard to say, "don't do it Greg". That incident still rears its head when differences arise between Aussies and Kiwis and it will be a long while before it goes away. Its importance overrode all topics. It wasn't a good experience to be an Aussie in New Zealand at that time; the barrage of verbal abuse was a bit unfair really, as not all Aussies were happy with the decision to 'cheat'. There has always been intense sporting rivalry between the two countries; the contests always hard fought, but generally, with respect. Greg Chapell did not do that down under thing, he did not give a 'fair go'.

Chapter Twenty-One

At last, the final leg. We are on our way to Auckland in New Zealand's North Island. This sprawling city, though not the country's capital, boasts its largest population. Its growth is fed by the migration of young people from the country towns, seeking the excitement and opportunities lacking in their own small communities. It perches on the banks of the gorgeous Waitemata Harbour, the Maori name means sparkling water. Our journey from Sydney had taken us across the Tasman Sea and around New Zealand's lonely, but spectacular, North Cape. Then into the mighty Pacific Ocean to steam down the east coast of the North Island to the Hauraki Gulf. This huge gulf dotted with small Islands is the marine gateway to the home waters of Auckland.

The first sight that greets you as you enter the Waitemata Harbour is an imposing, conical shaped, extinct Volcano. This is the legendary Rangitoto that is synonymous with Auckland. It stands like a sentinel watching over and welcoming New Zealand travellers returning by sea. It signals that you are home and safe as it stands in guard over Auckland's harbour.

The amazing thing about Rangitoto is its perfectly symmetrical sides. These sculptured-looking slopes show Rangitoto to be the same impressive shape, regardless of the direction that you approach it from. It stands there, a commanding spectacle, presenting itself equally to all. Its message to the early settlers and all since, may well be, 'all are welcome here, all are equal' wherever in the world you come from. To me that spirit reflected all that was great and good in that contented society.

Entering the harbour you saw the lovely coloured wooden houses snuggling into the green hillsides. Coming from a lifetime of English plain and all the same, brick council houses, these wonderful sights from my previous trip to New Zealand on the MV Athenic, came flooding back. It was a sight that moved me then and has never failed to move me in the many times I have sailed into and around this magnificent harbour. At that time I had no knowledge of what awaited me, just a burning desire to be a part of this green and pleasant land. Entering the Waitemata Harbour for the second time reignited the warm feelings that had so intoxicated me. Every New Zealand port we sailed into had an abundance of the coloured houses set into the hills around the harbours. They seemed to sparkle and reflect an aura of happiness and contentment that was so new to me. It is a fact that colour enhances life and these wooden houses painted in different vibrant shades did exactly that. I notice now, with a degree of pleasure that fifty years on, this approach is spreading through the UK.

My previous trip to New Zealand on the Athenic had lasted about four months. On my return home a revealing incident had taken place, though I wasn't aware of its significance at the time. This was not a temporary flirtation, not an impressive interlude. This was something in my soul, which I had carried home to England and I unwittingly communicated the depth of it to my mother. The morning I arrived home I was sitting having a cup of tea with her, everybody else being at work. I was regaling Mum with the events on the ship and where I had been and the things I had seen. I was telling her about how I had been so struck by the coloured houses on the hills. I must have spoken with a longing, or something similar in my eyes, as many years she later made the statement that she knew at that moment, that to use her words, "she had lost me".

And now back to a fine September day in 1958. It was late afternoon and the day was still very sunny. Spring was just finishing and summer was about to say hello. What a great time to hit New Zealand. The order had been given and the deck crowd were on duty in our berthing stations. I was the EDH with two ordinary seamen, with the Fourth Mate in charge, tending the spring. The spring is a thick wire-mooring hawser. One is usually applied just forward of amidships, another just astern of amidships. The spring's function is to secure the movement of the ship forward or astern whilst alongside the wharf. The tugs were manoeuvring us into our berth at the Princess Wharf, the main passenger terminal in the Port of Auckland. We nosed in closer and closer. I had the heaving line coiled and ready to throw on the Fourth Mate's command.

"Wait for it," he said.

The foredeck party, commanded by the second Mate and the Bosun, where Dinger was the EDH on the winch, got the first line ashore and secure. The Fourth Mate got the signal from the Chief Officer to feed out the spring.

"Okay, throw now, Russell."

I threw the weighted heaving line. It snaked out to the wharf and was caught first time by one of the shore guys. Our end was tied off to the eye on the spring, which we then fed out through the fairlead, taking care not to let too much out, while the lads in the shore gang struggled and heaved it ashore and then secured it to the bollard on the wharf. Once they had completed that we turned our end round the ship's double bollards in the traditional figure of eight holding method, which would enable us to adjust it quickly if required by the Bridge. The ship was still, the engines were quiet. The exhilaration of the crew was almost palpable. A new life seemed to invade the ship. This was the moment that all had waited for on that long sweep down here, particularly those who had been here before. The evening was upon us and it was Friday night in Auckland.

Secured alongside Princess Wharf, we young seamen felt we were in Paradise. Our money seemed to go a long way here and we were often asked to help the 'wharfies' in loading and unloading the ship in our time off and we were very well paid for it. Consequently we had a lot of disposable income and we knew just where and how to spend it, something those lovely Kiwi girls also seemed to know. Our first night out was to an amazing club called The Polynesian. Well known to those of us who had been here on previous trips. It featured a really good band and illegally sold us watered down drinks. No matter that, as we always smuggled in our own. Everybody knew, but a blind eye was turned. There were huge bouncers on the doors, but they weren't needed, we just wanted a good time. As there were more than enough girls to go round, the main source of potential trouble was negated. Dinger and I were pretty successful and pulled two lovely looking girls. One of them, who was with me that night, will play a large part in this story, some thirty five years later. She was an extraordinarily beautiful half-caste Maori girl, who at the time called herself Billy. The other was a Pacific Island girl, equally pretty, who called herself Dianne. They were two lovely fun loving girls. Dinger and I thought we had died and gone to Heaven. These weren't professional working girls, of the type that often hung around for seaman. They, like us, just wanted to live a little.

That first night was fantastic and so were many that followed it. Dinger and I fancied ourselves as good jivers and we probably were, which made us even more popular with the two girls. We jived the night away; the music was great. It was a Polynesian band playing pop and rock songs of the time. Their very good version of the Bill Hayley and the Comets classic, *'Rock Around the Clock,'* brought the house down. They also played some romantic Platters numbers. They were very good. The Polynesians are very gifted musically. Anyway the Platters numbers set the mood for romance. Dinger and I turned on the charm and won the hearts of those two ladies. We were ecstatic. We left the club with them and they took us to a coffee bar/club not far away called the Bar X in Pitt St. In conversation with them, we found we had struck gold. The girls were live-in housemaids in an upmarket private Hotel called The Gables. It was in the suburb of Parnell, quite near the docks we were told, but more importantly where they each had their own private room. Well, nothing like that had happened in good old Mill End. Girl friends were available, but definitely not with their own rooms. Any courting that took place was in much more spartan surroundings. But that was 1958; how things have changed.

As luck would have it, the girls were pretty impressed. Dinger and I had to sneak out of the hotel early in the morning before the management were around. We found our way back to the docks and our ship, smiling and feeling very pleased with ourselves. We strolled along, through tree-lined, wide streets. This was Parnell, a very upmarket residential area. It was a lovely morning and we could see the Waitemata Harbour sparkling in the distance. On the other side of the harbour, we could see the Royal New Zealand Navy dockyards and the old fashioned suburb that I came to know so well in the years ahead. It was Devonport and in those days before the harbour bridge was built it was only accessed by a ferry service. Back then it was a middle-of-the-road sleepy hollow. Today it is a trendy, restaurant-driven tourist attraction; highly prized as a residential address.

The vista laid before our eyes as we strolled along on that fine morning, from our slightly elevated position, was a magnificent sight to see. To compliment it, the sun was just above the horizon to the east and was sending down that special, gentle, early morning, caressing warmth. It was almost intoxicating, I felt very lucky and happy to be just where I was. I was excited and felt absolutely confident in the future and sure that my decision to return had been the right one. Any niggling doubts were dispelled. I had reached a place in my mind that could only allow me to go forward. I was really up for the challenges that lay ahead. In our lives we all have special moments that stay with us and this simple one is one of mine.

I looked over at Dinger as we enjoyed that stroll back to the ship. We were both thinking that this life was a long, long way from what we knew. So different from the lifestyle of where we were from. Not just in distance, but also in concept. Dinger and I had often discussed the consequences of jumping ship and where it could lead us. Dinger was as keen as I was on the plan. He too had an adventurous spirit, but I think he was supporting me as well. In truth I had to jump, he didn't. Dinger wasn't just following me though; he was definitely his own man. I always thought his long-term destiny was in another direction from mine. He was level headed, less headstrong than me. He had enjoyed a good education. Though he missed out on the eleven-plus, he had won a place at a leading technical school and had acquitted himself well. In the long term he put it to good use and enjoyed a successful army career. In good times and in times of trouble, he was a true Mill End boy; a good man to have by your side.

Dinger and I enjoyed a wonderful two weeks or so with the girls. We told them of our plans to return. It all must have sounded very romantic, but I was pretty sure that they didn't expect us to carry them out. They had probably heard it all before, so they just went along with us. We all made the usual promises of youth, caught up in this passionate, exciting time in our lives. I think we all played out that time like it was a scene in a play. The girls promised that they would be waiting for us and said they would let us stay with them on our return. To their eternal credit they did; let us stay with them that is; I would not want to bet on the waiting for us though! When the DM left Auckland we called in to Wellington for a few days, then on to Port Lyttleton, which was a courtesy visit, as part of a celebration. We completely flagged the ship to play our part in the festivities and then on the Sunday had an open day for the local population to come aboard, which they did in great numbers. The visit was a huge success. I think our stay there was for about three days. Our departure was quite touching as the local citizens crowded the wharf and gave us a great send off. There were streamers, a band and a choir. The gathering on the wharf all sang *Now is the Hour*. The haunting melody and the lyrics always found a soft spot in me and caused me to take stock of things, but there again, it is fair to say I am a sentimental sort of bloke. The first port of call on our homeward voyage was Sydney and Dinger and I, although a bit nervous, were ready to execute our plan and jump ship.

Chapter Twenty-Two

So there I was, standing at the bottom of Queen Street, Auckland, having left a trail of destruction behind me back home. My stance belied the fact that I only had eight pennies in my pocket. I was nineteen, nearly twenty and wondering what my next move should be. I had my girlfriend Billy's phone number in my pocket. I had just walked through the wharf gates with crewmembers of the ship that I had secretly boarded in Sydney. I had my few possessions in Dad's old army hold all.

"See you later and good luck with that Sheila," Pete, one of the ship's crew, called out as we went our separate ways. They were going to their homes and families; I was heading into an uncertain world. Dinger and I had jumped ship in Sydney as planned. We had survived a real helter-skelter time. Sydney was a tough town, especially if you were a stranger and broke. We were there for about ten days. We had walked down the DM's gangplank with the princely sum of about three or four pounds between us. However we had that most prized of assets, the confidence of youth.

We had spent a night in a doss house in George St. It masqueraded as the United Services Club and was used mainly by down-and-outs and alcoholics. It charged one shilling a night, so you can guess what it was like. We had forlornly made our way down to the dock.   There we sat on a wharf bench and watched the Dominion Monarch being shepherded out into the stream by the busy tugs. She was turned and slowly made her way under the Harbour Bridge and then she was gone from our sight.   Suddenly the realisation hit.   Shit! We've done it. We're on our own and homeless. For non-seafarers this may be hard to understand, but when you join a ship it becomes your home. It gives you shelter, food, order and stability. As the Dominion Monarch disappeared, so did our stability and our home.

We made contact with some Kiwi seamen in an infamous dockside pub, the Piermont Hotel. It was a well-known watering hole that catered for dockers, seamen, crims, pimps and hookers and was a clearinghouse for stolen and pilfered cargo. It was noisy and rough and one could easily imagine Long John Silver holding court there. I had been in some dives in different ports, but this was something else. Almost anything could be bought or sold, any sexual persuasion catered for, any injury or murder easily arranged.   Welcome to Australia's dark underbelly, I thought.

During the miserable time Dinger and I spent in Sydney we were constantly broke, but even tough times seem to throw up opportunities and a little scam came our way courtesy of a chance meeting at the Piermont Hotel. We fell in amongst the seamen and dockers there and befriended a group who worked on a demolition site nearby, the Fort Macquarie Tram Depot that was later to become the famous Sydney Opera House. They were a rough but friendly bunch and using the ruse that we were thinking of applying for jobs on the site, we gleaned many facts about their employment and work practices. They told us how much they were paid and more importantly, how they were paid. Labour was in demand and wages were high. The work force was constantly changing and the pay clerks used a number system to identify workers when making wages payments. The system was backed up by a numbered disk. It gave us an idea. We got talking to one of the younger workers who was nearer our age and persuaded him to assist us in a bit of skulduggery. A couple of the Aussie workers were complaining about a fellow worker who owed them money. He hadn't come to work for a couple of days and they were wondering whether he'd come in to pick up his wages on payday. They worked a 'three-days-in-hand' system, so it would be a full week's pay with overtime and penal rates etc. just waiting to be plucked. The younger guy gave us the absentee's name and pay disk number and agreed to lend us his own identification disc. The pay clerks were always hassled and just used to ask "name and number" while the worker stood there with his disc in his hand and gave his name and his number, collected the pay packet and signed for it. It had to be worth a shot. We cut the young guy in on the deal. He thought it was a great lark and a bit of fun. For us it was the difference between eating and going hungry.

Fortunately the absent worker was about Dinger's build and colouring in case the pay clerk remembered him. So it was obvious that Dinger should have the honour of doing the job. I stood aside, selfless as ever, just as I had done for Ken Wilson with the school robbery. My strengths have often been in the planning department with these matters. And being an old Mill End boy, Dinger was up for it.

Payday arrived. We met our young accomplice as arranged and had about an hour to kill. We hung around the building site. Dinger and I had both worked on building sites before, but nothing anywhere near as large as this. A siren screeched to announce pay time and the young lad signalled Dinger to follow him to the correct queue. Dinger slipped into the line about ten back from the counter and watched the procedure, smiling and cracking jokes with the other workers. He volunteered the old saws of building sites worldwide, such as "Today the golden eagle craps". It seemed an eternity from where I was watching, but eventually Dinger reached the pay clerk and flashed him a smile. The pay clerk asked him the endlessly repeated question. Dinger gave the name and number and waved the disk in the pay clerk's direction. The clerk didn't even look at it; he just passed Dinger a pen to sign the wages book. Dinger copied the real signature as best he could. The clerk handed him the wages and as easy as that we were flush again.

Our worker must have been on a good rate and had worked a lot of overtime. Good for him. We now had the equivalent of about four hundred pounds in today's money and that was more than enough to tide us over until our respective ringbolts were available. Our accomplice knew we were struggling so settled for about fifteen percent of the take. I'm sure our benefactor would have had his wages paid after he moaned and complained to the pay clerk for long enough, so no real harm done I suppose and to this day I look at the Sydney Opera House with great affection.

Elsewhere in this story I mention George Porter. George was a Kiwi seaman who plied his trade on British ships. He had once been shipwrecked on one in a massive storm in the Irish Sea. All hands were lost apart from George and I think, two others. I had previously met George when he was a DBS, meaning a "Distressed British Seaman" a self-explanatory term used to describe a situation any British seaman may find himself in for reasons of health, accident, missing a ship etc. They are entitled to full support and repatriation from other

British ships, or embassies from whatever country they may find themselves in.

I met and assisted George, who was a real character, in Buenos Aires, where he had run into some trouble the details of which he never disclosed. He was nineteen at the time and a real handful. Anyway he was being repatriated to the UK on the *Highland Monarch* so he and I became friendly. He fired up my imagination with stories of New Zealand, his family and friends, most of whom I was destined to meet in later years. I liked him, but not everyone did and many thought him a bit mouthy. He really was an exceptional character as is evidenced by this following little story. We had made our way back to the UK via Lisbon in Portugal. Whilst in Lisbon George had gone ashore for some fun. Fortunately I was on watch, so I couldn't join him. Inevitably George got into a scrap in a brothel, causing him to miss the ship and we sailed off without him. I thought that was the last I would see of him, but nothing was ever that simple with George. A few days later, after calling into Las Palmas, we were being guided into our berth in the King George V Dock, Pool of London and there on the wharf, waving and shouting, was George, with a big smile on his face. He had hitched a lift with another British ship and beaten us home.

That evening we had a drink in the *Round House* in Canning Town, a favourite watering hole for us. George was thanking me for my support; he knew he wasn't liked by some. George told me most of his gear had been lost or stolen and he didn't have a coat. I was wearing a really sharp windcheater type jacket, which was superb for travelling in. I also had another jacket in Dad's holdall with all my other kit. I knew he wouldn't ask, anyway, but I couldn't leave him like that, so I took my jacket off and gave it to him, plus five pounds as I had just been paid off and was flush. He thanked me and we said our goodbyes. He said if ever I was in Auckland I could contact him through the New Zealand Seaman's Office in Albert Street. I didn't think much more about it as I made my way home. I thought that really was the last I would see of him.

Life is so strange. About four months later I was sitting at the pictures with a local girl and the Gaumont British News came on. As I previously mentioned, there had been a massive storm in the Irish Sea and a ship was lost with most of the crew and one of the few survivors was interviewed. He was dressed in a blanket, looking cold and dishevelled and battered. This sad looking picture of a survivor was plastered all over the newspapers. Yes, it was George, minus my good jacket. So there you go. Some people will do anything to get on the news. Which is what I said to him when I eventually caught up with him in Auckland a year or so later. George's name had been invaluable in our meeting with the Kiwi seamen in the "Piermont Hotel" and Dinger and I were soon organised for ringbolts to Auckland; all's well that ends well.

Me, at home, after my first trip.
With sisters, Jean and Joyce and
mum, Sarah.

Me at 17, 1955. I
don't think I was
ever quite innocent
even if I may have
looked it.

THE R.M.S. HIGHLAND MONARCH

My first ship. I sailed on her for three trips to South America,
October 1955 – Trip two highlight was boxing in Rosario. I also
sailed on her sister ship the, 'Highland Brigade', with Dinger
Singleton and Bill 'Onions' Horwood, Ricky boys.

BOXING TEAM ON R.M.S. HIGHLAND MONARCH

After the boxing night in Rosario, Argentina - R/L, Terry, A real boxer - Trainer, Inky – Boxer, Sleepy Fox - Me – Boxer - Steward – Trainer.   A lesson in life, never volunteer, I was KO'd.

THE R.M.S. DESIADO

Another trip to Buenos Aires where I met Maria, the Brazilian girl, 1957.

THE ATHENIC

This was my first ship to New Zealand, 1957. The Athenic was a great ship. I had an affair with passenger, Helen on her. Notice the foremast and yardarm that I had to ascend and clear a jammed flag.

THE Q.S.M.V DOMINION MONARCH

Over the side painting the hull in Lytleton Harbour. The ship I jumped with Dave Singleton in Sydney, 1958. The D.M. as she was affectionately known. She transported many immigrants to Australia and New Zealand in her illustrious life. Launched in 1938 she served until 1962. She was a troop carrier from 1940.

The New Zealand Scows, Rahiri and The Jane Gifford under full sail. I crewed on both of these vessels in 1959. The Jane Gifford now restored and berthed in Warkworth, a living museum and tribute to older ways.

Me on the deck of the Rahiri beached on Mototapu Island Hauraki Gulf, 1959. She was my home for a while in 1959-60. Truly great, carefree days.

Me, on beautiful Milford Beach, Auckland in 1961, aged 23. The times were a' changing. Not long after this I, "got of the bus". A few years later, I was living in a property I owned, that was on the beach.

Holiday back in England with family after eleven years. L/R Me, brothers - John & Edward, sisters - Jean, Joyce and niece - Denise.

EARLY BOXING PROMOTION IN Y.M.C.A. AUKLAND

THE Santos camp in Auckland, from left: Manoel Santos (British Commonwealth lightweight champion, 1967; to have fought for the title again in Brisbane three nights ago), Barry Hornblow (president N.Z. Boxing Association), Len Russell (co-manager of Joey Santos), Joey Santos (10th rated light-welterweight in the world by the World Boxing Council), Bob Scott (co-manager of Joey).

L/R Manny Santos – Commonwealth Lightweight Champion, ABA suit, Me, Joey Santos – ranked 10th Light Welterweight in the World, Bob Scott, co-manager and business associate, meet him in book 2. At this time, I was President/Promoter for the very successful, 'South Pacific Boxing Association.'

ME WITH FRIENDS, ALL AUKLAND CHARACTERS, 1986

L/R Me, Detective Inspector John Hughes; Ray Miller, my staunch partner; Rambo (Alan Harris), a real character and long time friend and Jerry Clayton at my daughter's 21st birthday party, at our Takapuna beach house. D.I. John Hughes and also Jerry Clayton, who will feature heavily in book 2, in a High Court case that I was involved in.

Me with Rainton Hastie, King of the strip clubs, in the Bay of Islands, Christmas 1984. Rainton and I eventually became friends and partners, after early threatening skirmishes.

THE 'AMALFI', THOSE WERE THE DAYS

Cruising the Hauraki Gulf. A 38-foot, Hartley design, she slept six comfortably, but usually 10, uncomfortably. All good things come to an end.

Chapter Twenty-Three

I made my ringbolt out of Sydney on the M.V. Wanganella and it took four days to get to Auckland. As the ship had pulled away from the passenger wharf in Sydney, I had deliberately taken up a position near the Chief Purser, who would be standing close to the gangway, generally his official station when leaving port. I enthusiastically waved and shouted goodbyes to the heaving mass of people on the wharf seeing off their loved ones. The purser smiled at me; just another young guy, waving to his family. He would have seen that many times before. Swizzo, the crewmember who was helping me, had fixed up an unused out-of-order bathroom as my accommodation. It was quite comfortable with a mattress on the deck and blankets if I needed them. Either he or his friend brought food to me, usually just after meal times.

I thought the safest ploy was to pass myself off as one of the passengers as far as possible. To that end I used to have a stroll around the decks and got quite chatty with two passengers. By the second day I had built up a bit of trust with them. As a result of our conversations I was able to disclose that I was a stowaway. This didn't faze them a bit, in fact quite the reverse. One of them was a leading New Zealand artist, who was returning from the UK. The New Zealand government had commissioned him to paint a full-length portrait of the then young Queen Elizabeth to hang in the Governor General's residence. Unfortunately, I can't remember his name now and I imagine he has passed on. However he and his companion, a nice young English chap, were very kind to me. They used to bring me fruit from the dining room, biscuits and chocolate. We sat in the deck chairs one afternoon discussing spiritualism. It appeared the artist was deeply involved in it. To this day I still remember him stating that Winston Churchill was a confirmed spiritualist. That statement made a great impression on me. From an early age I had revered Churchill and it caused me to have an interest in the subject of spiritualism in later years. On two later occasions I saw the young chap walking around in downtown Auckland and we always waved and shared a knowing smile. They were good people and I hope they had a happy life together.

We've safely cleared the wharf gates now and I breathe a sigh of relief. Standing there on the corner of Queen and Custom Streets my mood was helped by the lovely sunny October day that Auckland was providing. People were going about their business in a leisurely, unhurried manner. It was about mid-day and from where I was standing, only two hundred yards from the docks and the ferry buildings, I could hear the whine of the cranes and the shouts of the wharf foremen as they signalled the crane drivers overhead. The trams were busily clanking up and down Queen Street, discharging and then taking on new passengers and gliding off along the tram lines. The ever reliable trams were loved by the citizens and were a part of the fascinating kaleidoscope of downtown Auckland. Office and shop workers were sitting eating their lunches in the sunshine, on benches or in casual groups on the Central Post Office steps. The Post Office was one of those grand buildings designed to project steadfastness and stability, which it did; but I thought the assembled throng of people projected it even better. The thoughts pressing on my mind were that I might be broke, but I wasn't broken; I might feel a bit apprehensive for the future and things would be tough for a while, but I knew I would find my way and above all I knew and felt I was meant to be here.

I made my way across Customs Street and into, what was then, The Great Northern Hotel. It was later rebranded as the "Auckland Hotel". New Zealand pubs were so different from the traditional English type. They were huge drinking barns designed to dispense as much beer as possible in the restricted hours that their licences allowed. They had to shut by six o'clock in the evening, which gave rise to the infamous "six o'clock swill". The beer was served out of long pipes that the barmen could walk up and down the bar with. The ice-cold beer was mostly sold in jugs, as they were easier and faster to fill. It wasn't very civilized but the drinkers had a job to do and that's how they did it. I was on a mission by now and was about to phone Billy. I was fervently hoping that she still entertained a fondness for me. I was also wondering if I had been usurped by a more available suitor.

As I mentioned, I had the princely sum of eight pennies to my name, two of which I was about to use on a phone call.

"Hello, Gables Hotel, can I help you?"

"Err, yes, Is Billy there?"

"Billy? We don't have anybody by that name here, Sir."

"You don't? Are you sure? "

"Is it a guest or a member of staff you wish to speak to, Sir?"

"Staff. She's one of the housemaids."

"Oh you must mean Moana or Cathy Lee I think. Anyway, staff aren't allowed phone calls."

My heart was beginning to sink.

"Please don't hang up," I say with real conviction, "this is an emergency".

"They all say that, Sir."

My heart sank lower; I was starting to wonder where I would be sleeping tonight.

"Hang on a minute, Mate," he said in a much changed and friendlier voice. "I'll get her for you."

I could hear him laughing as he called out to her. I had to smile myself; I realised I had just been treated to a bit of Kiwi humour.

Billy, as I was still calling her, was coming down to meet me in the Queen Street Milk Bar, a regular meeting place for our group. As it happened I knew Maureen one of the girls working there, from when I had been in Auckland on the Athenic. I had been out with her for a couple of nights so I was able to sit there and enjoy a milk shake while I was waiting and I have to tell you, New Zealand milk shakes are something to die for. Another stroke of good fortune came my way. I asked Maureen, if she knew a George Porter and she did. It seems everybody did. Better still, she was going out with him now and he would be picking her up at seven that night when she finished her shift. I really couldn't believe my luck. I know it sounds unlikely, but thinking about it, the Auckland seagoing fraternity was so small and everybody generally knew each other, sooner or later in the next few days we would have caught up.

Billy strolled in looking great and seemed genuinely pleased to see me. We sat in our booth and chatted while holding hands and stealing the odd kiss. Everything was okay for me to stay in the room with her. What a relief that was and what a pleasure awaited me. I was looking at Billy when from behind me I heard:

"Hi there Len you old bastard," accompanied by a massive thump on the back.

I learnt that this was a high compliment in New Zealand. Only real mates can call each other a bastard. Naturally, it was George. Maureen had phoned and told him I was in town. Men weren't into hugging each other in those days, but we did. I went to introduce him to Billy but they already knew each other. We all sat in the booth for a while, George and I swapping yarns and checking on mates - where they were and what ships they might be on. Then George pulled ten pounds out of his pocket, gave it to me and proceeded to tell the girls why he owed it to me, throwing in a dollop of me being a good bloke, blah, blah... I have to tell you that those old sayings about being rewarded in life for kind acts, which we generally question, certainly felt true for me then and it couldn't have come at a better time.

"Right we're celebrating," said George.

"Yeah let's go to the Hi Diddle Griddle, it's great there," piped up Maureen. "It's great to see you back here," she added.

Maureen was a nice girl; she and I remained friends for many years, as did George and I. The Hi Diddle Griddle was the type of fifties/sixties dine and dance restaurant-come-club that did so well in those days. Drink was generally illegally served or you smuggled your own in. There were draconian licensing laws back then. Funnily enough though, it seemed to make the outings more exciting. We were greeted in a friendly manner and taken to our table by the headwaiter. It turned out that he was a friend of George's called Keith Morgan and he became a lifelong friend of mine.

Keith was another English ex-seaman; he had jumped ship a few years previously. Keith had been caught and had served a month in Mt. Crawford jail and was then allowed to stay, which was how the system operated at the time. The Kiwis seemed to feel that the month's jail was your punishment and that you didn't deserve to have the additional punishment of being deported. Unlike Australia, where in the old days you needed a conviction to get in, but was now grounds for booting you out. Keith had become a bit of a legend with the Poms in New Zealand. He was a very well built, strong guy, who kept himself in good condition. When he wasn't working as a waiter he spent his daytime as a lifeguard at Parnell Baths. I think his main reason for doing so was to get access to the flock of pretty girls who congregated there. I joined him there on many occasions.

Keith's moment of fame came about in a pub brawl in Dunedin, a city at the bottom of the South Island. This was the hometown of a certain Danny Glozier, a New Zealand champion boxer. He was nicknamed "The Southland Buzz Saw". Danny was a member of a famous boxing family and connected, by marriage and friendship, to another famous boxing and street fighting family, the McNally's. Two of them, Joe and Paddy, both held New Zealand amateur and professional titles. These guys were absolute legends in New Zealand and it took a brave man to cross them. An argument had apparently erupted over a girl Keith was taking out; some say it was Danny's sister. Whatever, the cause of the dispute was now lost and pride was at stake. Danny and Keith went outside for a 'straightener'. It was actually very brave of Keith. All the wise money would have been on Danny and eventually that proved to be the winning bet. But it didn't come easy. I first heard Keith's version. He was modest and not inclined to talk about it too much, you had to drag it out of him. Many years later certain events in boxing brought Danny and me into regular contact and we became mates. I felt I knew him well enough to ask him about that fight behind the pub in Dunedin, which was held in such great regard by the Poms. Danny told me that he had got the surprise of his fighting life, even though he had won. He said that Keith, although not a boxer, was quite skilled as a street fighter. Don't be surprised I thought; remember Keith was a Tottenham boy. Using that and coupled with his surprising strength, he had made it a very hard fight. Danny had to be at his best to win. They mutually called it a day. Keith was pretty battered, but had stayed the distance with a champion, hence the legend was born. Danny was a really good guy, who went on to be a very successful businessman. I spent many happy times in his company; he was the original 'rough diamond' and a real Kiwi bloke.

We had a wonderful time that night at the 'Griddle'. It became a regular haunt of mine and nothing was too much trouble for the staff there. Billy just loved it; she really let her hair down. She was so handsome looking, as were many half-caste Maori. She was also blessed with a fine sense of rhythm. Her dancing caught all the male eyes and I felt a glow of satisfaction over that. I really felt that I had landed on my feet. Thinking about it later, I realised that the unwritten law of assistance amongst merchant seaman had largely contributed to the situation I now found myself in. In all honesty, it couldn't have happened without it. As we sat chatting, George asked me what I had been doing since he last saw me. I told him of my problems with the girl in England and with her father and touched on the business we had started. It was an office and window cleaning business. I realised George was taking a more than usual interest in the subject. He disappeared into the office to use the phone. When he came back, he told me about his brother-in-law, Joey Garner and his friend Peter Thornton, both ex seaman. Peter was English, Joey a Kiwi. As it happens they had recently brought a cleaning business and they were struggling with it. George had phoned Joey and lauded my abilities to him and they wanted to see me to work up some ideas to get the business pumping and also to see whether I wanted a job. That night, while lying there with Billy, I thought about the day. It was like this - I had started off with no money, no friends, maybe no girlfriend and maybe nowhere to sleep. Everything was reversed by the end of that significant day. Some money, somewhere to sleep, new friends, a job, prospects and Dinger covered when he arrived. Funny old world.

When we were not dancing, the live entertainment was Australasia's top female impersonator, a hugely talented Kiwi called Noel McKay. Noel had been a founder member of the famous *Kiwi Concert Party*. They were the wartime entertainment party of service men, who toured the army camps and battlefield areas entertaining the troops. They enjoyed a high reputation for their wartime efforts in which they were often exposed to great danger. They occupied a similar place in the nation's esteem to that of 'forces' sweetheart', the great Vera Lynn, in the UK. For many years after the war they used to have nationwide reunion tours, which were always a sell out. I suppose they were great nostalgic nights out for the returned servicemen, who would have originally seen them performing in the Pacific theatre or the deserts of North Africa. What a pleasure it must have been for the service men, now returned safely home, to be able to share such an experience with their wives and families.

All good things do come to an end. The music had stopped and most of the other tables were cleared. Keith had brought us a round of special coffees, the method for giving alcoholic drink after licensing hours. George and Keith had a bit of a squabble over the bill. I tried to contribute with my tenner but was told to stay out of it. We sat around the table happily chatting away; the girls were into a deep conversation about some other girl who had done something out of order. Keith was coming over to join us. I asked George what was going on over the bill. He said not to worry about it. It transpired that he had a deal going with Keith. At that time transistor radios and other novelty products were unavailable in New Zealand due to overseas currency shortages. George being very much the entrepreneur was smuggling them into the country and Keith was his main outlet for them. Keith sold them in the restaurant, at the Parnell baths and to other shady shops and dealers. They had a very good thing going. A while later I became aware that Keith was also running a team of safecrackers, all English boys; one of them was in fact an ex-London bobby. I got to know them all quite well. One of them was nicknamed "Socks" as he always wore them on his hands when out on a job. They were successful for a couple of years, but the police were getting close to them, so they wisely decided to shut up shop. I used to call them, 'the gang who couldn't shoot straight'. They just laughed at me. I wouldn't name them now, but they know who they are, again all good blokes.

Chapter Twenty-Four

Writing this episode really brings back memories of those great days when we were young. I can hear the music and laughter; I can see and feel the atmosphere at the wonderful Dominion Monarch Ball. I am transported to the Auckland Trades Hall dance on a Saturday night. The Polynesian club in Pitt Street, the Hi Diddle Griddle in Karangahape Road. I will never forget the balmy summer days spent with Keith and the lads at the Parnell Baths. With Keith being a lifeguard there we were in a great position to meet and score with the bevy of young girls we met there. What fabulous days; what great memories to have and share. My mind is turning out images of faces from that distant past. Joey Garner, George Porter, Jill, Marion, Kim, Oriole, Tony, Leah, Jeddah, Billie, Tangi, Glenys, the Bell girls and their brother Frankie, Lucky White, Jake the Snake, Dickie McCourt, Long Tall Paul Towers - he was six feet six. They were just some of the friends from those very first days in New Zealand that I remember so fondly.

Then there was us. The Poms, a name we were known by and happy to accept. Dinger Singleton, Keith Morgan, Danny Burr, Shane, Mickey Joiner, Denny Grey, Bob Painter, "old blue eyes" as we called him, Ray Miller who became my partner in crime and Tommy Adderley, the singing Steward.

Then there was Peter Thornton, Peter Best, Marty Nunn, Gordon Gillespie and good old Phil Socks. I suppose everybody thinks they have lived a unique life, or lived in unique times. I think when people are as far away from home as we were and still relatively young, you tend to cling together and create a special time.

"Right" said Joe. I had been talking to him and Peter Thornton for a couple of hours by now. We had talked about making their business grow. They had been in business for five months and the honeymoon period was coming to an end; reality was stepping in. They had quite a lot of house window cleaning jobs, a few shops and four medium sized factories that had come as a part of the business when they brought it. They were nice guys, but I could tell they were not particularly hard workers. In fact they were the types who should never own a business. The easy going, well-paid, low responsibility life at sea in New Zealand, sailing on the coast and sometimes to Australia had spoilt them. The conditions at sea and the terms of employment were probably as good, if not better than anything else in the world. Similarly, with the Waterside Workers Union, New Zealand and Australia were very much Union controlled. The Unions were big, membership was compulsory and they were well organized. Employers and governments took them on at their peril in those days.

Joey and Peter were hardly cut out to be captains of industry and they had realised that business and all the responsibilities that go with it, was not to their liking. They had an old green van that had also come with the business and it was their only means of transport. It was lovingly christened the "green monster". Often there would be eight of us crammed into this little van, going out to a party, or the moto-cross on a Sunday, a form of bike racing that was very popular in Auckland. Joey used to ride in some of the races. He was popular because he rode spectacularly, either winning or coming off, invariably in a collision with other riders.

This was all taking place in my first months in Auckland. I had started to work for 'the firm' as they called it. It was difficult, as I didn't know my way around. We also had the added problem of transport. I had to drop them off on a job, make a couple of calls and then get back in time to pick them up. I netted a couple of good office cleaning jobs for them. That's where the money was as they could employ others to do the work and then supervise it. Sadly they didn't and the quality of the work always slipped and the contracts were lost. They carried on just cleaning windows; they made a living, but that was it. By this time I had rented a room in their house. Billy and I still saw each other, but it was coming to an end, nicely though. I was very grateful for her support and we remained friends, which had strange consequences years later.

Chapter Twenty-Five

I was living in an old inner city suburb called Freemans Bay. This was a famous area in Auckland; similar to, say, Stepney in London, the Gorbals in Glasgow, or, perhaps the Bootle and Scotland Road in Liverpool. A tough working class area populated by people who didn't care much for authority, minded their own business, cared for each other and never grassed. That's how it was in the Bay. I had a very early lesson in that, which was hugely to my benefit.

One Wednesday evening I was sitting in my friend Joey's rented house in Froude Street, just off Napier Street in Freemans Bay. I was listening to some music; I can clearly remember it was a Louis Prima record and he was singing a favourite of mine *Just a Gigolo*. I was looking forward to enjoying some 'me' time. It was a typical Auckland house, a single storey weatherboard dwelling. The living room was connected to the front door by a long passage off which there were several bedrooms. I was sitting at a table from where I could see right up the passage to the front door. I heard a car door slam outside. It sounded just a bit too determined. I felt uneasy. Living as I was, an illegal immigrant, your sense of danger is heightened. I was particularly alert as Dinger had been caught and was being held pending deportation. I stood up watching the front door. It was a patterned glass door; you could just see through it. I heard footsteps and then I saw the silhouette of a uniformed policeman and another burly man wearing a trilby hat. Though I couldn't see through the glass clearly, I instantly and instinctively knew who it was. This was the famous Detective Dickie Bird. I had heard stories of 'Birdie' even before joining ships bound for NZ. He was legendary amongst young Brit seamen. I had seen him two times before, when he did his sweeps through the downtown bars. He was an ogre and the sworn enemy of British seaman, whether they had jumped ship or not. It was his sole responsibility and job, to pursue and harass us. He didn't like us and we didn't like him, probably because he was good at his job. He was reputed to have a sixth sense when it came to spotting ship jumpers. He called us young Pommie snots. I have to say he had run up an incredible record against us.

In old Freemans Bay, the houses were all jammed together on very narrow plots of land. Sometimes the house would completely cover the land frontage and access was only through the front door, or a very narrow passage down the side of the house that was often permanently gated off. It was a downtrodden working class area. This, however, had bred a fantastic community identity. To be from the Bay was a thing to be proud of. So there I was, living in the Bay, sitting there minding my own business, thinking of how I would approach that pretty girl I had seen coming and going from the house on the corner, when the calm was replaced by the realisation: "Christ, it's Birdie". I almost yelled it out, even though I was on my own. They started banging on the door and yelling. It had been a fine day; the sun was still warming us with evening rays. Fortunately I had showered and was dressed. I was in light cotton trousers, singlet and boat shoes. As I could see their image through the glass door, so I knew that they must also have seen mine. I had to run for it. I turned and sprinted out the back door. I ran across the small garden and scrambled over the high back fence.

The house, behind us was occupied by an Island family just arrived from Samoa. You learnt early in Auckland, you don't mess with Samoans. My only way out was through their house. Their side path was blocked. I heard shouting behind me. I had no choice. Their back door was open; they were sitting around the kitchen table having dinner. I went straight through and I called out, "sorry, very sorry", as I ran round their table. It's amazing the detail that the mind can record, under such circumstances. I was even aware of what they were eating. I vividly remember the smell of boiled pork. I just kept running up the long passage to the open front door and out onto the road. They were so surprised they didn't offer so much as a word or a yelp as I crossed the room. The dad didn't even have time to get out of his chair and he was so shocked he didn't say anything until I was halfway up the passage. Then he let out a roar you could have heard back in the Islands. I would have been in real trouble if he had caught me; he had a knife and fork in his hand and those Samoans weren't into 'Marquis of Queensbury' rules. "What a mad Palangi," [white man] he must have thought, "I'll get him," but by then I was gone. It must have looked like an old Keystone Cops movie. I have often chuckled to myself over that incident, the memory of the Samoan dad coming out of his shock, then charging up his hall, knife in his hand, roaring anger and abuse at the skinny Palangi who had appeared out of nowhere and run right through his house. I should imagine he kept his back door shut after that. To him or his children, please accept my belated apology; it surely was a case of 'needs must'.

I found myself out on a back street. I heard a car start from the direction of Froude Street. I turned and cut back through the Napier Street School. I knew a car couldn't follow me that way. I kept running and doubling around most of the roads in the Bay. Eventually I finished up in Franklin Road. The car was circling the surrounding roads. There were two constables with Birdie; one must have stayed in the car when they burst in. From a hidden position I saw the car stop. They must have decided on a new strategy. The young constables got out while Birdie took the wheel. They took off their hats. They were preparing for a chase. Those young Auckland cops were all fit as buck rabbits; they were all rugby players, or sportsmen of one kind or another. This was mighty serious.

For Birdie, this was a hunt and I was the prey. Make no mistake about it; Birdie was a determined man and he wasn't going to give up easily. Seamen's scuttlebutt had it that Birdie's frustrations had steadily built up. He had been the target for lots of abuse; his reputation was common knowledge to the entire collection of young British seamen, whether they were ship jumpers or not. He was discussed in dockside pubs all over the world. To us he was public enemy number one. The dreams he had harboured as a young constable, of chasing and arresting major criminals were no more. He had become the permanent occupant of a demeaning little police hut on the wharf. The hut was dedicated to catching young ship jumpers and nuisance seamen. Its main arsenal being the rows of miscreants' photos pinned up on its walls and a thick file of corresponding names. Birdie's frustrations were increased by the level of his own success. The better he had become at catching us, the more he consigned himself to seeing out the remainder of his career in that little hut. His skill in catching us, coupled with his natural dislike of his quarry, had him, 'hoisted with his own petard'.

I slipped into the bottom end of Napier Street, hugging the left hand pathway. I couldn't see them, so I hoped they couldn't see me. I was beginning to tire, the adrenalin was wearing off. I had to keep moving, but I had to rest. My singlet was sticking to me; the sweat was running into my eyes, the light cotton trousers I was wearing were ripped down one side. For me it wasn't just a police chase; it was a fight for survival; a fight to stay in this country. I trotted down behind Gadsdens, the tin can manufacturer's factory. I only needed a quick breather, a pause and the nervous energy would return. I cautiously made my way up the side alleyway of the factory. I couldn't afford to be caught here, as it was a dead end. I had to round the corner of the factory not knowing if they were close by or maybe cruising Napier Street. It was a hair-raising moment, but I had to chance it. I came round the corner and breathed a sigh of relief. It was all clear. I started trotting up the hill of Napier Street; getting close to the junction with Union Street. I had to pass four tough looking young guys leaning over the veranda of the corner house. I'd seen them around, they were locals. I noticed that they all sported tattoos. A voice penetrated my heavy breathing.

"Cops chasing you mate?"

I nodded. I guessed they must have seen a bit of it from their position.

"Quick, get yourself up here."

Why not? I thought. There weren't many options and they seemed friendly. I stepped up onto the veranda. One of them said:

"In here."

I followed him into the house and he ordered me to get under the bed.

Then he turned and went back out onto the veranda with the others. A short while later, I heard a car pull up and a voice called out:

"Hey, Garry, you seen a skinny Pom snot running around?"

"Nah, nobody round here."

"I'll catch the Pom snot," the irritated voice shot back. I knew it was Birdie. The car revved up and pulled away. I breathed sigh of relief. I felt overwhelmed with tiredness. It catches up on you when the pressure comes off. Birdie never got me, but that wasn't the last time he came close.

"Okay come out now, they've gone."

This was the big guy of the group. I hauled myself up and we all sat down in the small lounge. We introduced ourselves and I thanked them for helping me.

"No worries mate."

A very welcome, cold beer was thrust into my hands.

"Swallow that, you look fucked."

I find out that the corner house, number one Napier Street, belongs to the McGlynns; an old respected Bay family. The big guy doing most of the talking is Gary Duffty, the youngest son of the Duffty family another well-known Bay entity. The other guys were Rocky McGlynn, a great guy, who became my brother-in-law, Allan McGoon, nicknamed 'High Noon McGoon' and Georgie Hogg, a Maori guy. All real Bay boys and proud of it.

Birdie had addressed Gary by name. He knew he wouldn't get any change from them, that's why he didn't bother to get out of the car. He knew the rules. We had a few beers and then they said they had to go to "footie training". Rocky and George went on to play senior rugby league and could have gone further into representative level; but they enjoyed the social life too much. There was a brief discussion. They knew I couldn't go back to Froude Street so they decided I should stay there till they got back from training and it was agreed I could sleep there that night. While we were talking, Rocky's older brother, Johnny McGlynn, came in and joined the discussion. It was all-okay with him. You have to admire them. They hardly knew me and Poms were not that popular in NZ at the time. Things changed later on, but that was the prevailing attitude then. But they had a code and they lived by it. If you were offside with the law, you were probably onside with them.

I stayed at number one that night as arranged. The McGlynn's house was always referred to as number one, as in, "see you at number one" or "the guys are at number one having a few beers". It was small and basic, but it reflected the openness and warmth of its occupants. The front door was accessed from the veranda that ran along the front of the house. The elevated veranda was butted straight up against the footpath. It served as another room. The family or friends always happily sat or leaned there, observing and chatting with people passing by, the majority of whom they knew. The front door, which was used as the main point of entry, opened directly into a small lounge. There were two bedrooms straight off the lounge; privacy was a luxury that was simply not available. But it wasn't something that troubled these contented folk. The walls were painted a flat yellow, over layer upon layer of years old wallpaper. There were coloured family photos on the walls; one of them I noted was of the pretty girl I had been targeting. One of them was of Johnny in his army uniform, taken when he was serving in Japan and South Korea, as part of New Zealand's artillery contribution to the Commonwealth Force. This photo competed with a medium sized and glass framed colour print of King George VI in full military regalia. It said so much about this race and their loyalties. I believe that New Zealand was amongst the first Commonwealth countries to declare war on Germany, in support of Britain.

Number One seemed to function as a friendly neighbourhood drop in centre. As I got to know them it seemed to me that all friends and family were welcome anytime. It was rare for the veranda to be unoccupied. Mary, the lovely mother of the family, was always sitting there on that veranda. She met everybody with a cheery wave and a smile, a cup of tea and a chat. She was a person who loved people and accepted them as they were. In all the years I knew her I can't recall her having a bad word to say about anyone. She lived an uncomplicated life and gave more than she ever got. She loved her Freemans Bay as Freemans Bay loved her and along with her family she invited me into the very heart of it.

On the day after the Birdie incident I left Number One early in the morning. Rocky had been round and scouted outside my house for cops. There were none. Birdie would have known it was a waste of time. I had a problem now and I had to move on. It was a pity as I had been settled in and was happy there. I went in and quickly packed my gear. There wasn't much. I deliberately travelled light, never knowing when circumstances like these could arise. The word stress didn't exist in the vernacular as it does today, so I suppose I never thought of myself suffering from it. But this life of living on the edge, while it may sound adventurous or romantic, was certainly nerve wracking. Dad's hold all was well worn and even more well travelled by now, but it seemed its capacity for good luck was holding fast. Joey had offered me a lift and had dropped me off in town. I headed for a café I knew in Lorne Street, just off Queen Street. I sat there and ate a great Kiwi breakfast of fried potatoes, lamb chops, a sausage and two eggs; I must have been considering myself a condemned man. The café always tempted its customers with complimentary copies of New Zealand Herald. I reached for one and turned to the classified section. I looked at 'Rooms to Let' and there it was. The heavy type heading caught my eye immediately. I spotted an advert that would suit me; it was for a boarding house in a nearby suburb called St Mary's Bay just off Ponsonby Road. It was only a ten-minute walk into town from there. I went there straight away and secured a room. It was a nice old two-storey villa set right on the road with a big garden at the back. My room was large and airy. It had a big bay window that looked out over the harbour and the marina. It was a superb location and I was very pleased with myself. I felt that I was settled again. The boarding house I had chosen belonged to a family called the Claphams who had just arrived from Wellington. Bert, the eldest son of the family was an extremely high profile bookmaker, which as you will no doubt know was an illegal profession, which provided an efficient and lower priced alternative to the government owned betting agency the TAB. In all societies, in all times, it is illegal to compete with the taxman. You will hear more of the Claphams and I have to say that, as often as not, when I am in Auckland, I pay a sentimental visit to Freemans Bay and to that boarding house in St. Mary's Bay where I met the Clapham family.

Chapter Twenty-Six

As a direct consequence of the police chase and my move to St Mary's Bay I had the good fortune to marry the McGlynn's youngest daughter, Mary and I lived in and around the Bay in the following years. The Bay seemed to breed and attract a particular kind of person. The men were very chauvinistic in many ways, but you have to couple that with the fact that New Zealand women were the first in the world to get the right to vote, many years prior to Emily Pankhurst and her supporters. The important difference was that when New Zealand women got the vote in 1893, several decades before either the UK or the US, there was great public support for it even amongst the male population. In a pioneer countrywomen had proved their worth and their equal abilities and it seemed natural to the Kiwis that they should vote. It was probably part of that "giving a fair go" mentality I mentioned earlier. The Bay girls were definitely daughters of those pioneer women and although they allowed men to act as head of the family they certainly never saw themselves as inferior. They all, men and women alike, had a clear distaste for authority and those who went overboard to wield it, did so at their peril. I suppose in a way, they reminded me of the 'traveller' groups in the UK. But these people seemed to have a special bond and an unwritten set of rules that they happily abided by. Disputes between males, when they arose, which was not often, could as a last resort be finalised with a 'straightener' behind one of the three pubs which the Bay patronised and it was only ever one on one. The pubs, for any old timers reading this, were the Robbie Burns, the Freemans and the Rob Roy, now revamped and renamed the 'Birdcage'.

These pubs all had a history, sometimes funny and happy, but often with dark interludes and happenings. There were some major industrial strikes over the years involving the Bay people, who were, tellingly, union minded. The most notorious of these was undoubtedly the long 'Wharfies' strike of 1951, which lasted one hundred and fifty one days. At that time a lot of the Bay men were waterside workers, as their fathers before them had been. It was a way of life for them, with Freemans Bay being the closest residential area to the wharves. During that massive strike there was heavy violence wrought by Bay people on strikebreakers and scabs. Then in return an intense level of violence was inflicted on them by the police and specials. These were mostly farmers and their sons, drafted in to support the strikebreakers against the wharfies and their supporters.

There were pitched battles fought on Victoria Park, skirmishes in streets off Freemans Bay and wherever the unions held their meetings. The worst and most ferocious one is recorded as having taking place in Queen Street, Auckland's major street. The confrontations were used to settle a lot of old outstanding scores on either side. It was a dangerous and defining time for the residents of Freemans Bay. A point that still rankles to this day with the old crowd was the sweeping police powers, granted to arrest without warrants. It also became a crime to assist wharfies in any way, including giving food to starving families, even if it was just for their children. It was this and other times of unrest and official actions aimed at the Bay people, which bound them together and bred amongst them a feeling of 'us against the world'. As an example of their code, all that time I lived in the Bay I was a wanted man. My situation was commonly known, but never was I grassed up, or "topped off" as the Kiwis would say. In fact the opposite was true; I was protected by a leading member of the community, a prominent local Labour Party Councillor. My life on the run, although no 'Ronnie Biggs' epic, taught me many things about human nature. I was very aware of the falsehood of an everyday life that involves living a lie. I met good people, but my circumstances were such that our relationship was completely based on a falsehood and after a while it becomes dangerously easy to propagate the lie. I have to acknowledge that I lived it without too much difficulty and I suppose that I may have had a certain innate talent for deception.

The community wasn't generally criminally minded and they had a good work ethic. There were plenty of hard cases though and most of them were heavy drinkers and gamblers. I think that was a product of the hand-to-mouth existence they lived. Freemans Bay proper was defined by living, or coming from the area within the boundaries of College Hill Road, Nelson Street, Victoria Park, Wellington Street and Hopetoun Street. This included the Napier Street School. Two alumni of that school became notorious in both Australian and New Zealand criminal circles. One of them was Jimmy Shepherd, who later became a king pin in the deadly New Zealand 'Mr Asia Crime/Drug Syndicate' responsible for at least eight murders. Diamond Jim as he became known, was sentenced to twenty-five years imprisonment for his involvement in this notorious gang. The other was Jon Sadaraka, an armed holdup man who was twice convicted of murder, once in Sydney and once in Auckland. Jimmy Shepherd considered Sadaraka the toughest man in the Australian prison system.

Other characters from those days included Sammy Duffty and 'Slapsy' Bill Woolsey, both good amateur heavyweight boxers, who ran their own numbers rackets. Their version of the numbers game was based on the final three numbers of the turnover at the government betting agency, the T.A.B. They had tickets printed, each containing three numbers. The tickets were sealed so you bought the numbers blind. It was a pretty big business as Kiwis loved to gamble, it was a silly man who didn't support either of these two, or their sellers. I also remember Jack Niue (gambler and sly grogger). Sly grogging was running illegal drinking dens and New Zealand at the time still had archaic licensing laws. Other characters I recall were, Frank the Tank (sly grogger); Slippery Phil Winiata (greyhound trainer, race fixer, illegal bookie and an all-round crook); Jimmy Ross; 'Lugs' Mitchell; Maori Mac; Bryce Peterson and Mike Davidson, who was shot to death in the seventies by one of the Clapham brothers. Moving up the ranks there was Barry 'Machine Gun' Shaw; along with Frank Gillies, who had used a machine gun to murder two rival sly groggers. These were all faces of the day in the early sixties, some just run-of-the-mill crims, but others dangerous and desperate men; all with Freeman's Bay connections.

So there we have it. At that time I was a reasonably innocent young guy of twenty. I had left the sheltered life of my little hometown. I had been to sea and mixed with some pretty rough and ready types. However, there was nothing there that could have prepared me for rubbing shoulders with and living amongst, or knowing this crew.

Though I didn't realise it at the time. It was the beginning of a new path for me. As the years went by, I became deeper and deeper involved. I was aware of and party to, many criminal acts. Almost any crime that took place in and around Auckland was somehow connected to the Freemans Bay of those years. Plenty of action was planned in the back rooms of the 'Robbie Burns' or the 'Freemans', or in the 'sly grog' dens that prospered there. This was to change in later years as nightclubs and sauna parlours opened. They then became the meeting places of this clandestine army. And once again I was to the fore in that business and consequently, along with Ray and Jimmy, pretty much aware of what was going down.

There is an amusing story to tell about Jimmy. My first knowledge of him was from tales told in the Robbie Burns pub, or wherever the Bay boys were drinking and carousing. Whenever mention of famous or infamous Bay boys surfaced, Jimmy was always in the forefront. There were stories of his exploits from schoolboy days to the current time. I hadn't yet seen Jimmy as he was doing some hard time in 1958. His prowess at fighting, his unusual strength, his criminal activities, which included hold-ups and his successes with women were the stuff of legends around the Bay. These tales had really impressed me; such things seem to be important when you are a young man and I could not wait to meet this colossus. I was expecting a cross between Robin Hood and Rocky Marciano and a truly imposing specimen.

I had just returned from a weeklong trip on the Rahiri. I called into Number One to see Mary and her Mum.

"Where are the boys?" I enquired.

Mary, who had been at school with Jimmy, said, "They're all over at the Robbie Burns with Jimmy, he got out this morning."

"Did he?" I said, "Look, I won't be long. I'd like to pop over and meet him."

The ever patient Mary just smiled and said, "Okay then."

I sprinted across the road. I was about to meet a giant among men and a real celebrity. I strode into the bar and there were the boys in their usual position, laughing and drinking. Where was this Jimmy? I couldn't see him. He must be in the toilet, I thought. I joined the boys.

"Where's Jimmy?" I asked excitedly while looking around. Rocky McGlynn turned to the guy behind him who was laughing and joking with Gary Dufty and said "Jim, meet Len. He's a Pom, but a good bloke." I could have fallen over. Jimmy while well built and pretty good looking in a Mexican sort of way was the shortest guy in the bar. The giant from my imagination put out his hand and said, "pleased to meetcha Len, what do you want to drink?" He then said, "you look gobsmacked, what's the problem?"

I stammered, "I'll have a beer," then I burst out laughing, which could have had painful consequences for me. "Jim, don't be offended," I said and explained my difficulty before any tempers were lost. To Jimmy's credit he saw the joke. It came to be one we shared. Jimmy relates it to this day. He has pulled many a laugh with it at posh dinners all around the world and with the hierarchy of prisons in Australia and America. Like all good storytellers he happily makes himself the butt of the jokes. Good old Jim, he is now a respected author and worker for Aboriginal causes in Australia. Jimmy was a character I have been happy to meet and call a friend, 'through thick and thin; or should I say 'the long and short of it'. In the years ahead, in the massage parlour and night club businesses, Jimmy's association and friendship with Ray Miller and I proved invaluable in keeping the underworld scavengers in line. His name and reputation enough to scare off the dregs who thought they could operate in our territory, or cause trouble in our establishments.

On the other side of the social ledger was a man who did so much for the people of the Bay. He was that rare thing, an honest politician. I introduce Bob Elsender, an old fashioned Geordie. He was the 'Go-To-Man', everybody went to with their problems. He was a Justice of the Peace who signed all official documents; he was the unelected but respected leader of the community. He was a man of great standing in the Labour movement and his door was always open to anybody needing help. He did his very best for me and I was always grateful to him. In later years I was delighted when he and his family became very friendly with mine. His when they travelled to England, mine when my mother and brother came to visit me in New Zealand. He was a really good man, appreciated by all. Thanks for a very timely leg up Bob.

You may be wondering why I have included all this in the story, but I thought it important to show both sides of the life I lived and both sides of Auckland. My previous glowing reporting of Auckland may have presented it only as a glamorous upmarket easy life in leafy suburbs. At a later date that's what fortunately came my way. However, like all big cities, there are the richer suburbs and the poorer suburbs. The Bay in those days was the flag bearer for the latter. Believe me, in the early days things were pretty basic, it was a struggle, of that I can assure you. We are all products of the things and people that touch us on our way through life and this place and its people were hugely important in mine. Things change and Freemans Bay is now an in demand, very expensive, inner city suburb populated by the wealthy. I can't say I think it's an improvement.

But for me the memories flood back. I see the rubbish boys ('the dusties') making their way to work down Union Street to the Council depot. The Bay boys were mostly dusties. Their base was the huge Council Incinerator, which stood with its great landmark chimney at the bottom of Union Street, directly opposite Victoria Park. In its time that incinerator was responsible for the disappearance of some types of rubbish that the council hadn't bargained for. They worked together in tight little groups on the city council dustcarts; they never walked, they only ran. The Bay boys saw to it that they were the main group employed on the dustcarts, the job kept them fit and healthy. They were often joined in that work by established international rugby and rugby league players who wanted to work on the refuse carts as a means of improving their fitness and thereby their football careers. The boys never stood in their way, as they often played alongside them in club teams. They worked an honest system of 'job and finish'; they were out there running in all weathers and they all seemed to have a good work ethic.

Many times in life you hear the saying 'charity begins at home' and largely that is correct. But I think the greatest act of charity I ever observed was the constant generosity of those, amongst the poorest in material terms, who readily shared with those who had even less. And that's what I predominately saw and experienced in the Bay.

They had their nuisance drunks, their arguments and differences, but their bond overcame such mundane matters and for a time I was privileged to share in it.

A thing that struck me about the Bay boys in particular and Kiwi males in general, was that while they might not have been able to tell you who their local MP or the Governor General was, they knew for certain that Peter Snell was the world's best miler and they could tell you about his training schedule. They knew how many sheep All Black lock, Colin Meads, ran on his farm in the King Country and they could debate with great subtlety on an All Black selection. I think you could say they had their priorities right. It was a very different attitude and lifestyle from what I had been brought up with.

Chapter Twenty-Seven

So there I was in the Bay, feeling pretty much like a fox that had gone to ground to avoid the hunt, when a new door opened courtesy of George and Joey and the, 'Battle of the Britomart'. I had arranged to meet George on Friday night at the Glue Pot, a well-known pub on the corner of Ponsonby and Jervois Roads. It was just around the corner from my new home. We knew that Birdie did sweeps in the downtown pubs and bars on Friday nights, so we thought we would keep out of harm's way. Strangely, George was on Birdies' wanted list as well. George had jumped his British ship in Auckland, his hometown. His thinking was that he was a Kiwi so he was home and couldn't be deported back to the UK. "Not so" said the shipping company and the venerable Detective Bird. Unknown to George it was ruled that as he had signed on under British Maritime Articles he was therefore subject to UK regulations, Kiwi or not. That came as an unwelcome surprise to George.

George had been having a drink with some Kiwi crewmembers of a New Zealand ship that he had just signed on to. They were in a favourite pub of the Kiwi seamen; the infamous Britomart; a rough and ready pub, patronized almost exclusively by seamen and watersiders, many of whom were ex-seamen. It was conveniently situated on the corner of Fort and Custom Streets, not a hundred yards from the wharves. Apparently George was having a great time and drinking up large with his new shipmates. He was busy regaling them with tales of his exploits and enjoying free drinks. He was famous for surviving the Irish Sea sinking. The incident had received huge coverage in New Zealand, making George into something of a celebrity. Things were really livening up when Birdie came in and he was team handed, a wise decision considering the job that faced him. He had entered the 'Brit' with three constables and the firm intention of arresting Georgie boy.

Now I have to tell you that to have policemen entering a Seamen's pub with the intention of arresting one of the patrons, particularly one who was held in some awe, was more than foolhardy, it was demanding trouble. George was in full flow when Birdie attempted to arrest him. He came up behind George and he grabbed one arm, while one of the constables tried to grab the other one, with Birdie shouting:

"Come on, George; you're coming with me" and then belatedly "you're under arrest."

George who was a very strong and willing guy had struggled free.

"What the fuck do you think you're doing Birdie?"

"You're just another ship jumper and you have to be deported," Birdie replied.

The young constables went to move in on George.

"Fuck off I'm a Kiwi," yelled the incredulous George.

The constables rushed George and tried to cuff him. George immediately started fighting back and punching out at the cops. This was taking far too much of a liberty for the seamen in their own pub and they joined the fray.

This group was known as the "Buckos." Ordinary seamen mainly aged nineteen or twenty. They were led by a particularly tough guy, Lucky White, the son of a well known Auckland hard man and illegal card school operator, Charlie White. Among the Buckos were 'Jake the Snake', 'Tricky Dickie' McCourt' and 'Pete the Treat' McKinnon. There were another three or four of them in the bar. As George got wrestled to the ground, they rushed in and a general melee started. George scrambled to his feet. Lucky yelled "Fuck off, George, we'll take care of this." Which he quickly did. The scrap then started to subside. Birdie was threatening all sorts of repercussions. The constables, who hadn't really wanted to arrest and help deport a Kiwi, were smiling at the outcome. Lucky and the boys had realised this, so they had stopped the fight as soon as George was clear. Birdie knew he would have to try and arrest the whole pub if he tried to arrest anybody.

By this time, Jimmy Hewitt, had also involved himself in the skirmish, with the support of a couple of wharfies. Jimmy was a Waterside Workers' Union delegate; a powerful union man; an ex-boxer and ex-seaman. He would become a good and influential friend of mine. You will read more of this interesting character in book two. He was a great strength to me a few years later in my publishing scam days. By then, he had become a very important man in the Labour and Trade Union movement. Upset as he might be, there was no way that Birdie wanted to invite problems with the Union. He needed to keep a good relationship going there. Most of his work time was spent on and around the wharves. His life would have become much more difficult if he fell out with them. His bosses would be mighty unhappy if he bought a fight with the Union as in those days they controlled the waterfront.

So there it was, no arrests, no charges for anyone and George lived to fight another day. What a life; but George was still on Birdies list although for the present moment he was heading across town towards Ponsonby to meet me.

"Come on you Pommie bastard," was all I heard as Joey and George whacked me on the back. I had been sitting quietly sipping a cold beer while waiting for George to join me. I had been trying to interest a pretty girl on the next table in a date, but she was having none of it, which was probably just as well given my new status of suitor within the McGlynn household.

"Let's go," said Joey, taking charge, as was his habit.

"Where are we going?"

"You'll see; be patient ya Pommie prick."

This was Joey again. He had such a refined vocabulary. I could see that that was all the info I was going to get. George had a big grin on his face as we drove down College Hill Road in the old green monster. When we got to the bottom we turned down towards the Western Viaduct. This was a shipping area between the main wharves, the yacht clubs and the marina. The Union Steamship Company used it to berth their ships there between trips. The shore gangs would then be able to do their maintenance work unhindered. A part of this area was the Western Basin, which was essentially a harbour within a harbour. It was primarily for very small coastal vessels, fishing boats and scows. Vessels using the Basin could only access it when a swing bridge was turned. The bridge was part of the access road to the viaduct and the western areas of the port. The basin provided safe, secure births for smaller vessels. Busy ports have to cater for all shipping, not just the big cargo boats and the passenger liners. These little vessels play an important part in delivering and picking up small cargoes from the lesser and isolated ports that larger ships cannot access. In many cases they were a lifeline and prevented some communities from dying. This was particularly so as there were many small communities and towns that had been established in isolated coastal areas, on islands and on the banks of rivers. They had been established prior to passable roads being carved out of wilderness areas. Special vessels needed to be designed and built to access these isolated townships. A fleet of vessels had been built to cater for the unusual conditions. They were the New Zealand scows, originally constructed like two-masted sailing barques. They were mainly based in Auckland to service a huge area encompassing the far North Cape, the Hauraki Gulf and down to Whitianga and Mercury Bay, on the far side of the Coromandel Peninsula. Within this area was a host of small communities unserviced by road that needed to get their farm produce, special firewood for smoking fish, cattle, sand and shingle and all sorts of cargo to and from Auckland. The scows had been built with a flat bottom to allow them to be beached to cater for loading or unloading cargo in the communities that had no wharf. To compensate for the flat bottom and to make them more seaworthy, they were fitted with a centreboard, which operated as a keel that could be winched up and down. They were all originally built as sailing scows with a small diesel engine to assist them in entering rivers and creeks, but the sails produced their main movement. These scows were built in Omaha by the boat builder, Darrochs.

Omaha was a small settlement near Leigh, north of Auckland, populated by a group of Scots who had originally emigrated to Newfoundland. Because of this they were quaintly known locally as 'bluenoses'. Their life in Newfoundland had been harsh and not as they had hoped it would be. This caused them to move on again and this time their destination was New Zealand, to a small settlement, which came to be named Matheson Bay. Their particular skill was in boat building. It was a marriage made in heaven. New Zealand needed them and they needed New Zealand.

Joey, who was driving the green monster at her top speed of about fifty along the Viaduct, suddenly slammed on the brakes. We came to a juddering halt. I was in the back on the floor and got hurled forward crashing into the back of the front seats. Joey and George got out of the car laughing; this was one of Joey's favourite tricks. I got myself untangled from vacuum cleaners, floor polishers and buckets and climbed out of the back door as if nothing had happened. Joey used to love a reaction to his jokes. I didn't allow him that.
"Right guys what are we doing here?" I enquired brightly, though I was hurting a bit.
Joey snorted, "I know I got you." He looked quizzically at me.

"You're putting on a fucking act, you weak Pom."
But he couldn't be sure. While all this was taking place George had called out "Okay, Dick, we're here," in the direction of a scruffy, unkempt looking scow which was gently pushing against the wharf pilings. I looked her over, she was about sixty-six feet long and her beam was about twenty feet wide. She had a wheel house, a large open hold and one mast for'd fitted with a boom and heavy canvas sail that was hanging loosely to dry in the late afternoon sun. I could see that the main mast had been removed. In the stern she had a little companionway leading down to some cramped accommodation that I could look into from where we stood above her. She was well down as the tide was out.

"Okay, okay, I'm coming up." A voice drifted up from the accommodation. George then turned and said to me," We've organised a job on here for you, it's a great number, just say yes and I'll explain later."

I was bemused but fancied the idea.

"Sure thing," I said.

A young, athletic looking guy of about twenty-one or so climbed up onto the wharf. We were introduced. George said, "Dick this is that good Pommie mate, Len, who saw me right over there."

Dick turned, put out his hand and said,

"Dick McCourt, pleased to meet you," with a really genuine open smile. "George and Joe have been bashing my ear about you. I don't know how you put up with George on that Pom ship, he moans more than a Pom and he never stops yakking."

George stepped forward smiling.

"Careful McCourt or I'll have to drop you again."

Dick pushed into him, smiling.

"You only got me 'cos I was drunk," he said.

I learnt later that Dick, although of only average height and build, had the heart of a lion and never backed down.

"Okay, this is the story," said Dick. "I've sweetened Jock the Skipper and he's okay with it. There was a problem with Len not being in the Union, but that's sweet now. I got hold of Jimmy Hewitt to put some pressure on and he did, so they are just going to leave it for a while and quietly slip him in later. I told Jimmy you guaranteed him, Joey and that Len would keep his mouth shut. You okay with that?"

"Yeah, he's staunch," said Joey.

George was quietly standing there, smiling the smile of a satisfied man. I realised they had really pulled off a top move for me. There were long waiting lists to get into the Union and to get away to sea. I was impressed. It had been well worth giving that jacket and the fiver freely, with no hooks and no thought of being paid back. Dick interrupted my thoughts:

"Right, Lenny boy" (most Kiwis called me Lenny, I suppose it's less formal) "this is the 'Morning-Glory' (story), have you got your AB's certificate?"

"Er ... yes, an EDH one."

"That's fine it's just for Jock to look at. He likes to play Master Mariner even though there are only four in the crew."

Everybody laughed.

"This is the plan; I want to do a trip or two over to Aussie on one of the Union boats; it should be for three or four months. I might want to slip back into this job, so you will have to stand aside if that happens. The good thing is, by that time and if it happens, we will have you covered for the Union are you okay with that?"

"Sure thing, Dick," I said, "I just appreciate the leg up."

"Great, get your gear down here on Monday morning early. You'll be sailing at ten. The trip's out to Mototapu to pick up some wild steers and then run them up the Panmure Basin. They're probably going to the Westfield freezing works. Then Jock wants to make Kawau Island for a load of sheep. It's a good trip. I'll put you in sweet with the cook and the engineer and intro you to Jock. He's a real character, a real old time sailing man. By the way, are you okay with sails? We use that one there whenever possible, it saves time and costs."

I told him I was fine with sails, which I was. It was only a single sail and in truth I was really looking forward to it. A new chapter in life was starting. Me and the Rahiri. An old sailing scow; a new challenge. It felt good, like it was meant to happen to me.

Looking back it amazes me how one setback, the Birdie chase and then having to move on, opened a new vista and a fabulous experience for me. I spent all that summer on the Rahiri. It was such a simple, healthy life. I can only describe it as grand. We visited nearly every island in the Hauraki Gulf, running up on outlying lonely beaches to deliver farms supplies from Auckland. Then for the return trip we loaded cattle for the freezing works, or 'ti tree' wood that the fish merchants used to smoke their fish. We sailed as far out as the Great Barrier Island, so named because it served as a barrier between the open sea and the beautiful Hauraki Gulf. We delivered stores and supplies to Port Fitzroy and the whaling station, which led to another unique experience a year later. I was mesmerised by the natural beauty of the lonely bays and beaches we called into. The water was so clear and pure. The fish could easily be seen, some lazily moving in harmonized groups with occasional predators gliding in and scattering them. We often prised oysters off the rocks and ate them after sluicing them in the salt water. The farmers and fishermen gave us as many crayfish and snapper as we could eat. They stocked our iceboxes with home-killed lamb and beefsteaks. We lived like kings. The farmers and their wives always invited us for dinner if we were overnighting. There were pleasant long evenings, usually spent outdoors. I remember sitting in a farmer's garden one evening with a cold beer in my hand, looking out over the beach and listening to the seawater gently lapping on the sand. I was struck by the vast difference in my life now from a mere six months before. The family hassle, the car problem, the crash and the fight, the man I had sold the car to. All these things were now far away, not just measured in miles, but in the emotional distance a memory creates as it fades; like a slowly burning old black and white photograph.

Chapter Twenty-Eight

Amid these great times, sailing in the scow around the spectacular Hauraki Gulf, we also had some scary ones and plenty of hard work. We had one or two very bad and dangerous trips. One that was particularly, dodgy deserves telling. We had made a long trip up to Parengarenga Harbour in Northland; it was about as far as we could safely go. In fact it was close to the most northerly point of New Zealand's North Island. The purpose of our trip was to load glass sand for the new glass manufacturing plant that had been established with great publicity at Marsden Point, near Whangarei. There were great deposits of this valuable, high quality silica sand, which were needed in glass manufacture. I think it took us three days to get there; we only did six or seven knots, sometimes ten with the sail rigged. We went up almost empty, apart from a delivery for a farm near Wenderholm. The trip was uncomfortable. Scows weren't good sea boats. The Parengarenga Harbour sand deposits had been identified as the largest and best resource available for the manufacture of glass. This new factory was lauded as a great saver of overseas funds for New Zealand and as a figurehead in the drive to make the country less dependent on imported products.

We beached in the shallows of the Kokota Sandspit and set to work with the grab loading this fine sand. It was a long hard job. It had taken about six hours the evening before, then another six from early that morning. It took us twelve, slogging, solid hours to fill the open hold to brimming. At the end of the loading, we were all too tired to batten down and sail straight off. A short discussion and it was agreed that we would hole up for a couple of hours and then leave. I had got Keith Morgan a temporary job for the trip while our cook was off. I had told Keith all about life on the scows and how pleasant it was plodding around the Islands of the Gulf. My descriptions must have captured his imagination and he just wanted to experience it. Although I think he fervently regretted that wish when we hit the storm. Just plodding around the Gulf was all he had expected. The glass sand that we had spent all day loading made you feel very itchy. I decided I would go for a swim to freshen up. I scrambled into the dingy hanging over the stern and asked Keith whether he was coming. He hesitated and looked down. I saw a shocked look spread over his face. I asked him what the matter was as I positioned myself to dive.

"Don't," he croaked, "don't go in Len," and he grabbed me firmly by my legs.

"Don't fuck around, Keith," I said, feeling irritable from the itching.

"Look, look!" he said.

I looked down and there under the dingy, basking and moving gently in its shadow was a huge Mako shark. Makos are probably responsible for as many attacks as the feared white pointers and I nearly dived straight on top of one. I dodged a bullet there and I was very obliged to Keith for his powers of observation.

We all wanted to get back to Auckland as soon as possible. I was heavily involved with Mary McGlynn so I was keen to head home and the others probably had similar reasons. It had been a long hard day and we could have stayed overnight in the harbour and set off early in the morning, after a good night's rest. However we didn't do that, we secured the grab and boom secured off any loose lines and stowed away the shovels and assorted tools. Harold, the engineer, kicked over the dependable diesel engine.

There is something comforting about the steady throb of a diesel engine at sea. Jock took the wheel to take us out of the harbour. Keith got the galley stove heated up and started preparing a steak, mash and onion meal. A group of Maori kids rowed alongside us, like an official escort, cheering and laughing. They all knew Jock, as their parents and probably their grandparents had before them. Jock and the Rahiri were known all up and down the coast, he was a real live legend. His fame amongst the coastal and seagoing folk was such that, thirty-odd years later I was sitting watching TV, when Jock and the Rahiri appeared before me. It was in a very fine NZTV documentary showing how life had been back then and dwelling on 'the way we were,' as I think the show was titled. It demonstrated the importance of the scows and the men who sailed in them to rural coastal and township developments. As we were leaving the harbour our happy escort turned back with cheery shouts and waves. Those children may well have been living in a tiny isolated community; they may have lacked material things; but they were happy and confident. They used to ride down to see us, two-up on each horse, no saddles needed. Then they would drag out the boat and fish most of the day. No one ever got round to telling them they were deprived.

I stood bracing myself against the side of the cramped wheelhouse having a cup of tea with Jock. We had had many chats. He'd had an interesting life and he'd been a sailor for as long as anyone could remember. I think he had come from the 'Bluenose' community in Matheson Bay. He always wore those old light canvas three-quarter-length trousers at sea. I never saw him in shoes while underway. He must have been seventy plus. He was tall and raw boned and he must have been a great specimen as a younger man. I often saw him shimmy up that foremast. He took his trick on the wheel more often than he needed too. He was cut from the same block as Allan, the Bosun on the Highland Monarch and my uncle Bill Faulkner. A breed who perhaps are no longer with us. Compliments from such men are hard to come by. I think one of the most valued to come my way was from Jock. It was reported back to me that he had been holding forth in his favourite hostelry, Anna Powell's New Criterion in Albert Street. Apparently there was some critical discussion going on about the competence or otherwise of crews from the different nationalities. Poms were getting a raw deal from the mainly older Kiwi drinking school. Jock, the main man in the school, listened for a while and then said, "I don't know about that. My new AB, young Len's a Pom and he's up to it and he can sail with me anytime."

I probably shouldn't have recorded this, but I was really proud when I heard it. He was the real thing.

We were beating our way out to the open seas. Keith had done a great job on the steak, mash and thick onion gravy. Jock was hoping we could make it through, close to the Bay of Islands, then rest or shelter if we had to, before pushing on. He knew all the safe havens and bays up and down the coast. If we did that though, we would have to make any stop before nightfall. The alternative was to take a wider and longer course further out to sea, then chug on to Marsden Point over two or three days. That might not be too wise as the sand was a deadweight cargo and we were well down in the water. Also, because that would be a lot longer it would require more diesel. No sooner had we got clear of the Aupuni Peninsula and were heading south when the weather began to show signs of change. Jock gave me the wheel and a visual bearing to follow while he went below for a while. The weather really started to deteriorate; a storm was breaking out. A radio warning came out for all shipping in the area. The radio crackled out the warning, I think it was from the Station on Musick Point in Howick, Auckland. The lady, who ran the volunteer radio station in Houhora in Northland, came on with a further and personal warning for us. She knew we were out there; she knew Jock well and knew the rest of us from previous visits. On one trip she had kindly invited us all to Sunday dinner with her family. We were not well placed to battle a storm; and sand was probably the worst cargo to be carrying in a scow in bad weather.

Jock had to make a decision. He had considered turning and running back to Parengarenga. He decided against that as we were getting well down the coast by now. Also a full turn was not advisable in the large waves that were starting to surge faster and bigger. We didn't want to be caught turning and beam on by those seas. The wind was shrieking and hammering into the wheelhouse. All four of us were huddled in there wearing our life jackets. Jock kept us in sight of the sandy, jagged shoreline. We battled the storm for at least two hours as we jockeyed to get into, or close to the entrance to the bay and then the mouth of the river to Houhora. He had made the wise decision to run for Houhora. He was familiar with the entrance and the river and we wouldn't have to make any big turns until we were in a more sheltered position. He and I shared the wheel; he cleverly kept our head into the weather and then brought us back on course. His intimate knowledge from years of experience of the tides and rocks of that area allowed us to make it to safety.

The kind lady who operated the Houhora radio service stayed in contact with us, which could well have been a lifesaver had there been a disaster. We received a real banging around. It wouldn't have been such a problem if we hadn't been carrying sand. I had seen at sea before how the weather can be so treacherous and can change so quickly. But previously when I had been in those conditions, I was in ships of a minimum of eleven thousand tons, much better equipped to deal with the forces of nature, than a single screw, sixty-six foot and sixty-ton scow. We were safe. We holed up until the storm blew over. We gratefully hunkered down for the night; there were sighs of relief all round. The storm took three days to blow itself out. After that wait we gingerly nosed our way out and continued down the coast, eventually making Marsden Point. The strange thing was that when we had unloaded the sand, our orders were changed. We picked up some general cargo for Great Barrier Island and from there we had to return to Parengarenga for another load of the vaunted glass sand. To old Jock it was all in a day's work. There were no protests from him, no claims that he deserved a rest after that testing time. The trip that was supposed to take just less than a week, eventually took nearly three. The fifty-year-old Rahiri played no small part in the successful outcome in the storm.   Shortly after that hammering she went in for her annual survey, which she passed with flying colours; her timbers pretty much as solid as the day she was built. Between old Jock and the Rahiri they saved the day. And thanks to them I'm here today to write the story.

By now my friend Dinger had been caught and deported. He was caught through a strange set of circumstances.   First he was approached by a policeman in the street who asked him to take part in an identity parade, which he dodged by pleading being late for work. He was working as an 'off-sider', a term used to describe the driver's assistant on a lorry in the transport business. The company he was working for was City Haulage.   The company was a specialist in waterfront collections and deliveries. For Dinger the job was a good one; the money was good and he knew his way around ships and their handling gear. He was a valuable employee and the job wasn't too taxing for him.

As we all did, Dinger always had an eye out for old Birdie, which given Birdie's particular skills, was a sensible idea. Poor old Dinger had gone into work on that day and had been assigned to a truck that was heading for the wharf to collect a consignment of goods for a company out in Henderson. Dinger knew he had to be alert, but all the wharves were busy, so he quite naturally thought that if he kept his head down and didn't speak too loudly all should be well. Life can be cruel and play some awfully unfair tricks. Dinger and his driver had located and loaded their consignment. They were proceeding to leave the docks through the inspection gates when it started to rain. This caused a delay, as the gatekeepers who had to check the paperwork etc. wouldn't come out in the rain. Dinger's driver could see a queue forming so he stopped the truck to wait for his turn. Unbeknown to him he stopped right outside Birdie's window. Well I have said it before and I'll say it again, Birdie had an instinct for us. Apparently Birdie looked out of his window and poor old Dinger dropped into his lap.

He had no reason to suspect Dinger, who may not even have been on his list. We hadn't jumped ship in New Zealand, so Dinger probably wasn't in his pile of photos. Though there was some talk that he was liaising with Australian authorities. He walked to the lorry, asked Dinger to come with him and that was that, another nail in his tenure of that little wharf shed come office. Poor old Dinger couldn't give his home address, as that would lead Birdie to me and another guy. He stayed 'schtum', did a little time in Mt. Eden jail and was promptly deported. The story doesn't end there though; Dinger being a very resourceful, determined guy, jumped ship again when his deportation ship berthed in Sydney. Using the same undercover network, he returned to New Zealand, but this time settled in Wellington. Although he claimed he liked Wellington I think he just wanted to put some miles between himself and the redoubtable Birdie.

Chapter Twenty-Nine

Something like twelve months had slipped by since the police chase in the Bay. The romance with Mary had blossomed; I was in very tight with the Bay folk. I was never much of a drinker, but it went with the territory, so I became a regular in the Robbie Burns in Union Street on Friday nights. I was spending most of my shore time at Number One Napier Street nowadays. Sometimes I had been crewing on other scows if the old Rahiri wasn't busy, but always with Jock's agreement. Dickie McCourt, who had made way for me, had decided to stay on the Aussie run, so my tenure on the Rahiri was secure. Interestingly, one of the other scows I temporarily crewed on has become a well-deserved celebrity. She was the saved and brilliantly restored Jane Gifford. She was built in the same Darrochs yard and near the same year as the Rahiri. Incidentally the Rahiri was originally built, launched and spent her early days as the Daphne. The Jane Gifford after many years of painstaking renovation and financial crises was finally restored to her original state. In celebration she was ceremoniously re-launched in May 2009 and sailed up the Mahurangi River to Warkworth, her spiritual home, to a tumultuous reception. She now resides there enjoying a retirement much like a champion and well-loved thoroughbred racehorse. She provides a very successful tourist attraction taking visitors for nostalgic cruises up and down the beautiful Mahurangi River and out onto the Hauraki Gulf. She has been a tremendous success, being marketed for weddings, events and youth training programs; once again paying her way, but in a more sedate manner, as befits a gracious old lady of around one hundred and three years at the time of writing. The Jane Gifford restoration and the resulting huge interest in her, proves once again, the public's fascination for sailing ships and their contribution to society. It's pleasing and gives me a strange comfort to know that in my seesawing, often wayward, life I served on the very last sailing trading ship that operated in New Zealand waters. I'm not sure why, but it does seem to balance the book of life a little for me.

"Hi, how're you doing," said Johnny.
He was sitting at the kitchen table.
"The wanderer returns," Gary joined in.
They were sitting with Rocky and they were ferociously attacking a big bowl of Mary Senior's stew. There was a great bowl of mashed potatoes in the middle of the table and a plate piled up to overflowing with thick slices of buttered bread. This was a typical meal time at Number One, plain no frills, everybody welcome.
"Grab me a beer," said Johnny, "and grab one yourself."
"Okay," I said moving towards the old fashioned big fridge.

"Me too,"
"And me," chimed the others in unison.

I had just walked in the door after returning from a trip to the Great Barrier Island. We had taken out a cargo of bagged fertilizer to Port Fitzroy. After unloading it with the help of the local farmers, we had moved around the coast to a little beach where we had deliberately grounded ourselves as high as we could. The local farmers had caught a massive wild bull and it was going to be our job to help load it and get it back to Westfield, the Auckland freezing works. To do this we had to rig the cattle rails up the sides of the scow and make a secure pen so he couldn't move around too much. We then had to rig a strong enough gangplank to drive him on board. This had to be fenced as well and we had to rig the fence in a funnel shape to lure him in and then keep him moving with shouts and electric cattle prodders. It was a dangerous undertaking, but those outpost farmers were up to it. They pulled a cunning old trick on that big old bull though. To help lure him on board they drove one of their tame cows into the enclosure first. He, like all males since time began, fell for it and followed her onboard, but far from quietly. I think he may have realised he had fallen for the old five card trick, because he went berserk, but we soon got him penned without too much room to move. As soon as we got underway he quietened down completely. He got seasick and consequently his aggression just disappeared. I'm not one to judge, but I was told she was a pretty cow! For me, it was like I was in one of those black and white cowboy films I used to be so keen on. I felt like I was in one of those rustler's branding scenes, working feverishly before John Wayne and his posse came galloping heroically amongst us to save the herd, kill the bad guys (us!) and win the rancher's daughter.

Mary and I were engaged by then. I can't recall actually proposing, I think it was something we both wanted and agreed. We were doing all the usual things, saving hard and Mary was doing what seemed so popular with New Zealand girls, I think it was called putting a bottom drawer together. I can however recall the reason for getting engaged. Mary's Mum had unexpectedly come into some money, which was burning a hole in her pocket.

I haven't previously mentioned it, but Mary had two older sisters and both had married American servicemen, US Navy guys whom they met when they were down there on US ships. I think if I hadn't come along Mary may well have finished up over there as well. I think that was the family plan, for her to join her sisters. Mary was the baby of the family and that was thought to be the best option for her, to be with her older sisters. At that time New Zealand was a well-considered member of the ANZUS and SEATO treaties and so had regular goodwill visits by American defence chiefs, war ships, planes etc. New Zealand was a valued friend and ally. That wasn't going to last however as New Zealand fell out with the States in a mighty big way. For those readers not aware of the cause of it, I will explain. The dispute though serious came to be known as 'the mouse that roared'.

The 1972 General Elections in New Zealand brought a change of Government. This resulted in a Labour government being elected. As a result of this a major political change occurred that became enshrined in New Zealand foreign policy. Following its Party Manifesto, the new government declared a nuclear free policy; although it wasn't until 1987 that Labour passed the New Zealand Nuclear Free Zone Disarmament Act. However this initial policy proclamation caused New Zealand to cancel visits by US nuclear armed or powered war ships. You can easily imagine the major diplomatic incident this became and how it was viewed by the American State Department. New Zealand had been seen by them as a very strategic country in the ongoing crusade against communism in South East Asia. The row bubbled on and on. The American State Department and Secretary of State, George Shultz made and carried out many trade threats and sanctions against little old New Zealand. The government bravely stuck to its guns. Following American pressure, New Zealand was downgraded in the ANZUS treaty and it was many years before a New Zealand Prime Minister was invited again to the White House. So there it was, little old New Zealand against the world's greatest super power, the mouse did roar. I have included this little bit of New Zealand history as I think it important. To me it illustrates the character of the country and its people so well. The cost of sticking to its principles, right or wrong, was expensive to New Zealand in more ways than just financial, but they did. Maybe there is a good lesson there for politicians of today. Principles seem long forgotten.

There is one more recent action by the New Zealand government and its people acting independently of it that endorses my previous assertions. This involved a similar stance against the arrogance of the French government's nuclear testing in the Islands of the South Pacific. "They don't test anywhere near their own backyard," was the angry shout that rang out amongst protest groups throughout the land. The New Zealand Prime Minister suggesting that they might like to try their testing in Corsica. Their incredibly high-handed actions caused mayhem and illness amongst the Island people. They uprooted entire populations and the French explosions levelled islands such as Mururoa that they had lived on. The testing caused long lasting ecological damage and seriously interfered with the food chain. Then there were the shocking events of the Rainbow

Warrior bombing saga, arrogantly executed by members of the French Secret Service in the Auckland Harbour. A policeman friend of mine was a leading light in the pursuit and arrest of the French agents who carried out this atrocity. Most of the detail surrounding this event are now in the public domain, but it remains an interesting and in many ways a sordid tale.

Chapter Thirty

The story now goes back to Mary and the money windfall. Betty, the eldest sister, lived in Torrance California, while Delma, the next eldest lived just in New York state. Mary's Mum, with considerable encouragement from Mary, had decided to invest the windfall in a visit to her daughters in America. Mary was travelling with her mother of course, for a four-month holiday. Lucky Mary. Mary and I had decided to get engaged prior to this exciting trip to California. I suppose our young thinking on this was motivated by our wishing to declare a public commitment to each other. This being especially so with our being aware of the family's underlying wishes. Eventually the departure day rolled around, dreaded and wanted at the same time. After the obligatory drinks at the send off party in the Robbie Burns we all went off to Princess Wharf. A large raucous crowd of family and friends, which included half of the population of Freemans Bay, had congregated down there.

Their passage was on the MV Orion of the P & O line. The atmosphere on the wharf and on the ship was electric. All the buzz and rush of a ship departure that I remembered and knew so well could almost be tasted in the air. Truth be known, it made me almost yearn to be a part of it again. "All persons not travelling with the ship please leave now," came over the tannoy; the message accompanied by a blast on the ship's siren. A last minute rush of kisses, tears and goodbyes were exchanged; it was such an emotional time. Happiness and sadness stirred together in the same cup has a difficult taste. The emotion I felt was very strange for me. I was now the one on the other side; for the first time I was the one being left behind. I felt similar to the way I had felt when Dinger and I watched the Dominion Monarch sail out of Sydney Harbour, leaving us behind. My secret thoughts were entirely selfish, I had felt secure and a part of a family. I wondered whether this relationship would survive the months ahead.

The wharf was packed. Mary and her Mum were waving furiously, we were waving back and streamers were being thrown. Then the moment arrived, both beautiful and sad. The siren blew again and the gangway was lifted. A long-standing New Zealand custom of farewell commenced. I think it was born from the isolation of New Zealand, as people leaving were generally gone for a long time. A Maori Choir started to sing *Now Is the Hour*. The first words are 'Po Atarau'. It was written in 1913, almost thirty years before Gracie Fields' lovely version. This haunting song was taken up lustily by the throng on the wharf and those leaving on the ship. She slipped her moorings; the Auckland Harbour Board tugs nursed her out into the stream. They slowly assisted her to turn and start her voyage. We were able to see her pass Devonport and round North Head and then she was gone, out of sight and on her way. I felt I was once again facing an uncertain future.

The first morning after Mary left was a grey one, probably made greyer by her departure. I was sitting in the kitchen at number one. Johnny and Rocky had gone off to work. I had heard them leaving much earlier. I contemplated the future and decided to throw myself into work, save some money and address my difficult status in the country. I would need to sort it out, particularly if Mary and I were going to marry. I was to find out that that problem was also exercising Johnny's mind. That night he put it to me in a typical blunt Kiwi way, roughly as follows:

"Len, I've been thinking. We like you and all that, but what if you knock Bubba up (Bubba being Mary's baby nickname) or get married, then get caught and deported?"

He paused, "What then?" Another quizzical look and he added, "then we'd be stuck with the kids and Bubba'd be pretty fucked up and we don't want that. Have you thought about that?"

Well it was straightforward and fair.

"Yes, Johnny, I have for some time now and strangely enough I worked a plan out for it this morning."

"Let's hear it," he said.

Just like that. In all my life I never heard anyone straighter or more direct than a Bay boy.

"Okay this is how I see it. I've decided to save some more money and then use it to get my passport and then travel legally into Aussie. Then stick around there for a few weeks as a tourist. Then make my way to Melbourne and from there re-enter into New Zealand legally. I'm not registered over here in any way at the moment. I'm not under my real name on the scows wage and crew books. I think that's a pretty good plan."

In any event I wanted to fix it. I had decided it would be better not to be continually living on a knife-edge. I also decided there and then to lift myself and face whatever lay ahead. I thought the next few months would drag on, but in fact they flew by. Letters and photos arrived every week from Mary. I haunted the Western Viaduct and took every trip available, if not on the Rahiri then on other scows. I sailed on the Jane Gifford, the Owhiti and the Success, but the Rahiri remained my main interest and job. I was getting to know Jock really well and he entrusted more and more of the administrative jobs to me. Mainly to do with cargo arrivals and loading. I suppose that was giving him more time with his gang of old salts in the bar of Anna Powell's pub. It was no problem for me. It suited me, I always enjoyed a bit of responsibility. With all the extra scow trips I was doing, my life was full and busy. I was saving the extra money feverishly; my planned trip to Aussie and hopefully back, was getting closer.

Summer had given way to autumn. For me it had been a wonderful experience plodding around the waters of the abundant Hauraki Gulf, delivering and picking up such a wide range of cargo and getting to know those resourceful people who lived and enjoyed their isolated lives. Len Matheson, one of the Matheson Bay families, a crewmate on some trips, had introduced me to the delights of eating oysters straight off the rocks. Then we gathered scallops washed up onto the beach overnight, took them back on board and lightly grilled them with some onion and bacon for a breakfast fit for a king. I recall waking one morning when we had beached late on the previous evening ready to discharge a cargo of building materials in the morning. The morning was one of the most beautiful I had ever experienced then and probably still to this day. We were in a little isolated bay on Mototapu Island. It was about six o'clock in the morning and the warm sun had just risen over the horizon. I was struck by the clear sky, the clear green water and the silence, apart from the chatter of the birds waking in their nests on the cliff and the surrounding green bush. I thought if there was a paradise it must be near to this.

However, the seasons were changing and that would all be behind me for a while. Winter was on the way and life on the scows would be cold, rough and difficult. There was an upside though, Mary would soon be home. The time apart had not caused us to break up and we were getting married. I had looked into the procedure for buying a house under the flourishing group housing schemes. Len Matheson had recently bought one in the new estates being developed in Henderson, in northwest Auckland. This had whetted my appetite and given me the opportunity to investigate the procedure required to apply for one of the generous State Advances mortgages, which made this scheme work so successfully. I was alarmed that the application documents and subsequent disclosures required would make the path too difficult and dangerous and lead to discovery and arrest. Life continually throws up obstacles on the way through, more so if you are outside the mainstream and living by your wits. This was going to be some test of nerve and ability. I decided that I must act and sort the situation out, one way or another. I decided to take the bull by the horns and do what I could to legitimise myself.

Early one evening I was sitting on the veranda at number one, waiting for my future brothers-in-law and turning over the options in my mind. I was miles away in my head when a screech of tyres brought me back to earth. It was Joey Garner and he was with his wife, George Porter's sister, Cathy, a nurse and a really nice girl. We all liked her, but we all knew she was far too straight for Joey, who was a good guy but a real loose cannon and dangerous.

"Over here, Len, jump in."

He was looking mighty serious. Froude Street and his rented house were just across the road. He virtually ordered Cathy out of the car with a curt "go home"; which she wisely did.

"What's on, Joey?" I asked, knowing it was a serious matter.

"That bastard Lucky White has been putting it around that he can beat me," exclaimed Joe, with rage in his face. I had better explain this situation, as the seriousness of it will probably be lost on most readers.

On New Zealand ships and in the New Zealand Seamen's Union great store was set by who was the toughest man on the coast and recognised as such. To those who aspired to that title, it was as important as being the national heavyweight champion. Joey clearly considered himself a contender given his successes in some very tough battles, usually behind the Britomart pub. This position was something Joey was very proud of, particularly because his father had held the same rank in his younger days. Lucky White, by making those statements, was making a challenge and quite frankly pushing his nickname. Joey had to respond to it. It probably sounds childish but it's unwise to judge the social structures of another time unless you were there and can see everything in context.

I had been introduced into these circles by George Porter and I had no option as to whether I would join in or not; however this was a million miles above anything I had ever known, Christ, I was a country boy; this was a cultural thing with them and would be discussed in the same breath, as a world championship. This was considered a dangerous challenge; there would be heavy betting amongst the seamen and the wharfies as to the outcome. This was a real bare-knuckle, knock down and drag 'em out, bitter contest. Tough guys fighting for something they badly wanted. If this had taken place in the YMCA it would have been a sell out; but it wasn't one of those fights with a referee, Marquis of Queensbury rules and a doctor on hand. This was a bare-knuckle biff fest. The last man standing was the winner; no other outcome could decide it.

The question was what Joey wanted me for. It transpired that an arrangement would be made as to where the fight was to take place and when. This was too important to be decided by a chance encounter. Lucky and Joey had agreed to appoint two guys each to make these arrangements on their behalf. Joey had picked Peter Thornton his business partner, a tough Londoner and Johnny Holmes, another Londoner, who could handle himself, though there was no suggestion that they would have to fight. Lucky had picked Jake the snake and Dickie McCourt, so in the respect stakes it was about all even and nobody could take advantage. My role was never quite defined, but I ended up driving the old green monster and that was as close as I wanted to get. Don't shoot the piano player or the driver.

It was all on. The word had spread like wildfire. Apparently this had been on the cards for a while and it had just been a matter of time before it was settled. Here you had two sturdy well-built young guys. Lucky was twenty-one, Joey was twenty-five and they were similar in size. The venue was set in a park just off Dominion Road at ten o'clock the following morning. We got there at about nine forty-five. Lucky and his party were already there, plus a crowd of seamen and wharfies. There was no discussion, Joey just walked up to Lucky and asked whether he was ready. Lucky nodded his head, the same time as Joey nailed him with a head-butt, which drew blood. He had caught Lucky cold. They fought a savage fight for about four minutes, Lucky put up a good account of himself, but he never really recovered from the head butt. He went down under a flurry of heavy blows. Joe moved in to really finish it and luckily Peter Thornton jumped in between them, I don't think Joe would have stopped for anyone else.

"Jake," called out Peter, "if Lucky gets up, he's going down again. He has to swallow it and give in." Joey was screaming at Lucky, "get up or I will kick the fuck out of you."

He certainly would have and he was trying to get around Peter to get at Lucky on the ground. Jake knew the danger and said:

"Lucky turn it up, he is too good for you."

Peter added "Lucky, give it up. Have you had enough? Better say yes, or I'll let him go."

Thankfully Lucky lifted his battered face and said one important word "enough". That incident left an impression on me, but not a very positive one. These guys, though laid back most of the time, settled their differences as they felt they had to. There were no 'I beg your pardons'. Once again I was able to see that it wasn't all paradise in these old fashioned conservative Islands. There can be dark clouds even on the sunniest days was the lesson for me. And I drove the winner home.

Chapter Thirty-One

There were about two months to go until Mary and her mother returned from the USA and there had been an interesting development. The Rahiri had been ordered to deliver a full load of coke to the land-based whaling station at Whangaparapara. This was a sheltered little bay on Great Barrier Island. The island had been discovered by Captain James Cook in 1769 and after sailing right around it he supplied its highly appropriate name. It forms a natural and important barrier between the might of the Pacific Ocean and the relative calm of the Hauraki Gulf. The whaling stations used coke to heat the huge steel vats in which they boiled whale blubber into oil. The vats were positioned under massive flensing decks.

Killed whales were towed back to the processing stations. Their gargantuan bodies were winched up onto the decks and dismembered manually by the flensing crews. This gruesome task was accomplished using long-handled, razor-sharp, semi-circular knives and hand-held power saws. Large sections were stripped off the bodies and they were then diced into pieces about three feet wide and five or six feet long. This blubber was then dragged by the flensing crews across gore-laden decks, slippery with blood, with the aid of long steel hooks. The huge pieces of blubber were then pushed down through cavities into the vats below.   The vats were like insatiable demon mouths that demanded feeding. The roaring of the furnace fires; the rising, hissing steam; the awful smell; the mutilated carcasses and the blood-splattered, grim faces of the men on the flensing deck as they chopped and hacked with their long knives all flowed together to create a surreal, infernal tableau. I had the feeling of being there, but at the same time being strangely distant from it, much like Dante's Virgil viewing the rings of Hell. And appropriately for this local hell, work went on twenty-four hours a day while there were whales to be, 'processed', a terrible euphemism for that repugnant activity. Under the nighttime arc lights rigged above the flensing deck the scene would have graced any modern horror movie.

I regret to this day that I participated in such madness, but at the time I passed it off to myself as a necessity for a young man about to marry and purchase a house.   The whales caught and slaughtered were the beautiful humpbacks whose misfortune it was to follow the same, predictable migration routes that their ancestors had done for millennia before humans arrived in New Zealand. They were easy prey for the whalers. These great big sea mammals who, outside of the fictions of Moby Dick and Jonah, had never harmed a human, were hacked down from their sixty ton prime to scraps of meat and then to oil, all in a matter of hours and later burned thoughtlessly by humans as if they were an infinite resource that we had every right to squander. The pages of my book are populated with regrets, but few as haunting as this one. This episode took place in the late fifties to early sixties. Whaling, like actions such as drink driving, was considered normal back then. They weren't considered anti-social in those more innocent days. The protest movement against whaling gathered momentum a decade or so later and I'm pleased to record that New Zealand played a significant part in the reforms achieved.

The Great Barrier land-based station and the catcher craft were managed by a well-known South Island family named Heberly. Our manager was Charlie Heberly, a tough, dour man not given to laughing or light-hearted behaviour. He had one purpose in life and that was to catch and kill whales and he expected everyone who worked for him to fall into line with that. He brooked no opposition, succumbed to no obstacle. He had to keep order and discipline amongst a crew of tough and violent men in an isolated place where the arm of the law barely reached. The workers were mainly local Maori or Pakeha farmers, all physically strong men and well suited to the job. The loneliness of the location, the relentless and boring repetition of the work and the violent nature of the industry created an environment in which knives coupled with a small slight, often unintended, could have disastrous consequences. Those long sharp knives were always to hand. It was a tinderbox and you had to be very careful about what you said and did and how you were perceived.

I had joined the outfit as a deckhand on the MV Colville. She was a fast ex-Navy boat of wooden construction, built for patrol duty in the Pacific Islands during the Second World War. They were known in the Naval Listings as 'Fairmiles' and were modelled on the British torpedo boats. The Colville's main function was to act as a support vessel for the two killer boats, fast open-decked chaser boats equipped with harpoon guns. The Colville also carried a harpoon and had a compressed air generator used to pump air into the dead whales to keep them afloat. This had to be done promptly as the humpbacks tended to sink once they were dead. The floating whales would be towed back to the station and parked near the flensing deck, which extended down below the waterline. This eased the task of winching the carcasses up to where the crew could set about dismembering them.

I was never happy working on the Colville. I lacked the necessary commitment to the gruesome tasks and just didn't fit in with the rest of the crew. I sailed on her for a couple of weeks and then it was mutually agreed that I would do a few weeks on shore working on the flensing decks until the season ended. I would then get the top wages that had been the incentive to join and any bonuses due. Even at the time I regarded my sojourn on the Colville and the whaling station as a nightmare experience. But I was following the money trail setting myself up for marriage and house ownership.

The whaling station was eventually closed in 1964, largely as a result of whaling in the northern hemisphere greatly depleting the number of humpback whales that made it to New Zealand on their annual migration. The herds were so savagely culled that the industry was no longer viable. Its passing was not a cause for national mourning even though New Zealand had had a long tradition of whaling, going back as far as the 1790s when American whaling operations are recorded in New Zealand waters.

Chapter Thirty-Two

Mary and her Mum were home. They'd really enjoyed the trip, but I was pleased to see that they were genuinely glad to be back. We settled down into our routine and made a date for the wedding in about twelve months' time. It was a quiet affair held at her Aunty Rita's house in Point Chevalier, then a tidy working class suburb and now a very desirable, expensive residential area. The ceremony and party went off without a hitch. Strangely I felt that I was in a parallel universe and looking in on things, although I probably wasn't the first bridegroom to have that feeling. Mary and I had to pay for everything and we had no money left for much of a honeymoon, but we did the best we could with the help of a borrowed car. In the early days of our marriage we rented a house from Freemans Bay's main man, Bob Elsender. His daughter, Rona, was a friend of Mary's. She was a nice lady and was married to a chap who pops up later in this story, Kenny Young, a wild seaman, turned fireman. Our lives became entangled for a few years.

I had nervously acquired a State Advances Corporation loan and we had bought our first house, in Beach Haven on the North Shore. So there I was, married and the owner of a house, all within two-and-a-half years of my surreptitious arrival in New Zealand. Not a bad effort and my eight pence arrival kitty was growing.   As part of the housing loan requirement I had to show regular, steady employment. To achieve that, I had to come ashore. Mary's cousin had wangled a job for me and I was unhappily working in a well paid, but going nowhere, job in the Fletcher Steel fabricating works in Nelson St. I was reminded of my short-lived attempt at becoming a plumber when I'd left school not many years previously. I stuck this out long enough to get the house loan and a bit longer, as I thought that now I was married I should join that dreaded 'eight to five' brigade.

We had been in our shiny new, freshly painted house for about six months. My job required me to be on the same bus every single boring morning at seven o'clock.   On that bus were the same guys every day.   They all seemed happy enough with their lot in life. I had tried to think along those lines. I'd tried to rationalise it.
'Okay Len, you're married, you've got a mortgage to worry about, you have to buy furniture, you'll need a car, in a couple of years there'll be kids.'
It's just how life was. One morning I was on the bus and nearly at my stop for work. I looked around at the other guys, nice enough people; one of them caught me looking and smiled. He was a guy called Tom. He was about ten years older than me and lived down our road. He had four kids, a frazzled

wife and nothing that made any discernable waves in his existence. He was probably happy, but I wasn't. I knew at that instant that I could live this charade no longer. I jumped up, the bus stopped, I got off. I didn't know what I was going to do, but I knew what I was not going to do and that was get on that bus to work ever again. It was the plumber's workshop syndrome all over again, but once more I was saved.

Getting off the bus was a scramble, but I made it. This was not the only door I stepped through. I stepped through a door in life. This was the first step, from the old to the new, from the straight and narrow, to boundless possibilities, from constriction to freedom. From boredom to excitement, I entered a world of temptation and was tempted. A world of double-dealing and illusion, but a world I could not resist. That was the real door I had stepped through.

I found myself in the Birkenhead Shopping Centre about two miles from home. I found a little café, ordered some breakfast and thought about my new situation. Mary had quite a good job as a beautician in the cosmetic section of Eccles Pharmacy in Queen Street, Auckland's main thoroughfare. She was happy and settled and only pregnancy when it came would cause her to leave there. Eccles was an Auckland institution; it had served the needs of the business and shopping community for longer than most could remember. It had a fantastic position on the corner of Queen Street and Her Majesty's Arcade which also housed Her Majesty's Theatre. It was one of those lovely, historic old theatres, reeking with show business atmosphere and is now sadly gone, a victim of property developer greed in the 1980s. The seats may have seen better days, the amenities were outdated, but she was a lovely old girl, still full of character and precious memories stretching back across one hundred years of entertaining Auckland. Now, in the 1960s, she was hosting a new generation of eager theatregoers. *My Fair Lady*, *The Desert Song*, *Oklahoma*, *South Pacific*, all featuring very good overseas leads, spring to mind, conjuring up really wonderful memories. Among other famous names Vivienne Leigh and Sir Laurence Olivier performed there. As a consequence of this location the performers were always in and out of Eccles buying make-up and supplies. We regularly met the overseas and local stars from the touring shows. We always had tickets for their performances and were often invited to after show parties. I always suspected a contributing reason for the invites was the fact that Mary was a very attractive young lady and I'm sure that she aroused interest in the young males in the touring companies.

A little custom that had grown up around Eccles was Friday night drinks in the back room. As a regular visitor there I'd met a few of the company reps who sold products to the shop and who also gathered there for the Friday night late shopping 'in the know crowd' hospitality, which at times was very entertaining. The company reps were a pretty happy bunch and I wondered whether I could forge a career in selling. I'd certainly done well with it back home in England.

Reflecting on my life in that little café in Birkenhead I started to see the way ahead. There were only two things I had really enjoyed and been good at in work terms, one was selling and dealing with people and the other was going to sea. Now I was married, the sea option probably wasn't available. Mary understandably didn't like being on her own, especially at nights, in the little house in Beach Haven, which was a bit isolated. I really couldn't handle the norm of going to work every day, doing the same thing and seeing it stretch before you in the years ahead. Don't get me wrong, it wasn't work or effort that I was averse to, it was the feeling of being trapped, that the system had won, that that was the sacrifice you had to make for the misconception of security. In fact I think security blunts ambition and gets in the way of enterprise; in any event, that path wasn't for me, I couldn't do it.

Selling, that's where my mind immediately went. I suppose when you think about it, that's what it had to be, I had no trade to fall back on. Becoming a good or great salesman is one of those things that demands, or springs from an innate persuasive ability. Couple that with a strong survival instinct and you have a person of real ability. It can be a dangerous talent. Clever people can be carried away by the rhetoric of a talented salesman and find themselves investing in schemes they wouldn't normally touch. The salesmen are generally the ones who drive most business endeavours, straight or otherwise. Fortunately, I had both of those rascal requirements of a successful salesman in bundles, as future events would prove. Salvation was at hand. I knew straightaway things would be okay. It might not be easy, but things would work out. A departed customer had left a copy of the New Zealand Herald at the next table. I took it and turned to the Situations Vacant section. The Auckland economy was bustling at the time, which was reflected in the large number of jobs advertised, ranging from builders labourers to printers and drivers and all stops in between. There were opportunities for shop-based sales people, but that would have just been swapping one life sentence for another. I was looking for a repeat of the Freddie Graves, 'Greengrocer of Ricky', employer. The sales reps jobs were all in specialist areas requiring technical and engineering skills. No freedom there. I was more, you give me a product, leave me alone and I'll sell it' sort of guy. I ordered another cup of tea. Never got into coffee; I've been a cup of tea man all my life. Further down the page and there it was:

> *Personable salesman wanted to join young expanding company on commission basis in the Wedding and Bedding trade. Great potential. Own car essential.*

In retrospect the wording of the advertisement alluding to 'bedding' certainly had ramifications. Read on and you may smile.

I wasn't going to let a little thing like the, absence of a car stop me. I phoned the number given in the ad and made an appointment to meet the Managing Director at noon the following Monday. I had to spend most of the weekend assuring Mary we wouldn't lose the house. Mary had read the ad and focussed on the car requirement. She then added a comment to the effect that commission jobs never worked out; but to be fair to her, although she was sceptical about the job she never tried to stand in my way. It never occurred to me that I might not get the job. As far as I was concerned I just needed a car. Monday morning rolled around and I dressed formally for the interview. I'd talked a local car dealer into letting me have a car on trial, or 'appro' as we called it. I'd assured him I'd buy one of his cars, but just needed to make sure which one was right for me. I settled on a 'two-tone' Hillman Minx. It was brown and cream and had all the hallmarks of a man on the way up in life. I was.

Mary and I set off on Monday morning; my wife quite warming to the idea of being driven in an expensive-looking car and getting a ride to work rather than taking the bus. Car ownership wasn't very widespread back in those days and Mary and I felt pretty excited as we headed for the city. Sometimes life reaches a point where there are just two options. I had to stay on the bus, or take a chance. Fate, genes, upbringing, I don't know what decides it, but I've always been one to take a chance.

"Good morning, Len. Sit yourself there, opposite me. Would you like a coffee?"
"Err, no thanks."
This was the MD, a Michael Tabuteau. I wondered whether that was his real name or whether he was just poshing it up. He was a little bit older than me, probably twenty-five or so. He was well spoken and seemed very confident. There was a woman named Mary in the room. I assumed she was his secretary, but she turned out to be his business partner. Also at work in the office was a very attractive girl of about eighteen who turned out to be his wife. Her name was Glenda and her role in the office was mainly to look attractive rather than to actually produce anything. Michael and I

exchanged pleasantries. He asked me some searching background questions, which I was able to answer, having had a number of backgrounds to use as source material. He explained the business and the products to me and outlined the demands that would be made on my time and income earned by previous employees. Basically the job was to sell bedding and linen, plus ladies' sleeping attire, to young girls engaged or hoping to be. It was an established New Zealand tradition of putting a 'bottom drawer' together that Mary had earlier been engaged in. The company provided a full range of samples and their products were top class. Leads were generated through advertising in bridal magazines and newspaper supplements. Would a good looking young man like me be suited to discussing lingerie and bedding with wholesome young unmarried girls? I thought I might well be. My skills honed on the veggie carts selling to housewives might have some application and I was always able to put women at their ease with my non-threatening manner. We talked for a while, but it was clear he wanted me to join and I was certainly keen. And what about Fate hovering in the background of this little piece of theatre? I think she was also quite keen to see what would transpire if I got the job.

"Righto Len." Said Michael, in his best C.E.O. style that I came to recognise. "I think you have the qualities needed, I just need to discuss it with

367

Mary," they disappeared into another room for about 5 minutes.

"Welcome aboard," said Michael on their return. He strode towards me with his hand extended and a big smile. It was a charade; the die had been cast when I walked in the door, maybe when I got off the bus.

It was decided that I would go out that evening with another salesman, David, who had an appointment on the North Shore. Michael took me into the training room to improve my product knowledge and Mary made me up two cases of samples. And so my new career was launched. No more steel working and dirty fingernails. I was a salesman in the challenging and spotlessly clean world of womens' bits and pieces. I went and borrowed some money from the lawyer who had handled our house sale and that day bought a car. I opted for a sporty-looking Sunbeam Alpine. Not the most practical of cars and I could barely get the samples into it, but it did catch the eye and with my new clientele, looks were going to trump practicality.

I immediately warmed to David, the salesman supervising me on my first outing. He was leaving to go to the UK to pursue a career in theatre acting. He'd had some success locally and was off to follow his dream. I admired him because I knew what it took to chance your arm, leave home and security and head for the opposite side of the world and the unknown. He was a competent salesman, but he worked by the book. Our client that night was a young woman who had just become engaged and who had invited along a couple of friends to join her for the evening's demonstration. David introduced himself and then me and launched into a very wooden presentation. Despite that, he got the sale and his commission was something like twenty pounds, which was probably more than half a week's wages for most people. I was impressed and I was sure I'd made a good career choice. I just thought we needed to put a bit more of the demon in the demonstration.

I drove to the offices in Albert Street the next morning, dropping Mary off in Queen Street on the way. If anything the Sunbeam Alpine suited her better than the Hillman Minx and I didn't hear any more words of opposition about my new job. I was wearing a really well made three-piece suit and I hoped I looked the part. I was early, so I parked the car in Queen Street and embarked upon what has become a life-long habit. I skipped up the sweeping stairway of De Bretts, one of Auckland's leading hotels. I hadn't made a sale yet, but I think you should always start out as you intend to operate. Mark out the territory you want to occupy and the means will follow. My pockets were a little light on cash, but I was full of ambition and expectation. I was free from doubt. I sat at a window seat overlooking the bustle of Shortland Street below and ordered a sumptuous breakfast and a copy of the New Zealand Herald. I knew that this was the start of a new life.

The first month rushed by and I had appointments almost every night. My sales and commissions were incredibly high and I'd eclipsed all benchmarks set by David or previous salesman. I spent my days trawling through papers and magazines looking for leads. I took our business into new areas such as lunchtime displays in shops and factory canteens. Almost invariably I would make a sale or get an evening appointment. And there was a common denominator to the evening appointments. The client would usually want someone with her and so, invariably, there would be the attractive single girlfriend in attendance. I learnt to exploit what I had in my armoury. I wasn't a great sportsman, I hadn't been to university, but I was six foot plus tall, impeccably dressed with a nice car and an air of success. I was ambitious and I could chat easily with anyone. Well, you've got to play to your strengths don't you?

Another month went by and I had become the wonder kid of the firm. I was helping the other salesmen on the basis I got a share of any commissions they made. I was making very good money and more importantly, I was really enjoying myself. Michael was ecstatic. It all seemed so easy, but something was changing; fate was in the corner of the room tossing her petticoat and setting something a little unfortunate in motion. If I was going to find a true starting point for the slippery slope I skated down, I would probably put a marker about here.

Michael approached me one morning and said:
"Len, Glenda wants to join the sales team. I think it'd make my wife really happy to feel she was more involved in the business. She wants a bit of independence too. Do you think you could train her up?"
I pretended to think about it for a few moments.
"I don't know, Mike. Do you think it's a good idea? I don't want to slow down my sales."
"Len, take her out, train her up and if she's no good at it then at least she's had her chance and she can't keep going on at me about it."
"Okay, Mike, you're the boss; but I assume it's the same rules about commission."
"Yes," he sighed, "but you're making more than me."
"Well get out and sell a bit yourself."
That stopped him in his tracks.

Glenda was slim and very attractive. She'd been runner up in a recent 'Miss Auckland Beauty Contest'. Her marriage was not a happy one. I was

24 and on a roll with an, 'every post a winning post' mentality. There had been a bit of light flirting between us around the office. We both sensed where this might go. I think it was planned, subconsciously or otherwise.

Sometimes, particularly when you are young, there can be irresistible electricity between two people. Wiser older heads may escape it, but some time or other lust can make fools of us all. From the first day of Glenda's training, we struggled on that slippery slope of temptation.

The affair started nervously. Glenda was keen to share everything she had with me, except for the commissions and she decided to do her own sales work. Not very successfully as it turned out, so Michael asked me to, 'top her up'. I know, it was an unfortunate choice of words. The evening training top-ups took up one evening a week in addition to our daily liaisons. Then came the inevitable opportunities and stolen moments that we exploited through that fine New Zealand Spring. After two months of clandestine meetings, we entered that acute danger area that lovers always end up occupying. Lovers become careless, perhaps it is a subconscious wish to be caught, a hidden wish to end a deceitful situation.

Late one morning we visited a hide-away, the secluded thermal pools at the Waiwera hot springs hotel. It was a fabulous facility, then about forty minutes drive north of Auckland. The visit was planned to be a final liaison between us. We were both scared of the intensity that had developed and the problems lying in wait. We did not want to endanger our marriages any further; this was to be the end of the affair.

Whilst enjoying the stimulating 'hot pools', an incident occurred that illustrated the careless attitude that we had allowed to develop. The magical surroundings, the warm water, the playfulness had brought about an intimate moment. We had got carried away when our pleasure was broken by a cough that was steadily increasing in volume. I looked around to find the owner of the voice, it was an employee of the complex and I recognized him, he lived only a few hundred yards from me, talk about 'sod's law'. With heavy diplomacy he suggested we carry on these activities elsewhere, saying, "I will give you five minutes."

Glenda, who was shielded from him, cut in with, "Make it ten".

There have been many times since, that I have wondered, did she mean she needed longer to get dressed and leave, or did she want more time to continue. Your guess is not as good as mine!

Once dressed, we retired to the loungers and I couldn't help laughing at the ref' giving us five minutes of extra time. It had been a close call and we realised that we couldn't go on like that. We were certain to get caught and so we agreed to end the relationship for the sake of our partners.

Chapter Thirty-Three

It's strange how things happen in life. A new Len was emerging and deep down I knew him. He was an extension of the Len who wouldn't work at the plumbers shop and an extension of the Len who loved selling for the greengrocer and chatting up the housewives. I was right on top of the sales game, but the offerings on the side were causing trouble. Increasingly Glenda was aware of them. In local parlance she was 'giving me gyp'. The employee position was getting too small for me and I was thinking of branching out on my own in a similar business. I was considering an improved stock range and some other selling methods. The new Len, a real chancer, was emerging. The genie had been let out of the bottle.

I walked into Michael's office and told him I was leaving to start my own outfit. I had put aside enough money to launch it. He tried talking me out of it with offers of shares in the business and bonuses. His blandishments fell on deaf ears. I was off and ready to start my own business. Surprisingly, Mary readily agreed with my plan. I arranged a tenant for our house who would cover the mortgage and I moved us to a really nice luxury apartment in an inner city suburb. It was stylish, modern and had parking for the van I would need. It was the perfect location for the business and a young couple on the way up in life. This new pathway engineered the final split with Glenda.

Looking back, the time spent working with Michael, even with the distractions and dangers of the fling, was a stepping-stone that had to be experienced. So there it is, getting off of that bus, chancing my arm with the sales job. The Glenda affair was like many other steps, I believe it was all part of a mapped out journey.

A month later I was the proud possessor of a caravan fitted out as a mobile shop. British readers will know what I was up to. I was about to introduce the tallyman to New Zealand. Instead of battling my way into people's households with cases and display racks, I would pull up outside and invite guests into my regally appointed caravan where the goods were professionally displayed. Purchasers loved it from the novelty to the privacy. It worked so well that I extended the stock into general clothing. I bought end runs of stock from local manufacturers very cheaply and always paid in cash. Occasionally some really well priced stock would fall off the back of a truck for me. Business was booming despite the odd fracas with an indignant boyfriend who felt the fitting process had strayed into inappropriate areas. I provided credit facilities and sometimes the interest on deferred payments brought me more than the sales. I had a few bad debts but nothing unmanageable. I decided to put a second van on the road, but made the mistake of giving it to a relative of Mary's, an American brother-in-law who couldn't sell to save his soul. Eventually I got rid of him and put a sharp little operator in charge of the van.

I don't know whether it's been luck or shrewdness, but I've always been able to spot storm clouds well ahead of their arrival in my life. The stock that 'fell off the back of a lorry' was a regular part of the business, but I would only deal through contacts of the Bay boys. I never dealt directly with the seller of this type of stock. I knew that no matter what happened the Bay boys would never disclose to the police or anyone else who the end purchaser of the stock was. On more than one occasion this cautious habit of keeping a middleman between me and any illegality proved to be a life saver. However even working through the Bay boys I still began to meet a few really shady characters. I wasn't naive about what they were and did, but I found it an attractive and exciting world, or more appropriately, underworld. Some of them seemed to be clones of dear old Ernie, the Rag and Bone man, but there were some darker figures in the mix.

I had the business for three years and made some very good money, but I decided to get out and I arranged to sell it to Solly Lipman, a Jewish trader who ran a similar business in South

Auckland. I had no aspirations to break into the South Auckland market. It was tough territory out there. It had been a strong working class area built around the factories, but a wave of immigration from the Pacific Islands and the drift of rural Maoris to the city looking for factory work were changing the social make up of South Auckland. New suburbs like Otara were springing up, consisting of almost entirely State Housing and low rental accommodation. If you pushed too hard over late payments out there you were taking your life into your hands. Solly was a tough operator and he paid me in cash and didn't ask for a receipt. It wasn't a fortune, but I was pleased to have the money and to get out. It had been a good experience and I believe every venture you go into in life is a necessary preparation for what you'll encounter later.

I decided to take some time out and decide what to do next. I was cashed up and in no hurry. The old public golf course at Chamberlain Park out on the Great North Road saw a lot of me over the next six weeks. I hadn't joined a private golf club yet, but there were always plenty of work shy, keen golfers looking for someone to play with. And it was at the golf course that I met Ken, who gave me the idea for my next business venture, which was selling fire extinguishers. I know that doesn't sound like a very exciting or dangerous line of work, but as you'll see I have a knack of taking even the simplest business and giving it an interesting twist. As always a couple of slightly shady characters got drawn into the mix and the exercise ended with a major fraud investigation that I was lucky not to be dragged into.

I had always fancied myself as a pretty hot salesman and whenever there was nothing more rewarding on the horizon, or I didn't have the readies to set up with a new product, I would look around to find something that I could get out there with and quickly pull in some money with no capital invested. Ken had just been accepted into the Auckland Fire Brigade. It was a very hard selection process and you considered yourself safe in the job for life if you were accepted. Ken, who to his credit, had given up a life of carousing, drinking and brawling etc. was a real tough guy. This was a seismic life change for him. To try and tread the straight-and-narrow in such a disciplined calling would be a bridge too far for him, I thought. Ken, however, was absolutely taken by his new respectable career move and was enjoying the first flush of success. I used to meet him for drinks and the odd game of golf.

One afternoon I had just finished a round of golf and was sitting in what passed for a bar having a cold drink, when Ken walked in with one of his new fire brigade mates. They joined me with their drinks and we started chatting about the usual subjects. You know the ones; girls, rugby and past achievements; a bit of male bragging and bonding really. I naturally asked Ken how he was enjoying his new respectable life. Well that was like taking the top off of the fizzy lemonade bottle. He just erupted; he had been out on a couple of major shouts and was really enjoying the job. I think the risks and a bit of danger really suited his personality. He was the sort of guy who had no problem putting himself on the line. As I said, he was a rough and tough Kiwi and they don't come much tougher in my experience, though the Aussies can give them a close run.

While on that subject, it's interesting that whenever the Aussies play New Zealand at any sport it really is full on, no quarter asked or given. They both lift themselves and perform better than they normally can. Particularly New Zealand, as they're cast in the role of the poor cousins. That being true to a certain extent as Australia is certainly richer and supports a better and more affluent lifestyle, but that's not always the best way to measure things. Whatever the motive is for that intense competition, believe me it exists at all levels. It is most evident in sport, politics, entertainment and believe it or not, even amongst criminals. I know that's a strange one, but it's very true, though I think the Aussies had a definite advantage in that one, like racehorses, it's all in the breeding.

"Len, do you know that most fires could be stopped before they go too far if ordinary fire extinguishers were kept handy?" asked Ken, airing his new found knowledge.

"Yes mate, I can see that would be the case," I said.

Ken had just been on a big call-out for a major fire in Auckland's largest department store, The Farmers Trading Company. Rumours were rife around the town that it had been deliberately lit to cover a major shortfall in its furniture stock inventory. Funnily enough I knew a couple of the guys who worked in the furniture department. Their lifestyle seemed to be a bit exotic for average wage earners. They were always to be seen in the trendy restaurants and top bars. I was inclined to believe there may well have been a bit of truth in it, but it's just conjecture, even though most of the town larrikins seemed to have had their homes refurnished very nicely prior to the fire. Ken had also been a merchant seaman, working on both the Australian and New Zealand coasts where he had developed a certain reputation. Like many others, I was very surprised at his choice of career and was waiting with interest for the inevitable explosion; this guy was the original loose cannon. I knew there had been a bit of string pulling to get him into that job. Bob, his long-suffering father-in-law, was the local Labour party representative. He was a leading light in Freemans Bay. He was a JP and looked up to by all in Freemans Bay and his position carried a fair bit of clout.

"So Ken, are you still happy with the straight and narrow?"

"I bloody love it," said Ken very enthusiastically, "good money, plenty of time off and they've given me one of those cottages attached to the fire station, how about that? And what about this, the missus and the in-laws are talking to me again."

Miracles may well happen, but they don't always last.

Pete, who was with Ken and also a fireman, hadn't been saying too much, so I thought I'd better bring him into the conversation.

"How about you, Pete, do you like the job?"

"Yes, who wants another beer?"

Pete was a man of few words, but Ken wasn't.

"We had a call out for a little corner shop in Grey Lynn the other day. It was only half a mile from the station and we got there in bloody quick time, but it was too late to save it. All we could do was to stop it spreading. The dopey bastard was too mean to have a little fire extinguisher handy. It could have saved his business. My boss gave him a right bollocking. They're all the same," says Ken very righteously and warming to the subject, "too mean or too bloody stupid to buy the right equipment and have it handy. They should all be pinched."

The laconic Pete growled his approval.

At home the next day the conversation with Ken was tripping through my mind. 'There has to be an angle here,' I thought to myself. 'You had better have a look into this and it could be very timely.' I went straight to the yellow pages, an essential part of a budding entrepreneur's kit. The good old reliable yellow pages had it all, as simple as you like, under F for fire extinguishers. The main manufacturer was based in Christchurch, but fortunately they maintained a distribution office in Auckland. I phoned and made an appointment to meet the manager. He turned out to be a nice accommodating chap. He was middle aged and approaching retirement. I think he had lost any snap he may have possessed and was just filling in time, hoping for a peaceful life, but he needed to put some runs on the board and sales were desperately needed. It is generally the case in any company, you can have the best accountants, the best managers, the best product, the best premises, but they all come to nothing without that most essential of all ingredients for success, good sales staff. Without good sales people they might as well all stay at home, without the sellers nothing really happens and the top bosses know that.

Playing on that, it hadn't been hard to convince the manager Roy that we needed each other. I persuaded him to grant me an agency in writing for his products at a handsomely discounted rate. I in turn guaranteed him a certain amount of monthly purchases, which would keep his bosses of his back and keep him on track for his happy retirement. I had noted the half empty scotch bottle in his desk drawer and his over red complexion; it was a timely liaison all round. Once again lady luck was sitting on my shoulder, but I had gone out to help her, she doesn't just come into the living room.

The next move was to get out there and do a bit of test marketing, to sort out the objections and to find the most suitable products and price points; in other words how far could I load the prices up? Whenever opportunities like this arose I always went out there myself and did the initial work in the trenches. In fact I always stayed involved when it came to the selling. I was good at that, but poor on administration; it always helps to know your weaknesses. I had purchased some stock from Roy, mainly to use for demonstration purposes and to familiarize myself with the products and what they could do. Armed with a couple of the smaller units I stepped out into the great unknown of fire prevention. I had to pass myself of as an expert; easy enough I thought. I had taken the time to study some literature from Roy, which he had to dig out from one of his voluminous cupboards. They were covered in dust and fairly old, not having seen the light of day for quite some time. As you can probably tell the support material wasn't exactly cutting edge, but the units themselves were absolutely brilliant and bore the relevant safety standard markings required under safety regulations. I would be making a great play on those.

I shall never forget my forays and sales calls made on that first day. I was highly positive and motivated. Having spent most of the funds from the last venture I was nearly broke and that was always a good motivation for me. Well, what a surprise; it was an absolute flop, no matter what I tried and that included my absolute best lines of patter. I just got a stony silence and acres of negativity. I made eight calls, mainly on shops where I knew I would be dealing with the decision maker who could write the cheque. I managed to make one sale and it was bloody hard work. It was back to the drawing board, but I wasn't one to give up easily. In fact there were many occasions on other products and schemes when I should have done so, but I always found that very hard to do. I knew I needed a gimmick. I had been thinking about it since that first meeting with Ken and Pete. I had always had it in mind that I needed to be seen as an official and connected to the Fire Service in some form or another. I knew I would be treading on dangerous ground and had to step very carefully. But I had a plan formulating in my mind. It was tricky, a touch dangerous, but would prove to be very effective and I just couldn't resist it.

I knew from Ken that his station had a Sunday rugby team and social club. I had been to a couple of their Sunday games and they were always short of players so I offered to play for them the next Sunday. I wasn't any great shakes as a player, but they just needed the numbers. I had a drink with them all after the game as was the custom and after a couple of weeks of that I became one of the boys. I had casually told Ken and Pete about my new venture. They were very eager to help and air their superior knowledge so I was bombarded with technical information about compounds and different methods and equipment used for fighting different fires. Fat fires, electrical fires, petrol fires. I expressed admiration and gratefulness to them for sharing their skills and knowledge with me. I was successfully drawing them in ever closer to what I really wanted. At that time the Auckland Fire Brigade station was situated in the city on the corner of Pitt and Vincent Streets. I rented a room in a bed and breakfast type place in Pitt Street within a few doors of the fire station. This little manoeuvre gave me an address that was synonymous with the Fire Brigade. I had been given a Fire Brigade lapel badge while having a tipsy drink with the boys after one of the Sunday rugby games. This simple possession proved to be a little gem. I had also acquired an official tie of the firemen's social club.

The next bit of the plan was slightly trickier. I had purchased a number of small red suitcases, which I intended to emboss in gold leaf with an official looking title. I knew that just placing those on a counter or desk would save a lot of questions and create the required respectful and compliant attitude I was looking for. I researched the official operating name of the Fire Brigade as it was referred to in those days. I wanted something sounding official and looking close enough to pass light scrutiny. I came up with "The New Zealand Fire Safety Service". I couldn't find anything exactly like that, so it became the official title of my new enterprise. I had this name embossed very conservatively on the small suitcases. I then ran off some stationery featuring the Pitt Street address and particulars. I think this whole process had taken about a month from that first meeting and I was now ready for my next move.

Whilst familiarising myself with the extinguishers, I had discovered what proved to be a cute selling trick. On Ken's advice I had bought some white spirit. I would put a little of it in a small metal container and set it alight. The results were spectacular, the flames just leapt up. I would let it burn for a few seconds and then a quick squirt from an extinguisher and it went straight out. It was very impressive and there was no smoke damage, as white spirit doesn't create that. I knew I had the secret, the perfect demonstration exercise in the prospect's office or premises. I must stress that the white spirit when lit just shot up in flames very impressively and would look quite dangerous to the uninitiated. In reality however it only took a light blast of the extinguisher to snub it out. But as I said it looked very frightening. We all have a strong instinctive fear of fire. What a sales weapon that turned out to be.

I had brought on board a very good telephone salesman, 'a blower' as they were known in the trade. He had been around a bit and knew the rules. I put him on a good deal. His task was to phone potential customers and make appointments. His pitch was for: "one of our Pitt Street chaps to come out and do a safety inspection on the premises which we note is now due."

Calls would invariably go like this:

"Good morning, Sir, Roger Butler here from New Zealand Fire Safety Service Retail Inspections Unit. I need to speak with the manager or proprietor re your annual fire safety check which is a bit overdue."

"Is it really Roger?"

"I'm afraid so, Sir."

"Oh, okay then, what do we do next?"

"Well that's why we called you, Sir. We try to avoid problems and penalty payments. One of our chaps from Pitt Street has an inspection near you tomorrow morning if that's convenient."

And invariably it was.

If there had been a fire, we would phone prospects in that locality. The results were amazing. Roger would open up with his normal pattern of introducing himself and getting the punter nervous, but on side. After he had set the scene he would then go on to say: "Because of the recent unfortunate fire out your way, which between you and me Sir, could have been avoided, we are running some retail safety checks on fire equipment to see if it matches the regulations."

Regulations! That word really got the punters attention and then more references to "not liking to create problems or penalty payments" and the advice that one of the 'Pitt St. Boys' would be in that area the next day and an appointment was made.

Roger was one of the great 'blowers' and proud of his craft. He made very good money. He got a payment for every appointment made, plus a percentage of any sale concluded. He made a very good living working two or three hours a day, for two, or sometimes three, days a week. As I said he was good at what he did, but as importantly he had a close mouth and was recognised for that priceless talent by those who valued it. I certainly did. Over the years he worked on other projects for me and was always reliable, but I think he performed best on this one. Through watching him and observing the pleasure on his face as he secured the appointments, I was convinced he enjoyed it. He was a pro. He was a strange man in many ways. He really adopted the high moral ground in his dialogue with punters. I think it was his way of justifying his calling in life. Naturally I was the bloke from the Fire Safety Service who was going to be in their area tomorrow. I was hot to trot.

I will always remember my first call after the change of tactics. It was to one of the medium sized factory shops that were springing up at that time. The owner ran it himself with his wife and a small staff. I arrived dressed in a pair of black, sharply creased trousers; black, highly polished shoes; a white military-styled shirt with two buttoned down patch pockets, my fireman's social club tie and all topped off with my little lapel badge. Roger always got the Christian name and surname of the prospect, plus other snippets of information that might be handy or have a bearing on the sale. Consequently I was well armed for whatever might arise.

"Hello there, Warren. How are you going? Busy today I hope."

I introduced myself, shook hands and made Warren feel comfortable with me, leading off with a quick chat about some local issue, probably sport related. I would be completely clued up on the local rugby club and golf club. I would also know a bit about the local council and councillors in case that was needed. I was generally offered a cuppa at this stage; however I would put it off and suggest we had it after we had concluded the inspection.

"Have you got time for us to do this inspection now Warren? It shouldn't take long."

I made sure he could see the copy of the Shop and Factory Fire Safety Regulations I carried in a red folder. Warren was eager to please and to get this over and avoid any problems or unnecessary costs.

"I'm in your hands, Len."

"You certainly are," I thought.

"Warren, just before we do the assessment, I think it advisable to do a little demonstration showing how effective it is to have the correct extinguishers in the correct positions; it can be lifesaving."

"Okay, can you do it here and shall I get one or two of my staff to observe it?"

"Good thinking, Warren."

I laid out my metal pan and tipped a little white spirit in to it. I looked up in my best professional manner and requested that Warren and the staff all move back a little. I dropped a lighted match into the white spirit. Whoosh! Flames leapt up about six feet high. Everybody was startled and jumped back. A female staff member screamed and I thought Warren was going to have an accident. I hesitated and looked at him.

"Put it out for fucks' sake," he shouted.

I heroically and nonchalantly stepped forward and with one spurt from the small four-pound hand extinguisher, I doused the flame. I turned to him and his staff and said:

"I hope that didn't alarm you too much, but it's the policy of the Department to clearly show the danger of a flash fire and the need to have the recommended protection readily at hand."

Warren invited me to do the assessment 'post haste'. I walked around the premises with him accompanying me. I had studied the recommended and indeed the required extinguisher positions. And pointed out to Warren the considerable number of extinguishers he'd need. One by the fuse boxes, one in stairways, one or two upstairs, one in the kitchen and a few more here and there for good measure. Some of them were small four-pound units and a couple of the larger eight-pound types and two twelve pound models, which I strongly recommended. I had prepared an official looking diagram, which I filled in and made notes on. I assured Warren that I could readily sort out his problem.

"What about that cup of tea now, Warren?"

Well we had our tea and some very nice biscuits, over which we had a general talk about the regulations and once again the penalties. I impressed upon him that we tried not to be too heavy handed in these matters. We thought it more productive if somebody was a bit short on equipment to give the right advice on the correct requirements and put right the situation without recourse to further official corrective action, to which he gratefully nodded. The upshot was that Warren needed eight units of varying sizes to keep him within the regulations. We could, of course, organise it straightaway for safety's sake, not forgetting it would be a significant help with his insurance premiums. I also pointed out that having the correct equipment installed would be particularly helpful if he was ever unfortunate enough to have to lodge a claim for fire damage. Warren, who had winced at the cost he was facing, suddenly looked a little brighter. It's been said many times, there is no such thing as a completely honest man.

As time went on and I made more calls my patter became irresistible. Every call was a sale and every one of them remarked on how refreshing it was to deal with such a helpful chap. Nothing like the official grilling they'd expected. I was selling more and more units and making really good money. I had put on another salesman and he was coming along nicely. I was happy, Roger the 'blower' was happy, the State Advances mortgage company was happy, my wife and newly arrived baby daughter were happy and one of my customers became particularly happy. This next story shows just how wicked and dishonest some people can be and demonstrates how you should always be on your guard against these types.

Roger the 'blower' had been happily blowing away now for a month or so and like me his patter was now unstoppable. We were a great team and getting the results. Early one fine summer's morning I was feeling very satisfied with the business and the world in general, which of course is just when complacency can creep in. I had breezed into the Pitt Street office to pick up my appointments for the day. I could easily do four or five calls in a day now. To keep things motoring smoothly along and to avoid build ups I had Gary Duffty, one of the Freemans Bay boys, trained up to do the deliveries and also to do the attachments of the extinguishers to the walls where necessary. Gary charged the clients a fee for this service, which he kept for himself and did very nicely thank you. Roger kept the administration moving. He understood it left me free to do that most important function of any business, straight or otherwise and that is to make the sales. Nothing works without those. He knew his commissions were the better for it, so he made sure I wasn't tied down.

I have a lifetime habit and indulgence, which I intend never to stop. Wherever I am in the world or whatever I am doing, I always start the day in a coffee bar, hotel lounge, or dining room, where I leisurely read the paper, have a nice breakfast and then plan my day. It's a great pleasure in my life; I prefer it to pubs and restaurant dinners. I have never been able to stand around in pubs and chat and drink, that's never been my way of relaxing.

This particular day found me just finishing a lovely breakfast of salmon and scrambled eggs in my favourite hotel. I was in the upstairs guest dining room of De Brett's Hotel. Old world hotels like that have become very hard to find now. I noticed that one of my appointments for the day was out in the industrial suburb of Onehunga. I checked the notes Roger had prepared. The client's name was there and the address and name of the business. I thought this could be interesting as it was a well-known wool store and they would generally have been well up to speed as to their fire safety requirements. I drove out to Onehunga, which only took about fifteen minutes, given that traffic was relatively quiet at that time of the day. I drove up to the rundown premises and pulled into the parking area.

The building was one of those erected by, or for, the American Marines who were based in New Zealand during the Pacific campaign of the Second World War. New Zealand had been a staging, training and rest and recreation post for the Marines during that bitter conflict with the Japanese. The Pacific theatre was fought for control of the Pacific Islands airfields and shipping lanes, which were essential for the Japanese expansion plans. Though the Aussies fought in that theatre with the Americans, most of the New Zealand forces were otherwise engaged at the time with a certain Mr. Montgomery and a Mr. Rommel in North Africa and then Italy, where they acquitted themselves very well, according to both the above-named gentlemen.

'Office', was scrawled in white marker paint on a piece of black board balanced in the window of a small lean-to building, attached to what appeared to be a very large storage unit with huge double sliding doors on the front and rear of the structure. It had seen better days. It had in the past been painted black but this had now faded badly and the corrugated iron sheeting with which it had been constructed was failing. Into the office I strolled, dressed in my usual official-looking uniform. There was a very beautiful and stylishly dressed lady sitting behind the reception counter, trying to look busy. She flashed a dazzling smile at me; a lesser man would have fainted. I introduced myself and stated I was there to see Mr. A about fire safety. "Oh, he's busy for ten minutes or so, but would like you to have a cup of tea or coffee, while you're waiting?"

She returned with the tea and we exchanged pleasantries. Whilst this was going on I was making a detailed observation and health check on her well exposed cleavage and not giving great thought to fire extinguishers. The door into the reception area suddenly opened and I was greeted by Mr. A, a short chubby man wearing a pair of thick horn rimmed glasses. He was balding, aged about forty, but looking more like fifty. I noticed he was wearing a white silk shirt and sporting a pair of bright red braces needed to stop his trousers slipping below his rather large girth. Looking at him I knew he was a man used to the finer things in life.

"Hello, sorry to keep you waiting," he said with a friendly unforced smile, pushing his hand out to greet me, "I'm Maurice, call me Mo, but don't call me late for breakfast."

I wasn't going to have to use my make them feel comfortable routine as I normally did, he was doing a pretty good job of that on me. I have always had a very sensitive antenna for danger or trickery and it was really trembling now. This guy had 'shark' written on his forehead. Mo looked at my card and said without looking up, "come through this way Len and we can sort this out". I followed him to his office. We both sat down and went to speak at the same time. Mo pulled back, "Okay, Len, you go first."

"Thanks Mo," I said and then went into my spiel about overdue inspections, regulations and prevention etc. I explained that we thought it more advisable to assist and bring premises up to the required standard, rather than go down the road of prosecution. I was emphasising this while laying my red file with a copy of the Trade and Industries

Safety Act on top of it on to his desk. Mo looked at me long and hard and said, "Okay, Len what's next?"

"Well, this being a wool store, I'm pretty sure that you will have the required hoses etc." Mo nodded.

"And you probably have buckets and sand etc."

Mo nodded again. "Yes that's all correct Len, but you do your inspection. I'll come round with you. I want to be as safe as I can. I've just taken over this business and property, so I'd welcome your advice."

"Okay, Mo, but before we go and do the inspection, I need to demonstrate this latest type of hand held extinguisher. The reason being Mo, our research shows that the best chance of stopping, or beating a fire, is to have a piece of equipment handy and easy to use, which can stop a fire before it gets a hold. We all know the time it takes to bring your hoses and even sprinklers to bear; that's usually too late." Mo nodded his head in agreement. I went through the usual demo routine. Mo and his secretary, who had joined us, were suitably impressed. We walked through the cavernous, but dilapidated store. I pointed out where I thought cover was needed, making my official notes as I went. The whole process took about half-an-hour and we were back in Mo's office.

"Julie, would you mind making us a coffee or tea? I think we have a lot to discuss. Coffee or tea? Len"

I opted for the tea again. Julie obediently swished out of the room, flashing her smile.

"Well then, Len, let's get down to it. What, where and how much?" I was ready for him and after a quick calculation and referring to my notes and drawings I was able to give him the information including the rather high price. It would be my biggest sale to date.

"Len, that sounds very hefty. Shouldn't I get a discount for an order of that size?" I pointed out that this was a service we provided and that we only marked up a small amount to cover administrative costs. I started to relish the battle. Then came the Sunday punch and I'd known there would be one. "Okay fair enough," says Mo through gritted teeth, then smiling. "You will of course supply me with a certificate of inspection and compliance?" He paused, looking hard at me again.

"That would be normal procedure, Mo."

"On that basis we have a deal," he said leaning forward and shaking my hand.

"Right, that's fine, Mo. I'll attend to it straightaway. Our terms are thirty percent now, the balance on delivery within the next two days. That okay with you?" He gritted his teeth again.

"You firemen sure are tough," he said with a wry smile, he reached into the drawer for his cheque book and paid the full amount.

As you may have expected, this sale had a surprise ending. I was happily breakfasting in De Brett's about six weeks later. I had just finished reading the sports pages, which always got my attention first. I turned to the news section and there, a few pages in, was an article regarding Mo's fire ravaged wool store. Mo, in a later radio interview, spoke highly of the Fire Brigade's efforts to save his premises. He further stated that he fully expected to be back in business within a few months. As time drifted on there was talk that the wool he had stored may not have been lost in the fire; popular opinion suggested that it had been moved or sold, who knows? One thing I do know is that Mo knew exactly what he was doing; this was evidenced for me sometime later. I had expected to be dragged into the ensuing insurance bun fight and fortunately that never happened. I wondered did the Compliance Certificate; issued from our Pitt Street address, slip through the net. I think it must have and I think that's all Mo really wanted to buy.

A few months later I was in Cassel's, a great restaurant, well patronised by Auckland's characters, when a bottle of fine champagne was brought to the table by the proprietor Marc, a very nice Italian, whom I knew. Marc said this gift was from a guest who had just left and had asked Marc to deliver it personally. It had a note attached which read: "No discount needed. Keep on keeping on. Regards Mo."

The fire extinguisher caper carried on for a few more months and made some really good money. It could have been turned into a steady business covering more aspects of that industry, such as maintenance and other types of safety equipment, but it wasn't for me. As you may have gathered I lacked an appetite for the long haul and the incident with Mo had shown me that there were dangers in carrying on and issuing those certificates. I would however like to point out that although my sales methods may correctly be considered sharp, I think it should be noted they got the job done and people did end up with a product that they may have needed in a hurry. I firmly believe that ninety per cent of them wouldn't have bought that equipment without a 'gentle nudge' from me. I don't say that in any way from a guilt feeling or to vindicate myself. In fact truth be known, I am quite proud of my ability in that direction. My opinion may be thought biased, but I believe that once again, the end justified the means and it was great fun. Thanks Ken.

Chapter Thirty-Four

Old habits die hard and after I disposed of the fire extinguisher business I awarded myself some time off. After about a month of golf and general relaxation I was chaffing to get back to work. I'd had a couple of trips to Sydney with Mary and she'd taken a liking to Double Bay. She loved the amazing ambience of the place, the great shops, restaurants and coffee bars that were so far ahead of what we had in Auckland. For me it was a special place with its Jewish and Mediterranean owned businesses and flamboyant community of colourful residents. I was happy in Auckland, but being back in Sydney on my own terms gave me an inclination for something even better. Every day in Sydney I scanned the papers for sales and franchise opportunities. There were heaps of get rich quick schemes advertised and they always required a down payment to acquire the secrets to success. I cut out ads that interested me, made a few phone calls posing as a possible investor and had their sales material posted to me at a friend's address. I'd dabbled at a couple of mail scams but hadn't really given it the concentration it needed. Now, free of any distractions I was ready to give it my all, especially if it meant I was going to be able to spend more time in Sydney. I felt it was safer to base these upcoming capers of mine in Sydney, so that if things went badly I could bolt back to New

Zealand. As long as you weren't doing anything violent you could always pay Sydney's uniformed finest a fee to look the other way. What they called a 'tickle'. You have to remember that in the early days you needed a conviction, usually for dishonesty, to get into Australia and from thereon, scams of one sort or another were bred in the bones of Aussies. I think that then as now, Aussie is the spiritual home of the scam. And if they don't originate in Aussie they certainly get perfected there. At any moment in history the Aussie con man will be state of the art.

An early foray of mine was the 'Love Letter Scam'. I didn't invent it, but I certainly gave it a new twist. Often these scams lie dormant for a few years and then soundly bounce back. The timing of this one was perfect. Worldwide there were a large number of major construction projects going on which attracted workers from different countries. Single men, lonely and trapped at remote sites around the globe. I arranged to share an office with a fellow 'give-it-a-go' merchant in George Street and acquired that essential tool of the trade, a post office box. I then placed ads in the classified section of various Mining Magazines and suchlike. Remember this was before the advent of dating agencies and lonely-hearts clubs. The ads were very simple:

> *Jennifer, lonely lady*
> *aged twenty-five.*

*I am considered
attractive and want to
meet a caring man
with a view to a long
and genuine
relationship. I need a
loving person
to guide me in life.
Reply to Box 11111
Sydney, NSW,
Australia.*

The responses usually all came in within the first week. They were keen, but a little reserved. I had met an alcoholic ex-schoolteacher who had lost his job as a result of the drink. He turned out to be well suited to this job. His task was to write tear-jerking initial letters, containing a photograph, to the lonely respondents, designed to arouse their interest.   You could see them thinking about Jennifer and saying to themselves: 'what harm can this do?' and 'it sounds like she needs me and might actually like me.'

The important letter was the follow up. We had three standard versions for Tom the Teacher to use to hook the fish – letters A, B and C. We got responses from all over the world, but usually they were from professional types. A bearded scientist at an Antarctic research base; an engineer at an oil site in Saudi Arabia; a university lecturer at some remote outpost of the empire and even a missionary in Borneo. We attracted a very international clientele. If we had preponderance from any one group it was the Irish. Independence from Britain had put an end to deportation and they had to find new ways to acquire Australian citizenship. All of them were out there hoping for love and for one reason or another looking for Jennifer.

If a respondent was still with us by the time he received letter B, he was hot. Jennifer would by now be declaring a feeling of love and an inexplicable chemistry between them. If he was in cold climes he would receive a pair of thick, apparently home-knitted, socks from the caring Jennifer. If in the tropics he might get some linen handkerchiefs with a heartfelt plea to take good care of himself because a happy future beckoned from just over the horizon. Those little touches tended to close the deal. And now a meeting became necessary. When would the besotted letter writer be on leave? To where could Jennifer travel to meet him in person? Her wholesome photo no doubt adorned the wall of his lonely, bare sleeping quarters. They must meet, but there was the question of expense. Jennifer could get time off work but had no available funds given the need to care for her terminally ill mother. There would be the matter of her airfare and travel expenses and the cost of a housekeeper to look after her mother. Jennifer felt the break from her daily obligations would do wonders for her health and happiness. Only a miser could begrudge the two thousand Aussie dollars that was needed to arrange the rendezvous. If the target made it to Letter C it was almost certain he would remit the funds and often with a little extra for Jennifer's ailing Mum, to whom he sent his kindest regards.

We could count on closing about ten per cent of the initial responses. That amounted to about twelve transactions a month for four months until the bubble burst. We started to get newspaper reporters making enquiries as a result of complaints by disappointed bearded scientists. Often this was triggered by the letter telling them that Jennifer's mother had sadly passed away which had prevented her making the rendezvous.

Unfortunately this letter often arrived after the bearded one had commenced his journey to the Holy Grail. Bizarrely, the dead Mum letter often brought in further funds to help Jennifer with her grief. They exhorted her not to write again until she had had time to deal with her grief. Jennifer took them at their word and didn't ever reply, so deep-seated was her grief. The only real problem was that Tom the Teacher had become so immersed into the role that in his drunken state (when he wrote his best letters) he started to believe he was Jennifer. When he was really pissed he would often burst into tears at the loss of his beloved 'Mummy' as he wrote the cancellation letters. I reckon if we'd been malicious we could have sent him off to one of the meetings with a bearded one. It would have been hilarious, but of course two thousand bucks is two thousand bucks and I had a responsibility to the business.

There was an additional problem that we would often get letters from workers at the same construction site. Replying to these upped the risk level. After all, bearded research scientists are almost human and are just as likely as any other males to indulge in boasting about their new girlfriend Jennifer. As long as Jennifer confessed to them that she had used that name as a pseudonym and we made sure they got different photos from a differently named girl we were probably going to be okay. However, one day Tom was so drunk he sent out identical photos to three different men at the same construction site. It hastened the end of the con and I have to say it brought home to me the perils of drink that the Salvation Army chaps had always gone on about. We shut down the office, parted company with Tom who for years afterwards no doubt regaled people in bars with stories of the Kiwi called Mo who had introduced him to the elusive Jennifer. Well, you have to cover your tracks don't you? And let me offer a piece of wisdom to anyone foolish enough to get involved in these scams. Knowing when to get out is far more valuable than knowing when to go in. As I've said before, I've always had a sixth sense for danger and my continued liberty has been dependent on it on many occasions.

It was one thing to move businesses, but I saw no need to move countries or even cities. A new office and a brand new scam. I thought I should try my hand at the old 'bill them and they'll probably pay' lark. The best version of this had been done by three Kiwis in London who came back with hilarious tales and a lot of money. I heard of mailbags full of cheques and a lordly lifestyle. The boys had needed to beat a hasty retreat when 'The Met' decided that as they hadn't been paid to ignore the scam they weren't going to allow a bunch of colonials to take the Mick. Fortunately this team of Kiwi trailblazers made it home and lived happily ever after. Perfect examples of the motto – 'get in, get rich, get honest'. And having achieved that, they must remain nameless, especially their leader who is now a very prominent citizen, well known to me. The scam was called pro-forma invoicing. You sent an invoice out for work that had not yet been done or even been requested and as often as not the accounts clerk paid it. Time to work the Antipodean version.

I had the bright idea of promoting an 'Asian Restaurant register'. I designed the invoices to resemble a government request for information that required the proprietor to register the business. It was signed off by an Inspector Jordan who had a number of impressive letters after his name. Many of the restaurants were owned or operated by illegal immigrants and they didn't want to take the chance of offending officialdom and having some hard-nosed Aussie inspector calling. Some of them were actually pleased by the idea of having official registration. It's a numbers game. We sent out something like two thousand invoices all round Australia for an eighteen per cent return at about ninety dollars a time, about thirty-two grand. Not big money, but it helped the comfort fund. Still it wasn't enough money to be worth the risk of going to jail. I felt it was time to take a break from Sydney and let the dust settle. I said farewell to my Aussie partner and headed back to New Zealand being careful to leave a trail that suggested I'd gone back to the UK.

And in fact it was now thirteen years since I'd left England. It seemed like a good time for a trip back home. I had a few ghosts to bury back there and I wanted to re-establish myself with my family. It was summer in New Zealand and it was hard to interest Mary in travelling. She was a sunshine girl and her main pleasure in life seemed to be a strategically placed sun lounger. We had a great caravan site at Orewa, a very popular holiday resort about forty miles north of Auckland. Our site was next door to our old family friends, the Claphams, who owned the boarding house I holed-up in, after narrowly avoiding Birdie. It was lovely at Orewa in summer and I couldn't really blame Mary for preferring that to a cold English winter.

I don't think the word 'triumphal' would be entirely out of place when describing my return to Rickmansworth and the family hearth. The family came to Heathrow to meet me and I found I had a whole lot of nephews and nieces who hadn't existed when I left. It was an emotional moment returning home, although I can remember conjuring with the word 'home' in my mind and wondering which of the islands at opposite ends of the world was actually my true home. The furore over the car and my sudden departure weren't mentioned on arrival. I acted quickly to avoid any bother and tracked down the guy I had taken the deposit from and paid him back with a bit extra for his troubles. It was Christmas time and I'm sure the money came in handy for him. My other worry was the crash and the brawl but the police seemed to have lost interest in that episode. I relaxed and addressed the family problem. There was lingering disappointment over my selling of the cleaning business. It must have rankled seeing vans with my name included in the business buzzing around the area. I did my best to mollify my father who had taken it quite badly. I was quite happy to do this and often it could be achieved by funding all his betting. It cost quite a bit of money but it was nothing compared to what he had given me.

I looked up old friends. Dinger was overseas in the army. He was now a Sergeant and doing well. A few old girlfriends had married and were trotting up the high street with toddlers and babies in pushchairs. Not a situation that lent itself to chat up lines. I had a few nights out with the local guys, but they were all married and our nights were much quieter affairs than they had been. I realised how much my life and expectations had changed. I'd walked through a one-way door when I'd left Ricky and after what I'd seen and done in New Zealand and Aussie, there was no way I could settle back into life in the Home Counties. I was never a pub man and there wasn't much overlap between what I wanted and the life my mates in England enjoyed. I made a point of looking up my aunties. They were getting on in age and I knew I mightn't see them again. One was our lovable Aunty Grace who had so brightened our lives during the war and the austere years that followed it. I made it my business to tell her what a saviour she'd been for us and great tears of happiness welled up in her eyes. She understood how much I loved her and how important she'd become in my memories. It made me realise how important it is to tell people when you feel great affection for them and not just assume that they'll know. Hearing it said is the real reward.

Another favourite was Aunty Ruby, one of my father's four sisters. She had regularly sent money to my mother to put food on the table when Dad lost the week's wages at the greyhound racing. She was a throwback to the Bargee days of the Russell family. She had tanned skin, curly black hair, dark eyes and had been a Romany-looking beauty in her day. She rejoiced in the name of 'Roll your own Rube' owing to her smoking strong rolled up tobacco fags. She had a nice three bedroom Council house but preferred to sleep on an old handmade mat on the hard floor in front of an open fire in the living room with an old Navy issue greatcoat for a blanket. She spent most of her days with the greatcoat on as well. She presented quite a sight, riding around the village on her bike, very upright with the tails of her coat flapping behind her in the breeze. Unfortunately, she lost the softness that would have matched her early looks and her harrowing domestic circumstances had made her a gruff character in Mill End. These childhood memories have been seared into my brain and I remember my aunts in great detail and with deep affection.

A month flew by and it was time to return to my home down under. The trip had tidied up a lot of loose ends and my return seemed to have made up for my hasty flight. I was no longer a slave to guilt about my past misdeeds in Ricky. I also knew I could change and become whatever I wanted to be. I wasn't trapped by my past. I felt that those I was leaving behind in England were held in the tight grasp of habit and regimentation and that I had a freedom that was denied to them. There was probably a bit of the Bargee alive and well in my spirit.

On my way back I stopped off in Hong Kong for a few days. I had a contact there I wanted to meet. He was a friend of a business colleague of mine in Auckland, an interesting Kiwi named Adrian Harding. The contact was a jeweller who supplied cut-price fake Russian CZ diamonds, particularly diamond rings. Even established jewellery shops struggled to distinguish them from the real thing. I met up with him and he took me to a workroom at the back of his shop. Adrian had given him the necessary assurances about my trustworthiness. He showed me a selection of his CZ diamonds and the real thing. After he was satisfied with me he took me to a bar that I think was called 'Bottoms Up'. It was near his premises in the infamous Wanchai District. Over a few drinks we formed an association, despite the distraction of the dancing girls. Following this first meeting I went on my way with a clutch of fake diamonds. I sold some as soon as I returned to New Zealand. Others I kept and many years later used them as part of the purchase money for my lovely boat the *Amalfi*. I bought this from another well-known wheeler and dealer, 'Chappie', Paul Chapman, another rascal extrordinaire and a good bloke. They were always accepted as real and I'm sure were regularly checked out by experts.

The *Amalfi* was a stately, wooden-hulled, built for comfort, Cabin Cruiser. No speedy fibreglass gin palace. She was thirty-eight feet, diesel powered and slept six comfortably or eight if arrangements were 'friendly'. I had some wonderful holidays and weekends cruising on her. The main beneficiaries were often my daughter Sam and her friends and my son Lenny. Being the proud dad, I was always happy to indulge them.

My Hong Kong alliance enabled me to do a lot of business over the years. It concluded spectacularly with a run of fake Rolex watches. This was in the early days before they became known as 'knock offs'. Like the CZ diamonds they were almost indistinguishable from the real thing. We cornered the very large market for them in Auckland and Sydney for a while. We had such success with them that there were dustmen running around Auckland and Sydney wearing them. This eventually brought howls of protest from the agents, reinforced by the pillars of society and the posers who were wearing the real thing. Later I will relate a very humorous incident involving good old Adrian who really was your classic loveable rogue. It's a real 'gang who couldn't shoot straight' story and would have beautifully suited the George Daly character in the *Minder* TV show.

And so I arrived back in Auckland and joined Mary and the kids at the Orewa camp. By now it was December of 1971 and the middle of a stunning summer. On the way home I'd thought deeply about the events and significance of the previous eleven years. I was thirty years old and looking forward to new challenges, but generously decided to award myself a few months off. We spent the summer at Orewa and used it as a base for Mary and me and the kids to do some touring. Sam was nearly seven and Lenny was almost four. We had a powerful Chrysler Valiant that just ate up the miles. We travelled all around the beautiful Whangaparaoa Peninsula and then down to Whitianga and the fabulous Mercury Bay on the Coromandel. I had thrown off the shackles of rainy day thinking. It might have been necessary in England but it seemed out of place in this land of sunshine and opportunity. I was happy to spend money on the good life for my family. There wasn't a trendy restaurant we didn't try and no overseas show in town that we didn't see. Mary and I got on well together. She was very attractive, as evidenced by her winning a Sophia Loren lookalike contest in Auckland. Mary was quite shy really and only entered it for a dare. We were still all right in those years. I hadn't crossed the major boundaries that I was to in subsequent years. I keep a very happy memory of that summer when all was right with the world.

Unfortunately we often don't see what we've got until we've either lost it or imperilled it in some way. Two years on from that summer I teamed up with my old seaman mate Ray Miller and we delved into the world of massage parlours, strip clubs and all the nefarious activity that surrounds that world. Ray and I took to it like ducks to water. It was a relatively new industry in Auckland and we were its leading lights and of course attracted all the adverse publicity and gossip that comes with the territory. There were constant territorial disputes, fire bombings, threats and police pressure. I also had a successful boxing business, so one way or another I was always in the news. The years in that industry changed me and I lost track of the man who'd driven his kids around in the Valiant during the summer of 1971. There was a new man emerging inside me and he was starting to cast his own dark shadow. The new bloke loved the underworld and thrived on the constant mix of thrills, pleasure, danger, fast cars, boats, boxing nights, restaurants, parties and available women. But there was a price to pay if you wanted to survive in this dangerous and often violent world. I was prepared to take the risks but I couldn't expect my family to. You could point to specifics like one-night stands, affairs, constant late nights, gossip, but the marriage break up when it came was really because the two worlds – the sunny camp at Orewa and the dark and flashy night-life couldn't live side-by-side.

I deal with all this, the threats and the bombing, in detail in the second volume of this tale and at the moment my descent into darkness is still two years in the future. I cruised around for a couple of months, not doing much. I went to Sydney to check out new opportunities. I stayed at a great hotel, the Cosmopolitan in Double Bay. It was a marked contrast to the sorry shelter Dinger and I had stayed in the night before we jumped ship to Auckland. I tracked it down and then I retraced our steps down to the wharf and sat on the same bench from which we had watched the Dominion Monarch depart. I suppose I felt a bit boyishly like a returning hero, not on General MacArthur's level, but I felt that what I had achieved was definitely something to be proud of. I had left Sydney, anxious, flat broke and feeling vulnerable. I was now a cocky young 'urger' who could jump on planes and fly first class whenever I wanted to and although I had to watch out for policeman from several branches of the constabulary, Birdie's Immigration branch was no longer one of them. I'd become a Kiwi (with a bit of honorary Aussie thrown in for good measure) and I felt at home, in pretty much the same way Ernest Hemingway meant when in *The Green Hills of Africa* he said: "I loved this country and felt at home and where a man feels at home, outside of where he is born, is where he is meant to go."

I picked up a couple of excellent ideas while I was in Sydney. As they say, travel tends to broaden the mind. I headed home to Auckland to my family, looking forward to setting up a new business and getting on with my life. My descent from there to the world behind the neon lights, a world of guns and drugs, international crime, bent cops and villains, whores and hit men, humour and pain, high times and glamour, is all a story for another day, as is the incident concerning Elton John. I was asked to intercede on behalf of his manager, who had been detained in Mt. Eden, Auckland's notorious, dangerous jail. Having come with me this far I hope you'll join me for the second volume of my tale.

Looking back, I believe I was lucky. I was presented with some exciting but dangerous situations. Some eye opening events that I had to handle. I think that today's world has largely been stripped of adventure and new frontiers. It seems the height of risk taking in this day and age, is a gap year trip, or holiday in Spain, whereby you can Skype call your parents the minute you run into a problem. Strangely I think today's youth, equipped with their mobile phones and screens are deprived of the opportunity to chance their arm. The golden age of discovery, of pushing boundaries, sadly seems to me to be over and I think something valuable is lost. Life's experiences are now not lived, but borrowed from the screen.

At this point I'll simply bid you *au revoir* and hope to meet you in book two, where the second shadow blooms.

ACKNOWLEDGEMENTS

It could quite properly be said that writing a biography requires an inflated ego and a good dose of conceit. Be that as it may, the reward for having done so has been an amazing opportunity to almost relive my life. Although it brings to life many dark events that one would change given the opportunity, it also brings to the fore the better experiences, times and people that were a part of it. And that, my friends, is a gift far beyond the realms of valuation. That is how this enduring experience affected me, a first time writer.

For that opportunity and for bringing this other dimension of writing to my life, I have only one person to thank, my son-in-law, friend and editor, Dan Witters. I was encouraged and harangued in equal measure by him. My early efforts, keen, but amateurish, must have pushed the limits of frustration for an editor. I think it a testament to our relationship and Dan's patience that we did not split the family. I have come to believe that editing for a family member must be akin to teaching one's wife to drive. Anyway we got through it, thanks Dan.

I suppose I am indebted to all the people I met along the way; all of whom one way or another contributed to the experiences that came my way. In particular I must note the good old Mill End and Ricky boys I grew up with; they all know who they are. One I must single out, if you'll pardon the pun, has to be Dave (Dinger) Singleton, who jumped ship with me in Sydney. Like all those local boys, he was gutsy, as I hope my story shows.

Then there were my mentors, Freddie Graves from the green grocer times, Ernie Barter from the rag and bone fiddles. The schoolteacher, Mr Dan. Also Allen, the Bosun on the Highland Monarch. Plus an outstandingly good rock of a bloke, Bill Tierney, whose friendship has been massively encouraging to me. Each of them has touched me in a special way, leaving a mark that I think I put to good use.

From New Zealand I must acknowledge the late John Hughes, Rainton Hastie and Scow Captain Jock McKinnon. Also Ray Miller, Jerry Clayton, Sir Robert [Bob] Jones, Alan [Rambo] Harris, Bob Scott and Diamond Jimmy Shepherd, all of whom, one way or another, had an influence on my life and how I lived it.

Then there is my talented daughter Sam who, in her quiet way, has been a rock in an often-troubled world. Also I include my grandsons for whom I originally planned to write this book. Their interest has been an immense encouragement.

Inspiration can come from unexpected sources. Some of this tome was written in coffee bars, the 'Fat Aubergine', sadly now closed in the name of progress and 'Brown Sugar', owned by the ever supportive Louise, both in Rickmansworth High Street. While this location could never challenge the 'Montmartre' district in Paris, or other 'Bohemian' districts of art and writing, it provided a haven, a meeting place for like-minded people, to bounce ideas and concepts off.

Among them, the first I must name is, Ken Balneaves a talented Sci-Fi writer and author of 'The Greatest Gift'. Ken helped me in an unselfish manner in preparing this book for publishing. Thanks Ken, once an acquaintance, now a loyal friend. Also, Ken's wife, Sheila, who kept encouragement, drinks and coffee flowing through long hours of editing.

I also appreciate another man who gave me great encouragement and assistance through a down period, which greatly helped the production of this book, Gerard O'Connell. He too was once an acquaintance, now a loyal and valued friend. I think Gerry was partly driven to help, as his father, Tony, whom I had the pleasure of meeting, was himself an 'old salt'. He had trod a similar path to me; he ran away to sea at fourteen years old and had to do some tough growing up.

Then there's big John Gompers, 'the strolling minstrel', a man who loves music and books and sang at charity events, (well he would sing at any event, we couldn't stop him). Then, Dave and Pat, he a newspaper columnist, friends and always great sources of encouragement. Marc, the café part-owner and Danielle, his manageress, who always kept the 'welcome mat' out for me, no matter how long I sat with a single cup of coffee.

Further encouragement came from friends and drinking buddies, Tom, Phil, Robbie, Neil, Brent and Pat, a rugby and sports nut. All to be found in 'Druids' in Ricky High Street, a rugby and football pub/sports bar, par excellence. Alan the owner, a Welsh rugby player, now a noted coach and fan, always extending a hand.

Finally, there were my old Ricky mates, who could always be found somewhere in the High Street chatting, Dave and Olive, Gorgy and Vera, Greg and Taffy, plus a host of other old Mill Enders, all in their own way giving me a kaleidoscope of memories to draw upon, thanks.

Len Russell